Quality in Teaching

Quality in Teaching: Arguments for a Reflective Profession

Edited by
Wilfred Carr

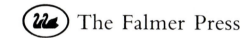 The Falmer Press

(A member of the Taylor & Francis Group)
London, New York and Philadelphia

UK   The Falmer Press, Falmer House, Barcombe, Lewes, Sussex, BN8 5DL

USA   The Falmer Press, Taylor & Francis Inc., 242 Cherry Street, Philadelphia, PA 19106-1906

First published 1989

British Library Cataloguing in Publication Data
Quality in teaching: arguments for a reflexive
  profession.
  1. Teaching
  I. Carr, Wilfred
  371.1′02

ISBN 1-85000-546-X

Library of Congress Cataloging-in-Publication Data
Quality in teaching: arguments for a reflective profession/edited
  by Wilfred Carr.
       p.   cm.
    ISBN 1-85000-546-X. –– ISBN 1-85000-547-8 (pbk.)
    1. Teaching. 2. Teachers –– In-service training.
    3. Teaching-Vocational guidance.   I. Carr, Wilfred
  LB1775.Q35   1989
  371.1′02 –– dc20

Jacket design by Caroline Archer

Typeset in 10½/13 California by
Chapterhouse, The Cloisters, Formby L37 3PX

Printed in Great Britain by
Taylor & Francis (Printers) Ltd, Basingstoke

Contents

Introduction:
Understanding Quality in Teaching

Wilfred Carr

The question of how to improve the quality of teaching is quite properly perceived to be at the heart of the contemporary educational debate. The main strategy used to stimulate public interest in this question has been to introduce a new rhetoric: phrases, slogans and metaphors which serve to create widespread public concern about teaching, and to make sure that this concern is expressed in a particular way. 'Standards', 'professional competence', 'accreditation', 'accountability' and 'appraisal' are part of the rhetoric now being employed to define 'the problem' of teaching quality and to promote certain practical proposals for its resolution.

The obvious danger of rhetoric is that it has the appearance of a rational form of persuasion while often serving to undermine rational argument and debate. As a result, many of the assumptions underlying the debate about teaching quality remain unexamined, alternative views of 'the problem' are being marginalized and unsubstantiated claims are beginning to acquire the status of literal truth. It is thus scarcely surprising that many teachers and teacher educators regard the current debate about teaching quality as uninformed and naive. Nor should it come as a surprise to find that it is becoming respectable to believe that educational theory has little to contribute to our understanding of teaching. But the more teaching becomes determined by rhetorical persuasion rather than rational argument, the more will it become an ideological activity governed by ideas and 'theories' which are unjustified, unacknowledged and undisclosed.

This book speaks to and for all those teachers and teacher educators who are committed to improving the quality of teaching but who are unwilling to accept that the current rhetoric offers an adequate understanding of what this means or how it is to be achieved. The book aims to offer to this audience a set of ideas and arguments which will help them to understand some of the limitations and confusions now infecting contemporary educational discourse, to develop a more defensible notion of what 'teaching quality' might mean and to devise practical means for its advancement.

Although many of these arguments are already well documented in the literature, their interconnections are often difficult to discern. Also, those advancing these arguments do so from very different theoretical perspectives and on the basis of different educational beliefs. The remainder of this introductory chapter outlines the general perspective on teaching quality that the book seeks to advance in order to help readers more readily grasp the book's central argument and more clearly perceive the significance of the contributions that follow.

A conspicuous feature of the government White Paper on *Teaching Quality* is the absence of any serious effort to say precisely what 'quality in teaching' actually means.[1] In consequence the ways in which the concepts of 'teaching' and 'quality' are used in the document are at best limited and partial but more frequently simplistic and naive. More often than not, teaching is portrayed as an unreflective technical process and 'quality' as synonymous with meeting prespecified 'standards' through a system of supervision, inspection and control.[2] *Teaching Quality* may use the rhetoric of professionalism, but in reality this amounts to giving teachers little more than the right to exercise a limited technical discretion within a restrictive framework of bureaucratic rules and managerial controls. Given this limited and limiting perspective, it is important to unpack the notions of 'quality' and 'teaching' so that the ways in which they are now being allowed to structure educational discourse can be better understood.

The concept of 'quality' has two quite different meanings. On the one hand, it can be used in a purely descriptive way to describe what the *Concise Oxford Dictionary* refers to as 'a characteristic trait' or 'a mental or moral attribute'. When it is used in this way, we may talk of somebody possessing the quality of courage or the qualities of a teacher. On the other hand, 'quality' can also be used in a normative sense to indicate a 'degree of excellence'; used in this sense, it signifies which of those 'characteristic traits' and 'mental or moral attributes' are to be deemed valuable or important. To talk of quality *in* teaching is thus to identify those qualities *of* teaching which constitute its 'excellence'.

In many cases the qualities constituting something's 'excellence' will be related to its effectiveness. For example, the criteria for judging the quality of a musical instrument will derive from its instrumental value: the effectiveness with which it can be used to pursue some particular human purpose or activity. In other cases, however, judgments of 'quality' can only be made by appealing to criteria derived from the intrinsic value of the activity being judged. The quality of a musical performance, for example, can only be ascertained on the basis of criteria derived from music itself. Any assessment of the quality of a musician's performance cannot, therefore, be divorced from some understanding of the values intrinsic to music. Although such an assessment may take the musician's technical and instrumental skill into account, it will depend primarily on criteria for discerning the musical qualities inherent in his performance.

What this brief and admittedly oversimplified discussion of the concept of 'quality' is intended to make clear is that identifying quality in teaching requires making explicit whether the criteria being employed derive from intrinsic or instrumental values.[3] To the extent that teachers and others who are directly involved in education invariably look upon themselves as professional educators, they will perceive quality in teaching to refer to its intrinsic value as a worthwhile educational process. From this perspective teaching will be of 'quality' insofar as it is perceived to be inherently educative rather than, say, a process of passive instruction or training. Indeed, if teachers and others involved in education did not perceive their teaching in this way, their conception of themselves as professional *educators* would largely disappear.

It need hardly be said that those who are not themselves professional educators — such as politicians, economists and employers — will tend to interpret and assess teaching quality in terms of values external to the educational process. From their perspectives, education is seen primarily as something which serves extrinsic purposes such as the national interest, the economic needs of society, or the demands of the labour market. Judgments about teaching quality in these cases will not be made by appealing to the criteria which serve to enhance teaching as an educational process, but by using criteria that enhance the effectiveness of teaching as a means to ends which are not themselves examined from an educational point of view. The important issues raised by the current debate about teaching are thus not simple technical questions about how quality is to be improved, but complex and largely contentious questions about how teaching quality is to be interpreted and understood. In *Teaching Quality* such questions are ignored and the document offers little more than bureaucratically framed specifications of 'quality' together with a series of control mechanisms — such as the inspection and accreditation of teacher education — for ensuring that these specifications are being met.[4] What is conspicuously lacking is an interpretation of 'teaching quality' which acknowledges the importance of educational values and recognizes teachers as professional educators, committed to enhancing their professionalism by improving the educational quality of their work.

If the notion of 'teaching quality' is to be interpreted in these terms, it is necessary for the rhetoric now dominating educational discourse to be replaced by a language which, will render the qualities constitutive of good teaching more intelligible, and so stimulate a more rational and enlightened educational debate. The important question to ask, therefore, is whether there is a language of teaching quality which is more compelling than the technical and bureaucratic forms of educational discourse which now prevail.

The most influential and eloquent contemporary advocate of such a language is undoubtedly J.J. Schwab. In his seminal paper, 'The Practical: A Language for the Curriculum',[5] Schwab argued that a general over-reliance on technical language had led to the fragmentation of educational thinking, a morally impoverished view of teaching and a failure to provide teachers with a capacity to confront the practical problems they face in their everyday work. These defects, argued Schwab, can only be overcome if the technical language now dominating educational discourse (which he refers to as 'the language of the theoretic') is replaced by the language of the 'practical'. In suggesting this, however, Schwab made it clear that

> By the 'practical' I do *not* mean the curbstone practicality of the mediocre administrator and the man on the street for whom the practical means the easily achieved familiar goals which can be reached by familiar means. I refer rather to a complex discipline relatively unfamiliar to the academic and differing radically from the disciplines of the theoretic. It is the discipline concerned with choice and action, in contrast with the theoretic, which is concerned with knowledge. Its methods lead to defensible decisions where the methods of the theoretic lead to warranted conclusions.[6]

In arguing for the interpretation of teaching as a 'practical' discipline, Schwab was explicitly invoking the Aristotelian distinction between technical and practical discourse.[7] For Aristotle, technical discourse is the language appropriate to thinking about how to act in order to bring about some determinate end. By contrast, practical discourse is the language appropriate to thinking about how to act in order to realize ethical values and goals. For Aristotle, as for Schwab, technical and practical discourse serve very different purposes and operate in very different ways. The overall purpose of technical discourse is to decide which course of action will most effectively achieve some known end — as, for example, when a teacher has to decide whether the 'phonic' or the 'whole-word' approach to reading is the most effective means of producing a specific learning outcome. The overall purpose of practical discourse, however, is to make a morally informed judgment about what ought to be done in a particular practical situation — as, for example, when an infant teacher has to decide whether it would be educationally justifiable to teach pupils the mechanics of language and arithmetic or whether it would be more appropriate to concentrate on responding to pupils' natural curiosity and interest. Practical discourse is thus required when teachers are faced with moral dilemmas about how to apply their educational values to a particular practical situation. Practical discourse is the language teachers employ when they have to decide what it would be educationally justifiable for them to do in some problematic classroom situation.

The essence of Schwab's argument is that teaching is primarily a 'practical' rather than 'technical' activity, involving a constant flow of problematic situations which require teachers to make judgments about how best to transfer their general educational values (such as 'the development of understanding' or 'the self-realization of the individual's potential') into classroom practice. Interpreted in the language of the 'practical', 'teaching quality' would have little to do with the skilful application of technical rules but instead would relate to the capacity to bring abstract ethical values to bear on concrete educational practice — a capacity which teachers display in their knowledge of what, educationally, is required in a particular situation and their willingness to act so that this knowledge can take a practical form. Without this capacity good teaching becomes indistinguishable from technical expertise. The teacher who lacks this capacity may be technically accountable but cannot be educationally or morally answerable.

Schwab's argument for the interpretation of teaching as a 'practical art' poses a serious challenge to received views about how teaching is to be developed and improved. In Britain this challenge was taken up by Lawrence Stenhouse who, like Schwab, insisted that teaching is primarily an 'art' in which general educational ideas acquire practical expression. 'In art', he wrote, 'ideas are tested in form by practice. Exploration and interpretation lead to revision and adjustment of idea and of practice . . . . That is what good teaching is like. It is not like routine engineering or routine management.'[8]

Given his view of teaching, Stenhouse faced the dilemma of mounting a national curriculum development project without resorting to the technical language of the then dominant 'objectives' model of curriculum planning and design. His response to this dilemma was to develop a theory of curriculum development and research which relied heavily on R.S. Peters' philosophical analysis of educational aims.

In 'Must an Educator Have an Aim?' Peters argued that the aims of education are not terminal endpoints to which teaching is the instrumental means.[9] Instead, they are attempts to specify the values to be realized *in* and *through* teaching and which justify the description of any teaching act as an educational process. Peters' own argument to this effect is worth quoting at length.

> Talk about 'the aims of education' depends to a large extent on a misunderstanding about the sort of concept that 'education' is . . . . Education is not a concept that marks out any particular process . . . rather it suggests criteria to which processes . . . must conform. One of these is that something of value should be passed on . . . . However, this cannot be construed as meaning that education itself should lead on to or produce something of value. This is like saying that reform must lead to a man being better . . . . The point is that making a man better is not an aim extrinsic to reform; it is a criterion which anything must satisfy which is to be called reform. In the same way a necessary feature of education is often extracted as an extrinsic end. People thus think that education must be for the sake of something extrinsic that is worthwhile, whereas being worthwhile is part of what is meant by calling it 'education'. The instrumental model of education provides a caricature of this necessary feature of desirability by conceiving what is worthwhile as an end brought about by the process . . . .[10]

Thus, educational aims such as 'critical thinking' or 'rational autonomy' refer to what Peters calls 'principles of procedure' — values to which any educational process governed by these aims must conform. To cite these educational aims as desirable is thus not simply to imply that role-learning, memorization or other forms of teaching which are incompatible with critical thinking or rational autonomy are ineffective methods of teaching and learning. Rather, it is to cite criteria for judging whether these teaching methods have any intrinsic educational value and hence whether they constitute genuine educational processes at all.

On the basis of Peters' philosophical analysis, Stenhouse was able to elaborate a view of curriculum development which avoided the techno-logical assumptions of the 'objectives' approach. In the 'objectives' approach the aim of curriculum development is to relate empirically verified principles of effective teaching to the need to achieve predeter-mined educational goals. For Stenhouse, however, curriculum develop-ment is understood as a way of relating the educational values already implicit in the teaching process, to teachers' professional obligation to improve the educational quality of their practice. Stenhouse thus advanced a 'process' model of curriculum development — a model which construed curriculum development as the process through which teachers deepen their insight into their own educational values and develop their capacity to translate these values into classroom practice.[11]

Hence, for Stenhouse, curriculum development was synonymous with professional development, and professional development was itself con-strued as a research process in which teachers systematically reflect on their practice and use the results of this reflection in such a way as to improve their own teaching. By relating this idea of 'teacher as researcher' to an analysis of professionalism, Stenhouse was able to argue that professional development required teachers to be provided with opportunities and resources to study their own practice through systematic reflection and research.

There can be no doubt that Stenhouse's work led to a more enlightened view of curriculum development and a more defensible notion of teacher pro-fessionalism. It is also clear that his 'process' view of curriculum development and his model of 'teacher as researcher' have contributed significantly to the advancement of Schwab's aspiration for the reconstruction of teaching as a 'practical art'. However, the developments generated by Stenhouse's ideas (such as school-based curriculum development and educational action research) have led to new questions which his own theoretical framework did not address. For example, although Stenhouse linked his idea of 'teacher as re-searcher' to the professional development of teachers, it is now obvious that the epistemological assumptions underpinning his notion of 'professionalism' need to be explicated and assessed in a more systematic way. What, in parti-cular, is required is a detailed analysis of the nature of the professional know-ledge informing the art of the teacher.

Donald Schon's book, *Educating the Reflective Practitioner*,[12] opens with a description of professional artistry which is clearly reminiscent of Stenhouse's image of teaching as an art:

Inherent in the practice of the professionals we recognise un-usually competent, is a core of artistry .... Artistry is a kind of

7

intelligence, a kind of knowing though different in crucial aspects from our standard model of professional knowledge.[13]

For Schon, 'our standard model of professional knowledge' fails to comprehend 'professional artistry' because it derives from a misguided epistemology of practice — an epistemology which is 'built into the very foundations of the modern university' and shapes our understanding of the relationship of research, professional knowledge and professional practice. Schon calls this dominant epistemology of practice 'technical rationality'.

Embedded in technical rationality, argues Schon, is the assumption that a 'profession' is an occupational group whose practice is grounded in knowledge derived from scientific research. In consequence, professional knowledge is taken to refer to theoretical knowledge about how to achieve given ends; professional practice is seen as a process of problem-solving, and professional competence as the skilful application of theoretical knowledge to the instrumental problems of practice. Within this epistemology of practice, notes Schon, artistry has no lasting place.

From the perspective of technical rationality, it follows that teaching is a profession only to the extent that it involves applying theoretical knowledge to the pursuit of fixed educational ends. The fact that much of the theoretical knowledge made available to teachers often lacks practical application, together with the admission that the 'ends' of teaching are always contentious and often conflicting, merely serve to confirm the popular view that teaching is only a profession in a limited and restrictive sense.

Schon argues that a view a professional knowledge based on technical rationality is inadequate on at least three major counts. First, by assuming that professional knowledge can be produced in isolation from the situation in which it is to be applied, it ignores the extent to which such knowledge always has to be 'embedded in the socially structured context shared by a community of practitioners' and 'exercised in the institutional settings particular to the profession'.[14] Second, because of its general indifference to the ways in which professionals actually work, technical rationality fails to recognize that they rarely 'apply' theoretical knowledge to their practice. Instead, they operate on the basis of their own, largely tacit, knowledge of what they are doing and what they are trying to achieve. Professional knowledge is thus not a systematically organized body of theoretical knowledge but a shared body of inherited 'practical knowledge', that is, ' . . . a common body of explicit more or less systematically organized knowledge . . . a set of values, preferences and norms in terms of which they make sense of practical situations, formulate goals and direction for action and determine what constitutes acceptable professional conduct'.[15]

Third, although technical rationality portrays professional competence as a technical problem-solving competence, the problems of the real world of practice 'do not present themselves to the practitioner as givens', but as 'messy', 'indeterminate' and 'problematic' situations which arise because of 'conflicting values' (such as the conflicting requirements of efficiency and equality or equality and quality).[16] Such problems cannot be resolved by the use of techniques derived from theoretical research but call for what Schon terms 'artful competence' — a non-technical process in which practitioners clarify their understanding of 'a problematic situation' in a way which enables them to redefine their problems in terms of both the ends to be achieved and the means for their achievement.

On the basis of his critique of technical rationality, Schon concludes that the question of the relationship between professional knowledge and professional competence needs to be turned upside down:

> If the model of Technical Rationality... fails to account for practical competence in 'divergent' situations so much the worse for the model. Let us search instead for an epistemology of practice implicit in the artistic, intuitive processes which some practitioners do bring to situations of uncertainty, instability, uniqueness and value conflict.[17]

In *The Reflective Practitioner* Schon puts aside the model of technical rationality and, through a careful examination of professional artistry, develops an epistemology of practice which places technical problem-solving within the broad framework of reflective enquiry. The central concepts used by Schon to construct this epistemology are those of 'knowing-in-action' and 'reflection-in-action'.

'Knowing-in-action' refers to the professional knowledge that practitioners actually use, which is implicit in their action, and often difficult to describe. 'Knowing-in-action refers to the sorts of "know-how" we reveal in our intelligent action. The knowing is *in* action. We reveal it by our spontaneous skilful execution of the performance, and we are characteristically unable to make it verbally explicit.'[18]

'Reflection-in-action' is the process central to the 'art' by which professionals deal with 'problematic situations'. It occurs precisely when a situation arises which indicates that the professionals' existing stock of knowledge — their 'knowing-in-action' — is no longer adequate. 'Reflection-in-action' arises, says Schon, when our

> ... routine responses produce a surprise.... Surprise leads to reflection within an action-present. We consider both the un-

expected event and the knowing-in-action that led up to it . . . . Reflection-in-action has a critical function, questioning the assumptional structure of knowing-in-action. We think critically about the thinking that got us into this fix. [19]

Thus, for Schon, 'reflection-in-action' involves reflecting on 'knowing-in-action'. It is the process through which the hitherto taken for granted knowledge implicit in action is made explicit, critically examined, re-formulated and tested through further action. In this sense 'reflection-in-action' is a research process through which the development of professional knowledge and the improvement of professional practice occur simultaneously.

When someone reflects-in-action, he becomes a researcher in the practice context. He is not dependent on the categories of established theory and technique but constructs a new theory of the unique case. His inquiry is not limited to a deliberation about means which depends on a prior agreement about ends. He does not keep means and ends separate but defines them interactively as he frames a problematic situation. He does not separate thinking from doing . . . his experimenting is a kind of action, implementation is built into his enquiry. [20]

By outlining the structure of 'reflection-in-action' Schon not only emphasizes the impoverishment of technical rationality as a basis for professional knowledge and practice, but also eliminates the familiar dualisms it sustains. From the perspective of technical rationality, means are separated from ends, knowing from doing and action from research. From the perspective of 'reflection-in-action' these dualisms are reunited through the single process of reflection.

The previous section has shown how Schwab, Stenhouse and Schon provide us with a language of teaching which is very different from our dominant educational discourse. It is a language which eschews the image of teachers as skilful technicians and instead portrays them as practitioners of the art of translating abstract educational values into concrete educational practice. It is primarily an ethical language which recognizes that teachers are guided by moral values and constantly under a professional obligation to justify their work in educational terms.

Once the language of teaching is construed as an ethical form of discourse, the division between 'professional knowledge' and 'professional practice' begins to break down. Professional knowledge no longer appears as an externally produced body of value-free theoretical knowledge but as that implicitly accepted body of value-laden knowledge which teachers use to make sense of their practice. On this view, teachers develop professionally by reflecting critically on their own tacit practical knowledge rather than by applying theoretical knowledge produced by academic experts. The acquisition of professional knowledge and the improvement of professional practice cannot be differentiated: each is constituted by, and constitutive of, the other.

When teaching is interpreted in this way, 'quality' has little to do with measuring up to a list of performance criteria but instead is something that can only be judged by reference to those ethical criteria which teachers tacitly invoke to explain the educational purpose of their teaching. This means that teaching quality cannot be improved other than by improving teachers' capacity to realize their educational values through their practice. It also means that this process of improvement can be nothing other than a research process in which teachers reflect on their practice and use the products of their reflections to reconstruct their practice as an *educational* practice in a systematic and rational way.

When the current rhetoric of 'teaching quality' is considered from this standpoint, three related conclusions begin to emerge. The first is that, by eliminating ethical categories from our educational discourse, the current rhetoric has so transformed our concept of teaching that it is now understood as a technical activity conducted for utilitarian purposes rather than as an ethical activity directed towards moral and social ends. The second is that in the course of this transformation, our conception of education is being distorted and that it is only by remoralizing our educational discourse that such distortions can be avoided. The third is that the task of remoralizing our educational discourse will only be achieved if we are prepared to raise critical questions about how teaching is now being interpreted and understood. Can our understanding of teaching remain intelligible once it has been separated from its moral, social and political roots? Why are we so keen to embrace the idea of teaching as a technical activity, and why are we misguided to do so? Do our current notions of professionalism and professional development recognize the extent to which educational values are part of the very fabric of teaching? Do proposed methods of teacher appraisal do justice to a concept of teaching in which the role of reflection plays a central part? Although these questions are by no means exhaustive, they serve to identify some of the central issues explored in this book.

The chapters in the first section, 'The Philosophical and Social Context of Teaching', explore the rationale for the view of teaching generally adopted in the book and the ways in which it is being undermined by various social and institutional constraints. In the first chapter Glenn Langford shows in some philosophical detail why teaching is only intelligible when it is construed as a form of 'purposive' action guided by a 'conceptual scheme' — an interrelated set of intentions and beliefs which enables teachers to grasp the overall purpose of what they are doing and what they are trying to achieve. For Langford, the overall purpose which serves to unify the multifarious actions of teachers is to enable others to become educated.

Because teaching is a purposive activity, argues Langford, it cannot be learned or understood in isolation from the social context in which it occurs. Since teaching is essentially a *social practice*, the conceptual schemes governing a teacher's 'way of seeing and doing' are derived from tradition and deeply embedded in the institutional settings in which teachers work. For Langford, this entails that teachers change and improve their practice by reflecting critically on the traditions of thought shaping their own practical experience. It is by revising the knowledge and beliefs inherent in their own conceptual schemes — rather than by applying knowledge produced via the conceptual schemes governing scientific or theoretical research — that teachers can best improve the ways in which they pursue their educational purposes and ends.

Langford's suspicion of attempts to use scientific knowledge to explain or direct a social practice is reinforced by Fred Inglis' analysis of the damage done to our understanding of teaching by the quasi-scientific language of managerialism, 'a language in which it is impossible to speak of the virtues... its absolute criteria of efficiency... cost-effectiveness, accurate evaluation of performance... [have] no purchase on the moral condition...' The major defect of a managerialist view of teaching is that 'it simply is not convertible into the real values of education'. Educational management (which is really nothing more than 'persuading others to assent to... ends which are systemic and unavailable to question') is now so popular because it embodies the dominant ideology of scientific rationality — an ideology that Inglis refers to as 'technicism'. 'For the technicist', says Inglis, 'to think well is to discover techniques.... Reflection and morality are displaced to the ivory tower. Thought and wisdom disappear; expertise substitutes itself.'

On the basis of what he calls a 'potted history of the teacher's formation', Inglis proposes that teachers in schools which still possess a modicum of autonomy may be able to resist the morally vacuous language of managerialism by embracing some of the ideas expounded in the classical political theory of republicanism. The practical expression of these ideas would entail that schools create self-governing forms of organization which encourage 'free and open discussion about the public, rational and moral justification of action' and which interpret the notions of 'responsibility' and 'accountability' as aspects of the moral dimension of teaching.

Inglis recognizes that those who try to organize schools as democratic communities will be frustrated by the fact that our dominant educational discourse is now so thoroughly infected by the logic and assumptions of bureaucratic rationality. In the third chapter in this section, Fazal Rizvi unravels this logic and these assumptions in order to show that bureaucratic rationality is both ideological and anti-democratic and thus impedes the promotion of democratic values in schools.

On the basis of an analysis of the key elements of Weber's theory of bureaucracy, Rizvi argues that while schools may display few of the defining characteristics of an 'ideal type' of bureaucratic organization, this should not be allowed to conceal the extent to which educational decision-making has become dominated by bureaucratic rationality — 'the rationality of matching means to ends with maximum economy and efficiency'. Understood as a form of rationality, rather than simply as a form of organization, bureaucracy can be seen to embody a range of epistemological and moral assumptions which not only stand in stark contrast to the requirements of schools as democratic institutions, but also serve the ideological function of eliminating serious debate about educational values. Rizvi concludes by showing that the 'means-end' and 'fact-value' distinctions, on which bureaucratic rationality depends, are both epistemologically untenable and morally objectionable.

All too often the question of teacher professionalism is treated as a question about the social status of teachers relative to doctors, lawyers and other occupational élites. The authors of the four chapters in the second section of the book, 'Teaching as a Profession', reject this line of enquiry and concentrate instead on the more important issue of what teacher professionalism means and how it can be advanced. Shirley Grundy approaches these issues by interpreting teaching as an occupation informed by the disposition of *practique*: a disposition to examine the assumptions underlying conventional forms of professional conduct and to reflect critically on the extent to which the educational values ostensibly guiding teachers' work are actually served by their professional practice. The development of this disposition is particularly urgent, argues Grundy, because the process of technologization is fast transforming teaching into little more than a technical expertise. The adverse educational effects of technologization cannot be resisted simply by teachers trying to preserve their 'professionalism'. Rather, they must develop that form of critical consciousness which will enable them to expose and challenge the technocratic assumptions now being made about the nature and purpose of their work.

Peter Gilroy also regards the preoccupation with the concept of 'professionalism' as 'little more than a piece of empty rhetoric'. He focuses his attention instead on how recent philosophical developments illuminate the nature of teachers' knowledge and so help us to understand some of the familiar 'theory–practice' tensions experienced by students on initial teacher training courses. Central to Gilroy's analysis is a distinction between two conflicting theories of knowledge: the 'autocratic' theory, which sees knowledge as objective and impersonal; and the 'subjectivist' theory, which sees knowledge in individualistic and personal terms. In the context of teacher education, the former leads to giving students a body of theoretically verified knowledge about teaching; the latter leads to encouraging students to develop personal knowledge from their own individual experience. Gilroy rejects both of these views and proposes instead a 'contextualist' view of teachers' knowledge — a view which is largely consistent with the ideas of Schwab and Schon as well as with Glenn Langford's idea of teaching as a social practice.

Gilroy's concern for 'context' is one which Hugh Sockett shares. Sockett's discussion of teacher professionalism, however, is organized around two very specific claims. The first is that 'views about educational theory and practice . . . provide different criteria for the knowledge base of practice which yield different accounts of professionalism'. The second is the claim that 'educational institutions are the political embodiment of epistemologies'. The central question provoked by these claims is thus, ' . . . What shape ought educational institutions . . . to have if the aspiration for increased professionalism is well founded and in the light of changing understandings about the nature of theory and practice?' Sockett pursues this question by reflecting on how the Centre for Applied Research and Development in Education (CARD) has tried to respond to teachers' professional aspirations by incorporating a particular epistemology of practice into its own institutional structures. The epistemological ideas to which CARD is committed are Schon's idea of the reflective practitioner and Stenhouse's idea of teacher research. In the remainder of his chapter Sockett identifies some of the lessons to be learned from CARD's attempt to give those ideas institutional expression.

The relationship between the epistemological and institutional dimensions of professionalism is also emphasized in Maurice Kogan's discussion of professionalism and teacher accountability. In the first part of his chapter, Kogan examines the epistemological assumptions implicit in professional models of accountability. He then shows that, because these assumptions can and do vary, professional models of teacher accountability can be either rigid or flexible, technical or enlightened. In the final section Kogan relates his analysis to recent educational policy developments. He concludes that the epistemological connotations of the 1988 Education Reform Act 'flatly contradict the professional accountability model' and 'seem to reinforce the contractual model of accountability'. However, this does not necessarily mean the demise of teacher professionalism. 'The issue is whether in the end', Kogan concludes, 'the professionals will be able to construe client needs, local authority evaluative criteria and National Curriculum perspectives in terms of their own epistemological assumptions about the generation and dissemination of educational knowledge and skills'.

The view of professional development adopted in this book draws heavily on Lawrence Stenhouse's compelling image of teachers systematic-ally improving the quality of their teaching on the basis of their own research. The practical methods most commonly employed in this research-based approach to professional development are the methods of action research. From an action research perspective, teachers develop pro-fessionally by collecting and analyzing 'data' about their own practice and reflecting on how to make their teaching more consistent with their edu-cational values and beliefs.

Since its emergence in the 1970s, action research has become a popular element in the INSET courses offered by many teacher education insti-tutions. In the early 1990s, however, it will be necessary to consider how action research can come to terms with the changing political and edu-cational climate within which teachers operate. This is the issue which the chapters in the final section of the book, 'The Professional Development of Teachers', all address.

Although the authors of the first three chapters are sympathetic to the general aims and aspirations of teacher research, they all take the view that it is time to review its past achievements and assess its future possibilities. In the first chapter, Martin Lawn argues that by seeing teaching as a practice which occurs in classrooms, the teacher research movement has neglected the extent to which teaching is now defined by political directives and by the structural changes being made to the organization of state education. For this reason, argues Lawn, teachers' work is best understood as 'school-work', that is, as a labour process which is controlled by the framework of rules and regulations within which schools have to operate. For Lawn, this means that claims for teacher professionalism need to be understood as an expression of the struggle to defend the quality of state education. It also means that teacher research needs to be reformulated as 'schoolwork' research — a form of research which is not limited to 'improving practice' but which encourages teachers to examine the wider social and political context which increasingly shapes their working lives.

Michael Golby also argues that teacher research needs to be extended 'beyond the classroom and school to investigate the contexts of power and control within which educational and social values are now being generated'. Golby asks whether the case study methods frequently used in teacher research can be used to confront issues which go beyond the confines of particular classrooms and schools. By drawing on the work of the Exeter Society for Curriculum Studies, Golby shows how the case study approach can provide the means for focusing on general educational questions and so enable teachers to sharpen their critical perspectives and make informed contributions to educational discussion and debate.

Like Lawn and Golby, Clem Adelman is concerned to re-assess the contribution of action research to teachers' professional development. As his title indicates, Adelman's aim is to emphasize that action research should not be seen simply as a research methodology but as a 'means of providing the kind of information essential to practical reasoning'. By drawing on Schwab's notion of 'the practical ethic' Adelman shows that much contemporary action research provides little of educational significance for teachers and is really no different from the traditional forms of educational research it is supposed to have replaced. Yet action research, insists Adelman, 'stands or falls by its demonstrable relevance to the practical ethic of education as well as whether it is reliable, valid and refutable as a methodology'.

The two remaining chapters in this section explore fundamental issues about the relationship between teacher appraisal and the development of teachers' professional knowledge. Both are highly critical of the kind of appraisal scheme currently being proposed, and both outline models of the relationship between professional knowledge and professional practice very different from the dominant managerial and bureaucratic models.

In the first of these, Richard Winter notes that most appraisal schemes are designed to serve two disparate purposes. On the one hand, they are designed as a means of achieving greater managerial control; on the other, as a means of providing reliable knowledge about teachers' professional activities. Winter explains that appraisal schemes incorporate these conflicting purposes because they are infected by the ideology of 'means-ends rationality', an ideology which combines a scientific theory of 'objective' knowledge with a bureaucratic theory of social organization. Winter shows that appraisal schemes governed by this ideology are incapable of collecting valid knowledge about teaching quality and that it is necessary to develop methods of appraisal based on a theory of knowledge which is free from the ideological assumptions of means-ends rationality. Winter proposes a dialectical theory of knowledge in which the notions of collaboration, reflexivity and critique play a central part. This theory of knowledge, argues Winter, can justify an approach to teacher appraisal which is based on the aims and methods of action research, and which is no longer tied to the 'assumptions of the natural science paradigm of knowledge which dominates the academic, political and institutional life of bureaucratized societies'.

In the final chapter John Elliott draws on many of the ideas and arguments running through this book in order to mount a critique of recent policy developments in teacher education. By reflecting on his own professional development Elliott also provides a non-managerial, non-bureaucratic approach to improving teaching quality in which the notions of self-reflection, practical knowledge and the teacher's professional culture play a central part. In this sense, both the style and the substance of Elliott's chapter encapsulate the central themes of the book and so provide it with a fitting conclusion.

Like most other contributors, Elliott is concerned by recent trends in teacher education. His analysis of these trends uses Foucault's thesis that conceptions of knowledge always presuppose particular power relationships in order to distinguish two conceptions of educational knowledge, each constituting different power relations. First, he identifies that form of reflective self-knowledge which enables teachers to develop themselves as professional educators and which presupposes that teachers legitimately exercise 'disciplinary' power in the pursuit of their educational values and goals. Second, he identifies that form of quasi-scientific knowledge which can be used to measure teacher performance in terms of a set of standardized competences and skills. This kind of knowledge, argues Elliott, creates the kind of coercive power relations that legitimize the external domination of teachers' work. Elliott shows how recent proposals for improving teaching quality call for forms of appraisal and research which undermine the teacher's ability to act educationally by producing knowledge that can be used to create hierarchical systems of teacher surveillance and control.

One of the purposes of this book is to offer a critique of this conception of educational knowledge. Another is to reconstruct the image of teaching as a reflective profession in which professional values, knowledge and practice are inextricably linked. In the present intellectual and political climate, the revival of this image of teaching is not an easy task. Technical rationality continues to provide the dominant epistemology of practice, and central government's predilection for technological views of teaching is inevitably creating conditions under which a reflective approach to professional development becomes impossible. It is the claim of this book that teaching is only a genuine profession to the extent that teachers are able to make the educational quality of teaching their central professional concern. By giving teachers access to a language and a set of arguments with which they may defend this view of professionalism, the book may help them to resist the rhetoric now being used to transform the nature and conduct of their work.

Notes

1 Department of Education and Science, *Teaching Quality*, London, HMSO, 1983.
2 A more detailed critique of *Teaching Quality* can be found in F. Slater (ed.), *The Quality Controllers: A Critique of the White Paper Teaching Quality*, Bedford Way Papers No. 22, 1985.
3 An extended philosophical analysis of the concept of 'quality' is provided by R.S. Peters' 'The Meaning of Quality in Education' in R.S. Peters, *Education and the Education of Teachers*, London, Routledge and Kegan Paul, 1977, Ch. 2.
4 This criticism has been expanded in some detail by John Elliott in 'Teacher Education and Teaching Quality', *British Journal of Sociology of Education*, 6, 1, 1985, pp. 97–116.
5 J.J. Schwab, 'The Practical: A Language for Curriculum', *School Review*, 78, 1969, pp. 1–24.
6 *Ibid.*, pp. 1–2.
7 Aristotle, *The Nicomachean Ethics*, tr. H.G. Greenwood, New York, Arno Press, 1973.
8 J. Rudduck and D. Hopkins (eds) (1985) *Research as a Basis for Teaching: Readings from the Work of Lawrence Stenhouse*, London, Heinemann, p. 97.
9 R.S. Peters, 'Must an Educator Have an Aim?' in *Authority, Responsibility and Education*, London, Allen and Unwin, 1966.
10 R.S. Peters, 'Education as Initiation', in R.D. Archambault, *Philosophical Analysis and Education*, London, Routledge and Kegan Paul, 1965, p. 92.
11 L. Stenhouse, *An Introduction to Curriculum Research and Development*, London, Heinemann Education, 1975.
12 D. Schon, *Educating the Reflective Practitioner*, London, Jossey-Bass, 1987.
13 *Ibid.*, p. 13.
14 *Ibid.*, p. 33.
15 *Ibid.*, pp. 32–3.
16 *Ibid.*, p. 5.
17 D. Schon, *The Reflective Practitioner*, London, Temple Smith, 1983, p. 49.
18 D. Schon, *Educating the Reflective Practitioner*, *op. cit.*, p. 25.
19 *Ibid.*, p. 28.
20 D. Schon, *The Reflective Practitioner*, *op. cit.*, p. 68.

Part One
The Philosophical and Social Context of Teaching

Chapter 1

Teaching and the Idea of a Social Practice

Glenn Langford

Any attempt to criticize, change or take part in the social practice of teaching, or to give an account of the relation between educational theory and practice, must rely, if only implicitly, on some conception of what a social practice is. It must also rely on a view of the *kind* of practice concerned, since there are other kinds of social practice besides teaching — for example, religious, medical and scientific. It must also rely on a view of what makes a social practice the *particular* practice it is, since practices of the same kind assume different forms at different times and places; for example, teaching practice in a fundamentalist Moslem country is very different from that in the United Kingdom. This chapter is primarily concerned with the first of these questions, that of how best to conceptualize the idea of a social practice as such, since the answer to that question must affect the answers given to the other two.

The traditional empiricist view of a social practice is strongly reductionist. Talk about a social practice is regarded as no more than a shorthand way of talking about interaction between individuals. All men, it is supposed, share a common human nature, man outside society being in himself no different from man in society. Given his nature, how a man acts depends only on the circumstances in which he finds himself. He will behave differently in the presence of other men; but only because, although he himself has remained the same, his circumstances have changed. Order may result from interaction between men; but, if so, only as the unintended consequence of the behaviour of individuals acting independently and without insight into the social consequence of their behaviour. For example, the price at which goods are bought and sold in the market is the unintended consequence of the actions of many buyers and sellers acting independently in their own interest. The social is reduced to the psycho-logical; and a social practice is no more than a logical construction out of the behaviour of the persons who are its practitioners. A practice of teaching, for example, is no more than the sum of the interactions between a loosely defined collection of individual teachers and their pupils, including any unintended consequences of their actions, for example un-intended learning.

Although a view of this sort may be adequate for an understanding of the social behaviour of at least some animals, it is inadequate for an under-standing of a social practice such as teaching. Persons are not contingently but necessarily social; and neither they nor their behaviour can be under-stood in abstraction from their social situation. Their relation to that situ-ation is internal, since what they are, as well as how they are situated, is determined by it. Teachers behave as they do, on this view, not only because of their own individual natures and understanding of their parti-cular situations but also because of their understanding of themselves as teachers in a social practice of teaching.

Social practices are themselves carried on only within the broader context provided by a society; and it is persons who provide societies with their members as well as social practices with their practitioners. The relation between a society and its members, and between a social practice and its practitioners, is internal, each depending on the other for being what it is. Although there are differences, and the individual is not in any straightforward sense a mirror of the social, our understanding of the one should inform our understanding of the other. It is necessary, therefore, to look at the concept of a person as well as that of a social practice and to try to understand the relation between them, since each must be understood in terms of the other.

Persons

Although persons cannot be identified with their bodies, they do have bodies; thus they can be identified as persons, and as the particular person they are, through their bodies. By contrast, social practices themselves do not have bodies and so can be identified only indirectly through the behaviour of the persons who are their practitioners.

Persons are also animals, although not merely animals; and the behaviour of animals is directed towards their survival as the kind of animal they are. The behaviour of most animals, however, is the result of evolution rather than reflection. They behave as they do not from knowledge but simply from a disposition to do so in response to the stimuli acting on them. Although their directed behaviour appears orderly to a third party, therefore, the animal itself has no insight into that order or the ends served by its behaviour.

In addition to the biological dimension which they share with other animals, persons possess a psychological dimension. Whereas the behaviour of animals is directed, the behaviour of persons is purposive. Directed and purposive behaviour are similar in allowing goals to be achieved through the changes which they bring about; but they are also importantly different. Whereas directed behaviour is simply a response to a stimulus presented by the environment, purposive behaviour is guided by beliefs and directed by intentions; and beliefs in turn are acquired through perception. Perception itself depends not only on the possession of the necessary sense receptors but also on the possession of an appropriate conceptual scheme.

Two related aspects of a conceptual scheme can be distinguished. First, it provides its possessors with a system of classification, or way of seeing, allowing them to see things and their properties as those things with those properties, and so making it possible for them to form beliefs about what they are and how they change. For example, it allows them to see a black cat as a black cat and, in doing so, to form the belief that the black cat which is now sitting on the armchair might move to the airing cupboard. Second, it provides them with a spatio-temporal point of view from which to see things. In seeing things from that point of view, persons make use of a unitary spatio-temporal framework which takes the person's own subjective location in space and time as its point of reference. Thus persons locate themselves in space and time relative to the things they are perceptually aware of at that place at that time, and locate other things relative to themselves. Consequently what they see from that point of view changes as they move about and as time passes, allowing them to see, for example, the black cat first as here (that is, where I am now) and later as there (that is, at some distance from where I am now), as I or the black cat move about. It also allows them not only to form internally tensed beliefs about what is now the case but also to acquire memories about what was and expectations about what will be the case earlier or later than now; for example, about where the black cat was or will be, again relative to the person's own position in time, that is, now. The primary function of such beliefs is to guide behaviour, of which they form an integral part, by providing information about how things are and how they might be changed; and since they relate not only to the present but also to the past and future, they give purposive behaviour an intrinsic temporal dimension which directed behaviour does not have. Persons, then, possess a way of seeing things and a spatio-temporal point of view from which to see them; and cannot but see their lives from that point of view.

Persons also form intentions which give direction to their behaviour, making use of the same system of classification which allows them to form beliefs. Intentions are like beliefs in having a content which is structured by the way of seeing which a conceptual scheme provides. Persons can form intentions, therefore, only insofar as that way of seeing allows them to do so. Intentions differ from beliefs, however, in that whereas the primary function of beliefs is to guide behaviour, that of intentions is to provide it with direction, making it possible for persons to bring about changes which are both foreseen and thought desirable. For example, my belief that the black cat is sitting on the armchair might well lead me to form the intention of removing it so that I can sit on the armchair myself. Since intentions are intentions to bring about changes in the future, they make use of the same spatio-temporal point of view as beliefs and, like beliefs, are internally tensed.

At any one time persons have sets of short-term, transitory beliefs about their own immediate situation which are constantly modified as changes in that situation are monitored through perception. They also have many other beliefs, including beliefs about how things are at other times and places, and general beliefs about the kinds of things there are in the world and the way in which they change. The totality of their beliefs thus provides them with a picture of an orderly world in which change takes place in a predictable way, and which constitutes a more or less stable background for their changing experience and short-term beliefs. They think of their immediate situation as no more than a small part of a world which is extended in space and time beyond their present experience of it. Thus the belief that the black cat is sitting on the armchair is part of a changing web of belief and can be thought of as having a separate, independent existence only with great artificiality.

Similarly at any one time persons have short-term intentions — changes which they would like to bring about in their immediate situation — which themselves change as circumstances change, both through their own action and fortuitously. They may, for example, decide to feed the cat when it is hungry. They also have more general projects which give direction to their behaviour over longer periods and which are themselves organized in a more or less orderly hierarchy. For example, feeding the cat is part of the project of keeping a family pet, which in turn has its place in the pattern of family life. Short-term intentions tend to form part of more general, longer-term purposes which give them significance or point. Persons have a sense, therefore, of both where they have come from and where they are going; and their behaviour on any particular occasion owes its direction as much to that as to their view of what is required by their immediate situation. In being persons, they live lives which have an internal unity over time which depends on the unity of their beliefs and purposes. They are temporally extended in a way in which physical objects, which merely continue to exist for a period of time, are not; they may be said to possess histories, whereas other animals have only life spans and physical objects have only pasts. Insofar as they are the result of their own actions, the succession of events which constitute a person's history will take place in accordance with the internal unity of their lives, although their lives may be affected by events over which they have no control.

In being aware of the beliefs and purposes which give unity to their lives, persons have a sense of their own identity through time; and the way in which they give shape to their lives through their actions depends very much on their sense of who they are. Their perception of themselves changes as their lives progress, since they see their lives from the constantly changing perspective which a spatio-temporal point of view provides. At any particular time, therefore, they necessarily see their lives from the position in them at which they have arrived at that time, that is, now.

Thus the behaviour of persons is guided by beliefs, both particular and general, and given direction by intentions and purposes. The acquisition of beliefs is made possible by the possession of a way of seeing and a spatio-temporal point of view from which to see things. The formation of intentions and purposes is similarly made possible by the possession of the same way of seeing, now functioning as a way of doing, and by the foresight which a temporal perspective provides. The possession of a conceptual scheme thus allows persons to form systems of beliefs which provide them with a unified picture of an orderly world, and to form hierarchies of purposes which give shape and meaning to their lives.

The system of classification which a conceptual scheme provides allows things to be seen not only as physical objects and animals but also as persons; and the behaviour of persons must be understood as a function of their beliefs and purposes, as described above. Moreover, persons may see themselves and others not simply as persons, but as persons of one kind or another, from whom a certain kind of behaviour is expected or required. For example, they may see themselves as teachers, and others as pupils, in a social practice of teaching; and in doing so not only form beliefs but also set the pattern for their interactive behaviour.

The behaviour of persons who see others as persons is guided, like all behaviour, by their beliefs, including their beliefs about the beliefs and intentions of others. Those beliefs may include beliefs about the other's beliefs about their own beliefs, beliefs about the other's beliefs about their beliefs about the other's beliefs about their own, and so on. For example, suppose Jill thinks that it is raining. Then Jack, seeing both Jill and the rain, may think that Jill thinks that it is raining. He may also think that Jill thinks that he thinks that she thinks that it is raining; and perhaps be aware that she is aware that that is what he thinks. Moreover, what is true of Jack's thoughts about Jill is likely to be equally true of Jill's thoughts about Jack. If so, each would be aware of the other's awareness of their awareness of the other's awareness of them. They would, therefore, be related to each other by what may be termed reciprocal self-awareness. Descriptions of such relations soon become difficult to follow; nevertheless, persons characteristically operate with beliefs which have this sort of complexity. Since behaviour is guided by beliefs, the behaviour of persons towards each other is affected accordingly. Moreover, a person's beliefs are likely to include beliefs not only about the beliefs of others but also about their intentions and purposes and, conversely, beliefs about the other's beliefs about their own intentions and purposes. These further beliefs will not only be used to guide behaviour, but will also modify the intentions which give it direction. A child's perception of her teacher's perception of her as clever or stupid, for example, is going to affect her behaviour and progress. Similarly the teacher's perception of the child's perception of his perception of her will affect his behaviour towards her, especially if her perception is mistaken; if, for example, he thinks she thinks he thinks she is stupid, whereas in fact he knows that he thinks she is clever. It will be argued in the next section that it is because persons can be related by reciprocal self-awareness that they can become practitioners in social practices.

Social Practices

As stated above, the aim of this chapter is to provide an account of the idea of a social practice as such, since any account of teaching as a social practice must rely, if only implicitly, on such an account. The view taken in the first part was that the relation between a social practice and the persons who are its practitioners is internal, each depending on the other for being what it is. It was considered necessary, therefore, to look at the concept of a person to understand why it is possible for persons to engage in social practices and, conversely, how a social practice reflects the character of its practitioners. Since social practices are carried on only within the broader context provided by a society, the relation between a social practice and the society of which it is a part also needs to be considered.

Whereas persons have bodies, social practices do not. They can be identified only indirectly through the behaviour of their practitioners. The relation of practitioner to social practice is that of part to whole. The idea of a whole in the relevant sense is that of something which possesses a kind of completeness which its parts lack; and the idea of a part is that of something which makes a contribution to the completeness of the whole of which it is a part. Things do not become parts in this sense simply because something is divided according to some external principle. A slice of bread is not a part of a loaf, for example, whereas a carburettor is a part of a car. Parts can be seen as parts only in the light of an understanding of their contribution to the completeness of the whole of which they are a part. Similarly wholes can be seen as wholes only in the light of an understanding of their dependence, for their completeness, on their parts. It follows that the direction of understanding is both from whole to part and from part to whole. It is not possible, for example, to know what a carburettor is without knowing what a car is; nor is it possible to understand what a teacher is without understanding the social practice of teaching to which he or she belongs.

A distinction was made earlier between behaviour which is guided by external stimuli and purposive behaviour which is guided by thought. Directed behaviour can lead to the formation of social groups because animals respond to stimuli provided not only by the environment but also by other members of their own species; and biologists commonly refer to the behaviour which results as social. Just as the behaviour of individual animals is directed towards their own survival, so too interaction between animals may lead to the formation and survival of groups of animals. A good example is that of insects such as ants which live in large, stable groups of apparently altruistic individuals, each acting in ways which contribute to the survival of the group. They behave as they do, however, not because they have any insight into the end served by their behaviour — the survival of the group — but because they have evolved to behave in that way in response to stimuli, for example distinctive pheromones, provided by other ants. They cannot be said to act for the sake of the survival of the group, therefore, since they have no conception of it, even though their behaviour is directed towards it.

A conceptualization of social behaviour which is adequate for ants is not equally adequate for persons. A social practice depends for its existence and identity on the overall purpose which its members share and are reciprocally aware of sharing; and it is their possession of beliefs and purposes which makes it possible for them to engage in such practices. Just as the life of a person is given unity and identity by that person's long-term purposes, so too is a social practice given unity and identity by the overall purpose which gives direction and point to the behaviour of its prac-titioners. An account of the overall purpose of a social practice of teaching would inevitably be contentious. My view is that it is to help others to become educated; and that to become educated is to learn to become a person in the society to which you belong. To do that, in turn, is to acquire the ability to take advantage of and contribute to the opportunities for life and living which that society offers, including the opportunity to take part in the various social practices carried on in it. The form which a practice of teaching took in a particular society would then depend on the detailed content given to the idea of a person in that society.

Persons can share and be aware of sharing a purpose and cooperate in pursuing it without being practitioners in a social practice. They must also be reciprocally aware of each other *as* practitioners; for example, they must see themselves and each other as and as seeing each other as teachers in a social practice of teaching. They can do so, however, only if they possess the social concepts needed to do so. Social concepts are applicable to social phenomena, just as physical concepts are applicable to physical pheno-mena; but social and physical phenomena differ fundamentally. Although we find out about physical phenomena through perception, they do not depend on our perception of them for being what they are. Social pheno-mena, on the other hand, do depend for their reality on being seen as what they are. The perceptions which bring them into existence must be shared perceptions, making use of a shared conceptual scheme; and they bring into existence a social reality which is objectively given so far as particular indi-viduals are concerned, about which they can be ignorant or mistaken. It follows that whereas physical concepts can be applied retrospectively, for example in descriptions of the world before the advent of man, social concepts cannot. For example, many of the concepts which structure social life in twentieth century Europe, such as that of a special needs teacher, played no part in the social life of the middle ages and cannot be applied to it retrospectively.

Social concepts are not simply descriptive but also normative. To be seen by others as a teacher in a social practice of teaching is not only to be seen as falling under a certain description but also as required to behave in certain ways, ways dictated in the final analysis by the overall point of the practice. There is no logical gap between what a person is in being a teacher and how he or she ought to behave as a teacher. How he or she actually behaves from time to time will depend not only on their commitment to teaching but also on their assessment of the particular circumstances, for example the situation presented by a particular class. Making use of the guidance provided by a conceptual scheme involves judgments about how the overall purpose of the practice would best be served in those circumstances. A person's ability to make good judgments and consequently their ability to formulate appropriate short-term intentions depend on the adequacy of their view of that purpose. Social rules, which may be explicitly formulated in codes of conduct, provide more specific guidance; but they cannot eliminate the need for judgment, since they need to be applied to particular situations. Good judgment in turn depends not only on an understanding of the situation but also on an understanding of the point of the rules and, therefore, of the overall purpose of the practice which they were formulated to structure. Thus an understanding of what it is to be a teacher depends on a corresponding understanding of the social practice of teaching and its overall purpose; and to see yourself as a teacher is to be committed to that purpose.

The most important thing which newcomers to a social practice need is an understanding of its overall purpose, since they cannot be committed to or guided by that purpose unless they have at least some idea of what it is. It was suggested earlier that the overall purpose of teaching is that of helping others to become educated, although what counts as becoming educated will depend on the particular practice concerned and the society to which it belongs. Once teachers understand, in general terms, what they are supposed to be doing, they are in a position to set themselves more limited and hence more manageable goals in the different situations in which they find themselves. Only when they have done that can they consider how best to achieve them, since questions about what to do are necessarily prior to questions about how to do it. Specific goals can be set for them by external authority, and rules of thumb can be provided to guide them in achieving them; but that is a poor substitute for understanding and commitment, especially in times of rapid change.

It was argued earlier that in living lives which are to some extent of their own making, persons have histories, whereas animals have only life spans and physical objects have only pasts. A person's history is the story, as they remember it, of the things they did and the things that happened to them in the past; that is, the story of how, according to their present understanding, they came to be the person they now are. Their perception of that story provides them with their present idea of who they are; and it is their sense of being themselves which allows them to make choices which they see as right for them and so dictates their future course of action. Thus a person's life has its own internal unity, which is unique to that person, and proceeds in accordance with its own internal rhythm, although it can be affected by fortuitous events, such as illness or loss of employment. Such events count as events in their life only because of the effect they have on its underlying unity and rhythm.

This aspect of the concept of a person is also mirrored in the idea of a social practice; but there are differences. Persons, like other organisms, have life spans which have their own biological character and rhythm. For example, their lives are of only limited duration and their bodies undergo progressive physiological changes as they become older; and they have to accommodate to such changes in the lives which they live. Social practices, on the other hand, are not themselves organisms, and so do not have limited life spans or bodies which undergo physiological change. They do, however, have members; and it is because their members are persons, and not simply organisms, that they have the same kind of temporal extension as persons and may be said to possess histories rather than life spans or pasts.

To understand another person is to see that person as they see themselves. It is, therefore, to see them as the product of their history and to have some insight into their hopes and fears for the future, and so to understand the pattern which they have tried to give to their lives and the frustrations and successes which they have experienced in doing so. Analogously, to understand a social practice is to see it as its practitioners see it, and so to see it as the product of its history and to have some idea of the way in which it is now changing. To do that is to have some insight into the overall purpose which provides it with direction and to have some understanding of its members' efforts to realize that purpose in the past and of their plans for doing so in the future. Their efforts and plans may be affected by external events and happenings, for example by financial stringency or changes in political climate. But such events are relevant to an understanding of a social practice and its history only insofar as they help or hinder the achievement of the fundamental purpose which provides it with its own internal unity.

As suggested above, it is a person's perception of their own history, their understanding of how they came to be what they now are, which provides them with their sense of being themselves and so puts them in a position to make decisions and choices which are right for them. They see their lives, however, from the constantly changing perspective provided by a spatio-temporal point of view and from their present position in them. Similarly it is practitioners' own perception of the history of their practice — their view of how things were done in the past — which gives content to their understanding of its overall purpose and so puts them in a position to make decisions and choices which are right for that practice. How a practice is carried on at any particular time depends on its practitioners' perception of its overall purpose at that time. The perspective from which they see that purpose constantly changes as time passes and events unfold; and it is their experience of those events which allows them to review and perhaps modify their perception of that purpose.

A social practice has a temporal dimension which is like that of an organism or person in allowing internal change while preserving identity over time; and one way of emphasizing that dimension is by introducing the notion of a tradition. A social practice may be said to be carried on in accordance with the way of seeing and doing provided by a tradition, which not only gives it structure at any particular moment but also maintains its continuity with the past and provides it with direction for the future. A tradition, therefore, makes both change and continuity possible. Change takes place in accordance with the way of proceeding which it provides; and continuity is maintained as that way of doing and the purpose which it embodies is transmitted from one generation to the next.

Traditions themselves can change. First, a tradition tells those who are guided by it not only what to do but also how to do it; and there are more or less efficient ways of doing things, for example of teaching arithmetic. In what Popper calls a closed society there is no understanding that things could be done differently. In an open society people are aware that they could do things differently if they chose to do so and may look for more efficient ways of doing them. The introduction of new skills and techniques may also lead to an expanded conception of what is possible and to different things being done. For example, the introduction of computers into schools may not only allow the same topics in mathematics to be taught more efficiently but also lead to the introduction of new topics. Second, reflection on their experience of taking part in a social practice such as teaching may lead its practitioners to change their conception of its overall purpose. Reflection may lead to fundamental change, even though the material for reflection is provided from within the practice. Third, external events may lead practitioners to change their view of the overall purpose of their practice. For example, restrictions in funding may make it increasingly difficult for teachers to maintain standards; and their perception of the public attitudes which lead to those restrictions may lead them to change their conception of what they are doing, for example from providing a good education for their pupils to providing a skilled workforce for industry.

Finally, something must be said about the relation between a social practice and the broader community to which it belongs. The idea of a social practice, such as the practice of teaching, medicine or law enforcement, is the idea of a part of a larger whole, the community to which it belongs; whereas the idea of a community is the idea of something which is complete in itself and, therefore, able to offer the possibility of a complete life for the persons who are its members. From the point of view of the community, the purpose of a social practice is to make its own special contribution to that way of life. The community could be expected to take an interest in the nature of that contribution and in the efficiency with which it was made. In the long run, therefore, a community could be expected to end up with the kind of education which it wanted, even if that meant that teachers had to change their conception of what they were doing.

Theory of Education

Social practices can be divided into those which are theoretical in being concerned with the acquisition of knowledge, such as physics and biology, and those which are practical in being concerned with bringing about change, such as engineering and agriculture. How a practice is classified depends not so much on what but on why it is done; that is, on its overall purpose. Indeed, many practices are both theoretical and practical, since knowledge may be sought both for its own sake and for the sake of the use to which it can be put, as in the exploration of space.

Whether a practice is practical or theoretical, as defined above, its practitioners need to know how to achieve its purposes; and what they need to know may be called the theory of that practice. The overall purpose of teaching is that of helping others to become educated; teaching, therefore, is a practical activity. Things can be changed, however, only by those who know how to change them, just as knowledge can be acquired only by those who know how to acquire it. Teachers need to know how to help others how to become educated; and what they need to know in order to do so is called theory of education. In their day-to-day practice teachers rely on tradition to provide them with the necessary knowledge and skills. Traditions, however, were divided earlier into those which, in being critical or open, make provision for reflection on existing practice, and those which, in being conservative or closed, do not; and insofar as teaching is carried on in accordance with a critical tradition there will be scope for teachers to reflect on their knowledge of how they do things.

The behaviour of persons, in being purposive, is guided by beliefs; and beliefs may be true or false. Behaviour is unlikely to be successful if based on beliefs which are false. If it is to be rational, efforts must be made to see that the beliefs on which it is based are well founded, making it appropriate to speak of knowledge rather than simply of belief; and such efforts will be made in a practice guided by a critical tradition. The knowledge concerned can be divided into knowledge of the present situation and knowledge of how that situation might be changed.

It was argued earlier that a practice, like a person, has a history rather than simply a past; and that its present situation can be understood only as a product of its history. The first sort of knowledge on which change must be based, then, is historical. However, it differs from history as ordinarily understood in that it is concerned with the present rather than the past. Knowledge of the present is in some ways easier to acquire than knowledge of the past, since the present is still available to be observed directly, whereas the past is not. In other ways, however, it is more difficult to acquire. The past is, so to speak, spilt milk; and while it may be regretted, it cannot be changed. The present, on the other hand, is the locus of change and the time at which plans for the future must be made if they are to be made at all. Consequently it is more difficult for enquiry into the present to possess the disinterested objectivity required for knowledge, especially when carried on from within a practice by those who are deeply committed to its purpose. It is not surprising, therefore, that educational research often combines an account of the facts with recommendations for change. But the facts do not speak for themselves; and they provide grounds for change only if it can be shown that they are not inconsistent with the purpose of education or with more general social values such as equality of opportunity.

A practice must also make use of knowledge of how things can be changed. In the case of a conservative tradition, uncritical use is made of knowledge which has been passed down unchanged from one generation to the next. For example, children may be taught in the way in which they have always been, and with more or less the same degree of success and failure. A deeper understanding of how things can be changed, however, may allow things to be done more easily or with greater success. A practice which is carried on in accordance with a critical tradition may seek to acquire such an understanding and to put it to practical use. Thus medicine looks to biology for a fuller understanding of how the body works in order to improve its practice and may, therefore, be said to possess a technology. It cannot be taken for granted that every practice is, or indeed could be, guided by a technology; and the central question which the theory of education raises is whether teaching could do so. Medicine is concerned with persons' bodies, and it is indisputable that there can be a science of body. Teaching, on the other hand, is concerned with persons themselves; and it is contentious whether there could be a science of persons analogous to the science of their bodies. It is similarly contentious whether there could be a technology of teaching which put such a science to practical use.

Disagreement about whether there is or could be a science of man stems not so much from disagreement about the nature of science as from disagreement about the nature of man. It would be wrong to dismiss claims made for the social sciences, including sociology and psychology, without examining them in detail. Nevertheless, the line of argument presented above suggests that the relevant knowledge — knowledge of how to interact with other people — is already available; and that it is acquired through ordinary experience of living and interacting with other people.

Conclusion

A satisfactory account of teaching as a social practice must begin with an account of a social practice as such, and only then go on to say what makes a practice a practice of teaching. Consequently this chapter has concentrated on what different kinds of social practice have in common rather than on how they differ. It has been argued that in general the difference between one kind of practice and another depends on the difference in their overall purposes; and that the overall purpose of teaching is to help others to become educated. I have not tried to give an account of what it is to become educated, although I have suggested that it is to learn to be a person. If that is so, then particular teaching practices will differ in the content given to the idea of a person by the society to which they belong; and if that changes, so too, eventually, will they. For example, in a materialistic society persons will be seen primarily as consumers and producers of wealth; and the overall purpose of teaching will be to produce such persons.

Chapter 2

Managerialism and Morality: The Corporate and the Republican School

Fred Inglis

It has not been part of the manners of educational theory to consider its relation to tyranny, and in the present climate of local financial management and curricular guidelines, to ask what is the state of the nation is to sound veeringly anachronistic. Darksuited professors and inspectors of education stir uneasily at the distant echo of 1968, the faint sound of running feet in the corridor and shouting outside, 'Ils pensent, donc je suis', 'La lutte continue'.

The struggle certainly continues, as teachers who have been stripped of working rights, instructed in what to teach, supplanted by the untrained, treated with open contempt by their own Secretary of State, and vilified and lied about by the most disgusting daily press in the world may certainly testify. When these amiable activities have gone along with the arbitrary amputation of their study time, whether for their pupils, their own academic advance, or for the sake of culture herself, then it is hard to tell the difference between the self-contradictory madnesses of catch-22, so prominent a structural feature of all modern bureaucracies, and the arrogance and insolence which come naturally to unassailable power. The intellectual and organizational level of the antagonism is measured by the fatuously detailed specifications of working lives which simply cannot be counted like that. (If I eat my sandwiches during the departmental meeting, shall I put it down as half of one of my 1265 hours?) The taste of it all rose sourly in one's gorge at a report in *The Times* in 1987 which quoted the Secretary of State (verbatim) as saying, 'Teachers are doing the best they can in difficult circumstances.' He smiled ironically. 'I believe that's the phrase, isn't it? Have you got that down?'

Neither educational theory nor professional training, neither much given to reflexivity, has had advice to give about these little difficulties. Indeed, glancing down the titles of contributions to administrative primers, at the list of in-service courses in local authority offices or university Schools of Education, the regulative terminology repeats the vocabulary of contemporary oppression, the inscription of the omnipresent techniques of surveillance and incarceration upon the harmless lives of classrooms, libraries, playing fields, school outings, camp. The currency of accountability, bureaucratic rationality, professionality can only be cashed at state banks. It is simply not convertible into what one innocently thinks of as the real values of education.

These brutal contradictions are a central part of the practical knowing and professional making of teachers. It is then the preoccupation of what is dignified in the literature as reflexivity to create ways of circumventing or cheating the contradictions and blockages imposed by the obduracies of power.

This is not mere name-calling. The state of all the advanced industrial nations (as they say) is in similar case. Offe argues that their twin, constituent institutions of production and welfare unstoppably diverge in their momentum.[1] The economic mechanism, notoriously unstable and uncontrollable whether in slump or boom, is driven by the standard criteria of cost-benefit, mass production and economies of scale, highly specific divisions of labour, the intensive allocations of capital and the commensurate reduction of those employed to a minimum. The concept which has been so effectively popularized over the past century that to study its historical formation and seek to unclasp its authority seems like flying in the face of nature herself, is *efficiency*. The system of organization by which efficiency itself is allocated and paced is *managerialism*.

Among the welfare and cultural institutions we obviously count education and the huge scope of its colonies from libraries to novelists, wordprocessors to school meals. At the same time, it is not surprising, given the power of the finance corporations, that they are looked to by all governments, but particularly those of the Right which have been enjoying their temporary season of power these recent years, to provide the planning forms as well as the ideological contents and meanings of all the rest of society, including culture and welfare. Offe, Habermas, James O'Conner[2] and common sense unite in contending that corporate models for culture and welfare are not merely procrustean nor simply irrelevant, but, colliding inevitably with the quite contrary motion and direction of those institutions, they make their difficulties and disorganization much worse. The adjacent but conflicting realms of economics and politics cross violently with each other, and cannot be reconciled. Whether liberal capitalism or market society can possibly resolve the clash of profit maximization with the necessities of human attention has been a question fought out in entirely literal bloodiness at each of this century's political revolutions.

It can hardly be answered here. Either you take the Fabian view, argued for in his civilized economics by Albert Hirschmann, that political economy is always a muddle,[3] and you sort it out as best you can; or you follow Offe and company and say it is structurally at odds with itself, and cannot ever sort this out. Either way, we live with a mess, and in the broad, visible but entirely subaltern realm of education, we have little choice but to make, in the short run, practical knowledge out of the engagement of theory with experience. These historical exigencies and our own nerve will make it possible to stand up for human ends and values as well as make sufficient accommodation with the unignorable demands of power; or they will not.

> What if the Church and the State
> Are the mob that howls at the door?
> Wine shall run thick to the end,
> Bread taste sour.[4]

Paying-on-both-sides is a baleful business, but teachers have lived with it for a long time, and in that time they have come a long way. It is a laborious point to make, but teachers in Britain now are better paid, more widely respected, more publicly visible and influential and, therefore, more completely an independent and self-made estate of the polity than ever before.

Take the simplest index, their pay: the headteacher of a sizeable primary school or the deputy head of a big secondary school are now paid more than most university lecturers, hospital administrators, middle management in coal mines and principal officers in the DHSS. At the same time, schoolteaching is now a fully graduate profession, a distinction still shared by only a smallish bunch of the city-suited élite and in class- and status-touchy Britain, a convincing mark of respectability to all issuers of credits and debits, moral and financial. The presence of Schools of Education with their powers of degree conferral and research chequebooks in most universities, however much they are doubtless condescended to in the groves of academic snobbery, is a further measure of privilege and power. Teachers have ranks of journals, national newspapers, holidays in France and fairly new cars. They are even, whatever they pretend to others, held in some honour by the parents who come so meekly to be told at parents' evenings by overworked departmental heads (not always sure what the child looks like) how their pride and joy is getting on towards attainment at 7, 11 and 14.

This last is probably the mark of their standing which teachers them-selves, in my experience, most dispute. It is, in the light of my ensuing argument, worth a detour. It is true that the yellow *Sun* debauches the good name of teachers when malignancy moves it, and during the programme of strike action in 1986–87, public opinion, so far as one may ever generalize about that protean monster, was most likely divided in its pub judgments on teachers. At the same time, parents could often be heard to say how staunchly they stood by the teachers of their own children, and certainly they turn to the teachers first and readily for their counsel on their children's careers, their conduct, their very safety.

This apparent discrepancy matches much that seems inconsistent in public attitudes and states of mind, discrepancies which opinion polling, necessarily conducted in the abstract, can rarely spot. On the one hand, people endorse the broad sweep of social relations and the commonsense view of their order. In doing so, they ratify the dominant slogans, proverbs and *bien-pensant* opinions of the day. This is the pollster's fodder. On the other hand, they (we) have no trouble in dwindling to the strictly situated diminuendo of their own lives when they abruptly must. 'I don't like *them* striking, but in *my* strike, see, we got a legitimate grievance.' The logic of the particular always comes out on top in any ideological contradiction. This is not to say that this logic is synonymous with self-interest: the doomed and gallant British miners' strike of 1984–85 is an instance of parti-cular logic and local knowledge lending extraordinary endurance to thousands of men in the teeth of their own wisdom. Instead we might think of people stretched taut as we all are between the large political canopy above our heads and the domestic arrangements whose loved and hated, ponderous weights tie us to our particular piece of ground. We argue for each according to the immediate demands of expediency and obligation. Power has a way with it, no doubt, but not all its own way.

This brief sally into the athletics of political consciousness has its exact enough bearing on the making of utopia in schools. For now, perhaps, it will do to vindicate my claim about the public estimation of teachers where the public is also parental at the time. It also returns me to my buoyant view of teacher progress with its eighty years of steady settlement since the celebrated 1902 Act, years in which teachers have come to the modest fulfil-ment and power of a class position on the topmost rim of the *petit bourge-oisie*. Such a point of advantage has given many of them a chance for pro-motion into the intelligentsia (purportedly hard to classify) and with the leisure, cultivation, self-awareness and social space to mark themselves decisively off as not to be trifled with, having minds of their own and a decided taste for telling others where they get off.

This is half the social formation of teachers. The other half is less sure of itself and much less obviously entitled to its seats in the Third Estate of the polity. In a rather compressed and brutal version of its shortcomings, David Hargreaves characterized schoolteachers as, rather too often, boring, exhausted and loathing their job.[5] Picking up Willard Wooller's overlooked and interesting speculations about the structures of action which shape professional style and its *being*, Hargreaves roundly claims that teachers talk too much, too loudly, too uncontradictably, that the terms of their work drive them, conscience stricken, to longer and longer, more enervating and unrestorative hours, that the meanness and narrowness of so much of their duties — collecting the dinner money, forbidding denim trousers and green hair, keeping pedestrian traffic in the school on the left of the corridors — that all this makes them, rightly and understandably, hate the job.

Well, nobody would turn on Hargreaves and accuse him of failing to stand up for teachers in our time: for twenty-five years he has spoken out on behalf of the quality of mercy and the creation of richer and more comradely relations in schools, some of them, in Ardwick and Tower Hamlets, the grimmest in unregenerate old England. But it may be objected, while taking the force of his comic cartoon, that not only *teachers* as an occupational group are bores, that Monty Python made the same point very vigorously about chartered accountants, and that many people may absolutely detest their job.

The difficulty with teachers as a class is to be found, as in all class analysis, by study of their structural location and the specific details of their historical formation. It is curious that a highly self-aware, even at times self-pitying, class fraction has not yet produced its own, full-blown history — *The Making of the English Teaching Class* as it were. The radical critique thrown up by 1968 — Grace, Willis, Giroux, Sharp and Green and the Birmingham Centre — spent so many years simply *blaming* teachers for fooling themselves that they were doing children-as-individuals any good at all, and calling them to phantom colours struck on a barricade at the far end of the playground. We could do with a history, doubtless versed in the theory of provisional subjectivities and the doubtfulness of class agency as *ever* to be spotted at effective work in social change,[6] which treated the formation of teachers with the inwardness and strength of sympathy demanded by any great work of history. Such a book would need to be less a theory than a world.

It would acknowledge, certainly, the unavoidably subaltern position of teachers, obliged by duty as well as by location in social structure, to prime the engines of social reproduction. The missing book would pick its way between the equal dangers of overdoing structural determinism and of overdoing voluntarism, allowing on the one hand that education as a social institution is inherently conservative and defined by function as an apparatus of the state, doubtless ideological as well as functional, and therefore bound to do all it can to ensure the docile stability of that state as the hungry generations pass through it. To say all this does not cast teachers as the stupefied lackeys of old corruption except (as we shall see) insofar as some of them not only acquiesce in lackeydom, but readily lend themselves to the dreadful procedures of toadying, self-seeking hypocrisy, and the suppression of an upright, critical minded manliness and womanliness which the state now asks of its civil, obedient servants. On the other hand, this great, imaginary work of somebody's historical imagination would precisely indicate what teachers could and did by way of the will: would take the measure of their voluntary contribution to the liberal values they are hired to uphold.

Either way, our history would deal faithfully with the experience and transformation of the children of one class fraction, the skilled artisans of the now moribund smokestack and heavy assembly-line industries, into the adults of a new class fraction, 400,000 members of the comprehensive school (primary and secondary) staffs.

Since the people's war and the 1944 Education Act provided both structural opportunity and ideological climate in which a moment of popular liberalism and democratization could flourish, schoolteaching has been the avenue of, as they say, upward mobility. It has promoted the coming-to-self-awareness and a true and sound emancipation, on the part of the children of the English, Scottish and (above all) Welsh skilled working classes.

Those children were, as children will be, very varied. The daughters went into primary schools where the few sons who joined them became the head; their sons went into secondary schools. In order to get there, they had to stick at education itself, being good, smiling back at those teachers who smiled at them, passing exams and doing homework assiduously when the homes in question were crowded and noisy and sometimes poor, needing the wages the children were not earning, but which their friends who came to the door and clattered off down the street were bringing home to Mum as well as spending on themselves, on suits and frocks and bikes and hair-do's.

According to their several lights and the traditions of their family, their college or their nation, when these children became young teachers, and then heads of departments, headteachers, advisers, deputy chief education officers, they did as they were told or they stood up for less compliant virtues. Some of them took seriously the great names of the liberal tradition which are the professed master symbols of British society: freedom, justice, equality. At times they added to them such excellent values of the home-grown Labour movement as solidarity, mutuality, bloody-mindedness. Others fell into the way of a quieter, more obliging life. They did their best for children and, as it happened, for themselves, by urging on pupils the old English and far from deplorable character traits of obedience, somnambulism, amiability, peacefulness, credulity.

That is the synopsis of our history. Nor am I speaking as the judicious objectivist of the social scientific observatory. Schoolteachers are my friends and forebears, my colleagues and successors. I am trying to speak to and for them, and to do so in an idiom capable of breaking through the horrible condescensions and oleaginous bullying with which education as an academic and administrative discourse has ingratiated itself with its superiors and taught the expediencies of accommodation to its pupils.

As I noted, it can hardly be a surprise whether to Marxist (if there are any left) or to Weberian (which we have all become for want of anything more plausible), that the welfare industries are subjugated to the productive forms and to the ideological contents of the giant corporations. I also pointed out, in Offe's company, that the tendencies and meanings of production and welfare radically diverge, and that they do so in a peculiarly headlong way where, as now, so much of the systems of production is dedicated to the wholesale and remunerative manufacture of world destruction, whether by anthrax, thermonuclear fission, or the trusty old bullet.[7] But a little thing like that persuades nobody of the unsuitability of teaching the lessons of the giant corporations to the guardians of liberal values in schools, in hospitals and in the offices of what are so compellingly called supplementary benefits.

'For much is lost between Broceliande and Camelot.' In 1965 when Tony Crosland, then Minister, sent out his famous circular asking for all local authorities to submit their plans for going comprehensive with all despatch, it seemed as though the steady advance of British education towards a confident, settled, even generous future was assured. There would be rows, of course, but between the vision of a just and creative education system and the actualities of, say, Leicestershire's and Cambridgeshire's community colleges, the gap seemed not at all wide, and available to the whole nation.

Fred Inglis

A rough beast was slouching, however, at that very time towards the House of Commons. For ten years it has done its considerable bit towards the destruction of that on the whole noble vision and its stirring, collaborative creation, the comprehensive school. It had always been sitting around, the beast, biding its time, for British political culture is a very mixed creature, and carries an odd bag of political values. Its progeny in this case came to power by declaring themselves on the side of a strong dose of small business economics and a brisk transforming of the dusty, shabby old incompetents muddling along in welfare and education into eager young representatives of business ideology.

The sociological cables were already in place for such metamorphosis. Given my potted history of the teacher's formation, the way forward was by their acquiring the credentials of a profession. Better salaries, degrees, control of working conditions, mortgages, house journals: these were the indices of status and influence. Unions, rule-books, collective voting, routinization of hours, wage labour: these were the signs of class they had battled to put behind them. Offered the desk and office space, the three-piece suits of management, more than enough of the teaching profession, as it gladly called itself, came enthusiastically forward. For managerialism has become the dominant ideology, and therefore the source of legitimation, for all the most powerful institutions of Western society. This much is truistic. The corporate and state bureaucracies alike fill the moral vacuum which liberalism requires them to leave at the centre of social activity for individual rights and freedoms, with the classically managerial criteria already listed: efficiency, productivity, cost-effectiveness, value-freedom and scientific rationality.

Managerialism, no doubt, may mean many things. In this chapter I shall simply dodge what Herbert Hart called 'the definitional stop' and take managerialism to mean whatever its conventional use purports or refers to in the varieties of administrative experience, in or out of the state, and in those countries generically referred to as the Western democracies.

Democracy, indeed, is part of my theme, at least insofar as it prefigures the forms of contemporary freedom. For my argument, in decidedly Foucauldian strain,[8] will be that in managerialism we have the latest and most successful systematizing of the 'carceral' society; that it contains and organizes to its own deadly end most of the alleged freedoms of liberal (or even possessive) individualism, removing the freedoms, as Foucault tells us, without the agents even noticing. The argument will further be that managerialism simply is the latest thing in the protean discourses of power, that it conceals the will to power by appeals to the fulfilment of purely technical imperatives (now the main legitimating ethos of politics), but that its inhuman, because structural, necessity is mere subjugation of its officers and its objects.

Moreover, my argument has the temerity to ignore Foucault's serene determinism, and, following Taylor's criticisms of Foucault,[9] to suggest not only that managerialism is self-contradictory and irrational, but also that far from being beyond the reach of the old-fashioned terminology of good and evil, it may be named as cruel, wicked and oppressive. Concludingly, and in candidly voluntarist mood, I shall suggest what may be *done* about this highly temporal state of affairs, and appeal, if only glancingly, to models of self-organization which may fight off the worst effects of the managers, and return to visibility a picture of freedom as both the condition and content of a virtuous citizenry.

If this last effort comes out a bit preachy, it will nonetheless immodestly propose how to remoralize the language in which the necessary debate about administration, public decisions, business and politics themselves is conducted. The blunt point belongs to Habermas, when he writes that 'for scientific rationality not to be ideological [which naturally it *always* repudiates], there needs to be public discussion of decision-making processes . . . .'[10] Habermas' solution is less petering-out than it sounds; it is my conclusion here that managerialism only retains its power by suppressing moral-political argument.

The narrow technicality or scientism of public thought, especially in relation to the maintenance of our political institutions, has, as is claimed by theorists of very varied doctrinal and intellectual dispositions, driven itself into one specific cemetery among the dead ends always waiting for the decadence of the Enlightenment. This critique is largely ethical. It is compounded, on the one hand, out of a highly plausible scepticism about progress theory. On the other, it appears as a revisionist republicanism, which points to the excellent freedoms of Renaissance city states as having much to teach present-day voluptuaries of consumer individualism, and which, in more analytic vein, rejects the preferred precipitation of moral worth as caught either in the sincerities of momentary feeling or in the play of blame and approbation over individual action. It intends to replace these with the grander, Aristotle-derived notion of *eudaimonia*, roughly translated as 'human flourishing'. *Eudaimonia* is that achievement known only in its fulfilment at the end of a life lived according to the virtues of which the man or woman in question is capable. Any such effort to restore a taxonomy of the civic virtues to our social theory rests inevitably on thinking in which the origins of *res publica* and polis, and their defenders, the citizens, come into relief at the expense of those more familiar figures, the voter, the tax payer, or indeed, the managers and managed. Let us refer to this argument as the return of Cicero.

At the present moment and in parents' meetings in school halls, with the audience hunched up on small school chairs, Cicero's return has an unexpected relevance. For schools, as everyone knows, are now required by law to organize their own budgets around a fixed sum passed onto them from the government by way of the local authority. In many places, no doubt, the consequences of this enormous change will crudely be another vast extension of the habits of bureaucratic rationality into the harmless, cash-free lives of 10- or 14-year-olds and their custodians. It should be added that, since these are the hard, exiguous limits of the managerial frame of mind as defined by our master corporations, this is exactly how the change is being taken by the aforesaid orderlies of Teachers' Centres and Schools of Education.

Nonetheless, the small shopkeepers and ledger-minders do not have to have things all their own way. Discussion of a budget leads naturally to discussion of the aims of education and the proper ends of society. All that is needed are a few Aristotelians and Ciceronians in the company. Although they may not so think of themselves, there are plenty of teachers and not a few parents who would answer to such principles. The principles include a determination to see lives and livelihoods as both figure and ground of moral meaning, and to affirm at the same time a due sense of the civic virtues, now in bad case.

The heart of this matter is the attack on technicism, which is to say, the ideology of scientific rationality.[11] Technicism is what vindicates (or legitimates) management theory and practice. For the technicist, *poesis* — which, very roughly, we may translate from Aristotle as 'creation' — and *praxis*, which no less roughly means purposive action — are not distinguishable. All making is instrumental; action for the technicist can only be described in relation to a product, or more broadly, to bringing about a state of affairs (readily conceptualized, most particularly by managers, as a product). By these talismans, making has no 'character' of its own; it becomes a sequence of techniques. Aristotle's *tekne*, which licence might allow us to translate as 'the skilful use of craft', is for the technicist absolutely and easily describable without reference to persons. The inquisitive consciousness of our official thought-forms typically seeks the solution of problems. To think well is then to discover techniques; to act well is to solve problems. The notion of a good *life*, lived in a livelihood, is expelled, along with responsibility. Livelihood is replaced by job definition, responsibility and accountability.

Responsibility and accountability are in turn stripped of their ethical and democratic associations, and turned into functions of state surveillance. You are responsible for having this done, and accountable to a superior (not your peers) if it isn't. It is desperate at this late juncture in the history of political thought (thought about the conduct of the good society) to have to point out the meanness and grudgingness, to say nothing of the oppressive cruelty, of this view of human productiveness and creativity.

Technicism offers itself as value-free; it begets the science of management. The monstrous child of the Enlightenment is the managerialism which the grisly collusion of late monopoly capitalism and the bureaucratic state has engendered in its local or Western version. Its assumptions are so imperial and pervasive precisely because it can draw upon that totality of the intellectual origins of the modern state which it is a commonplace pun to summarize as totalitarian. Over two centuries, its political scope has been extended by means of its administrative and moral mediations to enable and ratify the surveillance and control of total populations in the name of their own contentment and welfare.

Such, of course, is the barbarous movement of a whole civilization. It needs to be said again and again that the successes of technique and technology over things and objects have led people to suppose that they can gain the same successes over human beings and subjects. Thus, once you have a problem, you can devise techniques to overcome it. Techniques generate skills. Reflection and morality are displaced to the ivory tower. Thought and wisdom disappear; expertise substitutes itself. The expert sets up the aims and objectives. The research team describes the skills and techniques which will ensure their achievement. The implementation team comes in to show people how to reach these goals. Sometimes they listen to their criticisms in order to indicate why they are irrelevant. This is called feedback. Then everyone in the scheme goes away to do as they've been told. Such and such are the sequences of the planners and the plan. Management turns out to mean persuading others with a more or less good grace to assent to ends which are systemic and unavailable to question.

These ends are what are commonly called political realities. They are real enough, but they are not inevitable, except in so much as those with power, duly and democratically come by, have decided that this is what will happen. The managers are then hired to persuade people that what is real and nasty has its own necessary momentum, and it is not just an act of coercion. The manners of power are not to pussyfoot about in the hope that people will never catch power in the act. Either they will learn to be managed into assent, or they will not see power in action at all, only the old transparency, reality, as it assembles those easily recognized hardnesses, the facts.

Naturally, not everybody will oblige by seeing things the realistic way. After all the very words should ring like a warning bell. To be managed is to be persuaded of something against your better judgment. The huge tendency of industrial society is to devise ways of organizing agreement to its prior and determinate ends, and to find space for all its members within which they may be sufficiently quiescent not to challenge those ends but to leave the system to go on producing whatever it pleases, including its own destruction. Regulative practices exfoliate from the larger motion of this machine. Counselling is largely a process reserved in state bureaucracies for those who in one way or another have been chewed up and spat out by the system, and its administrations are intended to console or otherwise sedate its victim for his or her anti-social disappointment when life hasn't quite matched up to desires. The grander motions of scientific administration ensure everyone else's complicity in the ends of a system too vast and inaccessible for question.

These are the ways to control a world in which morality and politics are set in opposition as respectively the realms of subjectivity and of reality. Your morality is defined by your deepest feelings, and is, therefore, yours and immune to reason. Politics is defined by the hard facts of reality and is immune to individual action. 'You can't do anything about it.' Either way, there is no room for rational dissent, for the living out of moral judgment, or for the decisions about significant action.

The defects of managerialism are severe and threefold: in its rationality, its ethics and its politics. In the first case, managerialism is unexaminedly utilitarian, and like all utilitarian systems, irrational and superstitious. In the second case, the historical ambiguities of its origins in the alliance of utilitarianism and liberalism mean that managerialism structurally produces in its practitioners a tendency to hypocrisy and lying. In the last case, it is impelled by its theory of power to deny resistance and establish dominance; it is cruelly oppressive, and the enemy of freedom.

Utilitarianism is offered by its advocates as the taken-for-granted way of deciding on social policy in a mass society with a high degree of statutory personal liberty. In a negotiation culture, whose most characteristic social form is the committee, utilitarianism with Bentham's celebrated calculus to hand, 'the greatest good of the greatest number', can always measure up the best-thing-to-do-on-the-whole, especially in cases of conflict.

However indispensible some such ready reckoner is, the discontents it has brought to our civilization are familiar in the smallest details of school life. Human needs and wants are not only incommensurable: to go no further, questions of distributive justice cannot be *solved* by collective choice. (Collective choice may, of course, *agree* upon them.) But the local adviser blithely portions out his budget for in-service courses according to what he believes to be the utilitarian calculus; local financial management is carved up according to the same rough-and-readiness, always allowing for the natural principle of selection such that 17-year-olds are absolutely more expensive to educate than 5-year-olds.

It is so obviously more *sensitive* to the corrugations of social life not to insist on reducing everything to the calculus, and to expect (even under conditions which enjoin ordinality in ranking) that strictly practical rules for cutting down the risks of decision-making under which alternatives are 'ranked by their worst possible outcomes' come into play; that is, 'we are to adopt the alternative the worst outcome of which is superior to the worst outcomes of others.'[12] To compress fiercely, Rawls' so-called 'maximum' principle, expressed as it is within the limits of his classical liberalism, has far greater imaginative and logical reach than utilitarian rules of thumb exactly because it links the actualities of self-interest with a non-normative account of his two principles of justice. Self-interest, even primitively defined, has to take account of both chance and equity.

Of course, managerialists may insist that they are not utilitarians when it comes to collective choices, though such insistence will hardly survive a reading of such more value-laden classics in the field as Hicks' *The Management of Organizations*, Handy's *Understanding Organizations* or the ineffable reader edited by Bennis, Benne and Chin.[13] But if they do so, they have to concede themselves an entirely different seat at the negotiations. For if one professed goal of the business of management is less the maintenance of efficiency, or the allocation of benefits, and more the achievement of satisfaction on the part of members of their constituency, then they have to abandon value-freedom and the alleged 'facilitating' element of their role and its duties, and come clean that what they are practising is politics according to the customs and ceremonies of the power élite. Managers, we may say, invariably have purposes for others' improvement — or at least for their acquiescence; but power would prefer those others to come round to agreement of their own accord without entirely noticing how much less it will suit them than the boss.

If I am right, it is at this point that charges of lying and hypocrisy may begin to stick. At the same time, it is true that public is not private morality, and that understanding the place of lying in the politics of education (or on a grander scale) is not exactly the same as naming lies for what they are in domestic life. Good may come out of lying, whatever Kant said about the risks. Indeed, it is precisely the risk which distinguishes public from private lying.[14] Public office generally entails more risk-taking. Moral character in a public officer can only be relevantly judged according to the moral features of his or her institution. Ruthlessness in public life is axiomatically related to office. A prime minister may order the destruction of Dresden. A headteacher may dismiss a pitiful drunk. Even allowing for the diminuendo, however, the moral defects of public office only excuse the private character who exploits them, to the extent that he could not do otherwise. The more power, the more independence; the more independence, the less excuse. The public officer is indeed accountable, in a morally adequate society, in that he must be able to give rational and morally adequate accounts of what he has been up to, as morally adequate representative of the constituency.

This holds for his private actions as well. That is, the Chief Adviser or the deputy head have to accept, *as public officer*, moral obligations and limits on their individual actions. The deputy head who ignores this in her small compass, like the prime minister who ignores it in her large one, is a mere tyrant. The trouble with management and its theories is that it is exactly these moral and political matters which vanish from the structure of their central concepts. Accountability and professionality extrude morality from public policy as private and subjective. Efficient killing by soldiers in Northern Ireland or the Falklands is as much a sign of their non-moral professionalism as the efficient teaching of literacy or keeping the school's assessment profiles by the teachers.

The welfare bureaucracy, however, is enjoined by its masters and its doctrine to achieve its efficiency without the use of such entirely visible weapons as the Armalite and the stun grenade. Hence the charge of structural hypocrisy. Middle management in our time tries to hold together the exercise of power in the name of productivity and cost-effectiveness, while still claiming to act on behalf of the personal realm and the cherished values of human concern, sympathy and attention. Hypocrisy is the only way of reconciling the obliging niceness of the social class hired to do this work with causing those hurts their conscientiously denigrated power requires them to inflict.

Lying as routine is the next, inevitable stage in effecting the triumph of managerialism. It follows from the requirement I named that a public officer publicly justify his policies in order to maintain his support and what is betrayingly called his credibility. As, however, the domain of the state has swollen to take in the whole of the polity, those justifications and explanations become correspondingly larger. But the larger the state institutions, the less controllable — manageable, indeed — they become. Hence, to maintain credibility the manager must lie about the success of his policies.

The momentous energy required by power to hold this contradiction together has created the image-building and public relations industry, so much more pervasive and terrible than mere advertising. The language of image-building deeply penetrates the idiom, the categorical frameworks, the explicanda and systems of explanation, and the common sense of managerialism. The concern with 'presentation' goes from the Cabinet to the board of interviewers for promotion to deputy principal. It relies on the shrivelled clichés of carrot-and-stick psychologism, on such tropes as 'damage-limitation' and 'crisis management' whose contradictory linguistic form indicates the strain they bear, and on the fatuous pretence that all problems may be algorithmically resolved or numerically balanced in terms of purported percentages. As the *faux bonhomme* chairman will put it so spuriously, 'there is a 70 per cent chance that . . .' or 'on this scenario among three, this is the worst case (or best guess) . . . .'

What is at issue is not only the incredibility of such insane speech, its bluff and philistinism, but also its demoralization. It is a language which brings out starkly Foucault's lesson that power is always inscribed in claims to truth. It is also a language in which it is impossible to speak to the virtues, a task so clearly outrageous that no managerialist in the literature even attempts it.

To say so is not to lapse into what the realists would call sentimentality. It is to say that organizational thinking, with its absolute criteria of efficiency, clarity of communication (obedience), consent, productivity, cooperation (the eradication of conflict), cost-effectiveness, accurate evaluation of performance and so forth, has no purchase on the moral conditions which I claimed earlier essentially link character and role, individual and state, in the definition of institutions. Such a way of thought can only explicitly sanction two moral values: integrity and obedience. Integrity is a pot which will hold decidedly unattractive people, and obedience is hardly a value at all in a secular democracy.

Demoralization on the scale I allege not only makes for ill-health in the polity, as witness the toadies and hoodlums in the cabinets of the West. It also makes possible the totalitarian conditions of dominance and subjugation, a threat which has darkened as it has become less noticeable since the demise of its two first-born, Fascism and Stalinism.

Finally, managerialism is cruelly oppressive. Giddens notes that the clinching last of four features of the nation state and its modernity, after its setting up of capitalist enterprise and industrialization together with its protection of these by the formalized control of violence (police and the army), is its system of surveillance.[15] And Foucault describes the steady advance of the organizational matrices whose 'petty, malicious minutiae' mark out, measure and subjugate the innumerable varieties of productive behaviour. The disciplines of normalization — psychiatry, psychology, counselling, evaluation, profiling, time and motion study and the rest — mark out the dispositions of time, space, identity and attitude by which mass society maintains its order and dictates even the very terms which we count as spontaneous and fulfilling of our own true selves.

Within the social organization specifically intended to chastise recalcitrance, to teach how to labour and when not to labour, to organize time and the body (work and play, effort and leisure), to imagine within the stern bounds of social permission ('not *those* videos but these *books*'), to regulate complicity and cooperation, within schools, that is, the march of surveillance and subjugation is by now unstoppable. There is a rout of research, working parties and steering committees within the welfare institution closest to home which is by now entirely bent on extending and deepening the scope of surveillance. In education the procedures of assessment, appraisal, evaluation, staff development, management itself and most recently and forcefully legislation, all bear witness to the grand and extravagant surveillance of ourselves and our children in ways so invasive and pervasive we think of them as normal life.

These strictures hold, perhaps never more so, even when humanitarian impulses are on show. The manager's most contemporary visage is that of confessor-advisor: 'May I suggest early retirement and all its advantages? I *think* we can let you go.' The successful exercise of his power is to persuade others to find that they want what he wants on behalf of them and of superiors too distant to be argued with: 'There's nothing anyone can do, really.'

Political action, however, is almost always ambiguous. Its central, elusive commodity is power, and power is not analyzable by the instruments of zero-sum game theory. It is protean and without controllable limits. Power may be involuntarily created and given away. Thus, where managerialism seeks to subjugate by removing moral considerations and leaving only the unbiddable facts of plain, blunt old reality, remoralization insists on popping up again, calling for the hard facts of justice or fairness or mercy, and winning back power by resistance, evasiveness or mere procrastination. All department heads know those ropes and when to pull them.

By definition, the struggles between sources of power in a liberal society are wide open, which is no doubt why illiberalism has been so irritable and impatient in Britain since 1979. The struggle continues in terms of the traditions of value and action available to different class (or other) formations. Teachers, as my respectful potted history was intended to bring out, include in their kitty of popular mythology an active story of their own worth and freedom, their being-as-good-as-anybody-else, their ground gained and lost, their solidarity. The same story coexists with its negative turn, the one which tells of being-good and doing-as-you're-told, of not-rocking-the-boat and getting-on-quietly.

There is no saying which will win. But here we come to the non-Foucauldian point at which we might break with managerialism both in our private and public lives. One way out might be with Albert Hirschmann and his politicizing of the economic theories of consumer choice at those moments at which the vociferous expression of disapproval not only replaces a silently pedestrian vote — when 'voice' in his terminology replaces 'exit' — but also when such vocalism becomes a public good and a limitlessly consumable pleasure in its own right.[16] Staying roughly within the frames of economic theory, Hirschmann at least provides a much richer model of behaviour than the flow chartists of the market research and management algebra.

But I want to suggest a rather more drastic reformation of the structures of administration in those segments of the polity which may practise with at least minimal plausibility the idea of self-government. In as much as welfare institutions in general (and schools in particular) are my point of reference, I want to suggest that these are similar enough in form, as well as having enough substance in their characterizing moral and political features and traditions to learn from the political theory of classical republicanism. If they do, they may be able to foreswear the distortions of a narrow liberalism and its myopic defence of private freedom and rights together with the oppressions of utilitarianism in its massive forms, while still hanging on to the excellent vanity of human wishes. To rejoin freedom to duty is to *re*moralize the language of political realism without any of the sillier forms of romantic and socialist optimism about the human heart.

One way of putting the republican case is to return, as I began by doing, to Aristotle. The great name of human flourishing, Aristotle's *eudaimonia*, entails a canonical form of society arrived at by men's and women's reasoning about common ends and their virtuous rationality. In certain versions of republicanism, according to Skinner's summary,[17] achievement of this state must be enforceable: we have to be forced to be free. There is a legal duty to meet civic obligations in order to maintain the free state.

The stress falls in this account on freedom, and since, let us say, the instance to hand of a miniature republic is a school where attendance is compulsory, freedom is not perhaps the first value to think of. With the republicans in mind, however, we may think less of individual agents as free, and more of institutions whose *liberta* is grounded in the way of life of a whole community, where public spirit is the guardian of both social and personal liberty, and in which the *content* of freedom is the common endeavour for civic glory and prosperity.

Machiavelli's *Discorsi* on Livy's history is the classic text for these ruminations. At first glance his version of liberty and the free state is incomprehensible to contractarians in the liberal mould like ourselves. There is no place for what in cheery mood we call individual choice and what in harsher tones we refer to as egoism. But it is omitted not because Machiavelli is cheery — no political theorist of the present comes near him for the darkness of his view of human beings — but because egoism for him is the destroyer of liberty, not its risky and omnipresent embodiment. Corruption in human beings is the drive to egoism which destroys their own liberty; the only thing to do with it is legislate forcefully against it, so that human beings will not undermine liberty for themselves.

Any attempt to restore such a view of egoism in the world of the Western states and their rampant consumerism will founder anachronistically. The idea at this date of the city-state of school or college pursuing a glory expressive of its own freedom would stretch even the flashy new performance indicator systems a bit far. But it is not too far-fetched to say that the free state of a school seeks always, as milieu or culture rather than as productive mechanism, to live the great epistemes of freedom, self-criticism and the common good, so complexly carried in mutuality, welfare (indeed) and justice.

On one republican account of the conditions for the fulfilment of human beings, such fulfilment is only possible if citizens pursue those determinate ends which exercise the capacities and attain the goals which make us free. This is Berlin's 'positive' concept of freedom to perform freely. Obviously, educational establishments have a decided account of such ends and seek to coerce their members to pursue them in the name of fulfilment of potential, according to which the truly free man or woman is virtuous. By these lights, the institutional forms and their culture which we need will be those in which freedom to be the fully human creatures we are capable of being is realized. To achieve this, we may well need to be coerced into a life of liberty we will otherwise allow to lapse into a life of slavery. ('Turn off the television, now.')

The true republic is *self*-governing, and goes to great trouble to prevent any one faction getting its own way to the detriment of the common good. All the same, teachers in the liberal tradition are likely to be nervous about the idea of coercion of ourselves, even by ourselves. The point to grasp is that, while cultivating the civic virtues or public-spiritedness, we still insist that these are no less precisely the grounds of free *personal* liberty or 'negative freedom'. To do so, we must have the courage to defend our free state (against, let us say, the grander state itself) and have the necessary prudence, judgment and other civic attributes to govern, and to prevent others governing us. Once more the 'corruption' of egoism which makes us indolent or servile or expedient constitutes an irrational failure to see that its indulgence can only damage our very own freedom. That freedom turns on our public-spiritedness. We must, therefore, be coerced to exercise it (as, in a homely example, Australians are required by law to vote). Compelled by law to uphold freedom on the part of all, our private freedoms are thereby upheld in the only *free* way they can be. Personal liberty is necessarily linked to the virtue of public spiritedness, but quite without necessity or legislation covering what you do with it.

The practical expressions of these principles are reassuringly familiar. They include the everyday forms of political argument on the public, rational and moral justifications of action, with criticisms freely voiced where they are accurate; on the open recognition of cant, hypocrisy and bullying for what they are; on our old friends and enemies, responsibility and accountability, being attached justly and mercifully to the moral dimensions of teaching offices and *not* to the Taylorization of education (this means, at the least, the avoidance of logically impossible precepts — teachers cannot stick to rigid routines *and* show imagination and initiative). My favourite instance of a due republicanism was shown by the head of English who, in response to the management team's circular entitled 'What Employers Expect of Our Pupils,' sent round in perfect blitheness and no secrecy two memoranda of his own: 'What Employers Do *Not* Expect of Our Pupils' (e.g. critical-mindedness, clear knowledge of rights, commitment to trade union principles) and 'What Our Pupils Expect of Their Employers' (not much).

This is the active reciprocity of republicanism, perhaps not in the classic Ciceronian idiom, but at least in a Jeffersonian one. If it sounds to a hardworked, schoolteaching audience like little more than keeping schools up to the moral mark of liberal society's official principles, that in itself would be one in the eye for management. If we want liberty even to do as our little principality wants, let alone to do what we want for ourselves, we must restore mistrust in princes and our so princely managers, and take charge of the public arena ourselves. It follows from this that, in liberal parlance, far from being able to mark out a terrain of minimum interference by the state, it is only by seeing our public duties as the prior condition of our rights, that we can maintain our rights at all.

These rough notes must do to suggest institutional and conceptual structures entirely different from those of the broadcast managerialism which, in my argument, defaces and defames our polity. In the relative autonomy of a few instances, schools, colleges, hospitals, social security offices, cooperatives, power stations, there is no reason why we should not attempt the restoration of a latter-day republicanism which would sort well with some of the best of our libertarian and progressive traditions. Given that schools, colleges and universities are entrusted with the task of educating the hungry generations who will be the future, it might even turn out that to follow such a course would lead to a better society.

Notes

1 Claus Offe, *Disorganized Capitalism*, Cambridge, Polity Press, 1985.
2 James O'Connor, *The Fiscal Crisis of the State*, London, Macmillan, 1973.
3 Albert Hirschmann, *Rival Views of Market Society*, Princeton, N.J., Princeton University Press, 1987.
4 W.B. Yeats, 'Church and State', *Collected Poems*, London, Macmillan, 1960, p. 283.
5 David Hargreaves, *The Challenge of the Comprehensive School*, London, Routledge and Kegan Paul, 1982.
6 See Ernesto Laclau and Chantal Mouffe, *Hegemony and Socialist Strategy*, London, Verso Books, 1985, especially Ch. 4.
7 This is the main argument of Anthony Giddens, in Vol.2 of his *Critique of Historical Materialism*, published as *The Nation-State and Violence*, Cambridge, Polity Press, 1985.
8 See, most relevantly, Michel Foucault, *The Birth of the Clinic*, London, Tavistock Press, 1973; *Madness and Civilisation*, London, Random House, 1967; *Discipline and Punish*, Harmondsworth, Penguin, 1977.
9 Charles Taylor, 'Foucault on Freedom' in his *Philosophical Papers*, Vol. 2, Cambridge, Cambridge University Press, 1985.
10 Jurgen Habermas, *Legitimation Crisis*, London, Heinemann Educational Books, 1975, p. 106.
11 This argument in this and the following sections is fully developed in my *Popular Culture and Political Power*, Brighton, Harvester-Wheatsheaf, 1988.
12 John Rawls, *A Theory of Justice*, Cambridge, Mass., Harvard University Press, 1972, p. 312.
13 Herbert Hicks, *The Management of Organizations: A Systems and Human Resources Approach*, New York, McGraw-Hill, 1967; Charles Handy, *Understanding Organizations*, Harmondsworth, Penguin, 1976; Warren Bennis, Kenneth Benne and Robert Chin, *The Planning of Change*, 2nd ed., New York, Holt Rinehart and Winston, 1970.
14 See Thomas Nagel's essay, 'Ruthlessness in Public Life', in Stuart Hampshire (ed.), *Public and Private Morality*, Cambridge, Cambridge University Press, 1978.
15 In Giddens (1985), p. 5.
16 See Albert O. Hirschmann, *Exit, Voice, and Loyalty: Responses to Decline in Firms, Organizations, and States*, Cambridge, Mass., Harvard University Press, 1972.
17 In Quentin Skinner, 'Two Paradoxes of Civil Liberty', *Tanner Lectures on Human Value in 1984*, Cambridge, Mass., Harvard University Press, 1986.

Chapter 3

Bureaucratic Rationality and the Promise of Democratic Schooling

Fazal Rizvi

Throughout this century, the goal of democratic schooling has been vigorously promoted. In the 1920s and 1930s the progressive education movement was based on the belief that the notions of education and democracy were inextricably linked. In the 1960s and 1970s the ideas of free schooling, open schooling and deschooling were all informed by democratic concerns to make education less authoritarian and more centred on the interests of the child. In recent years the advocates of critical and feminist pedagogies (for example, Wood, 1984) have found the liberal-humanist notions of democracy insufficient, and have suggested that democratic schooling requires not only a more humane attitude towards children but also a fundamental restructuring of social relationships in schools. Others, like Watkins (1989), have argued that a 'stronger' notion of democracy implies that to be committed to democratic schooling is to be committed to a more equitable distribution of power relations than that which currently prevails in most schools. For Watkins, educational administration should be so structured as to give teachers, pupils and parents some political control over educational decisions. Such a view of democratic governance is justified on a range of moral considerations, including liberty, social justice and respect for persons.

Now while the moral case for the democratic administration of schooling is a strong one, its realization in practice remains elusive. There are few, if any, outstanding examples of democratic organization of education. Empirical studies (for example, Sharp and Green, 1975) have shown such innovations as have been tried to collapse after relatively short periods. Those teachers and parents who invest considerable effort in democratic experiments often become frustrated with the seemingly insurmountable intransigence of institutions. Many turn to cynicism, believing educational democracy to be practically unrealizable. Why is it so difficult to institute democratic reforms in schools? What is it about the nature of school administration and the way teachers approach education that thwarts democratic schooling?

In this chapter it is argued that the realization of democratic ideals in schools is seriously constrained by the dominant rationality which informs much of the theory and practice of educational administration. It is suggested that the contemporary tools with which we analyze educational problems, and even formulate programmes of democratic reforms, are invariably informed by the assumptions of bureaucratic rationality; and that unless we recognize this form of rationality to be fundamentally ideological and anti-democratic and begin to employ other approaches to solving educational problems, we will continue to be disappointed in our efforts to achieve genuine democracy in education.

The empirical data upon which the theoretical arguments are based are derived from research studies over the past five years conducted by members of the Social and Administrative Studies Research Group at Deakin University, Australia. These studies have been concerned with issues that schools and bureaucracies have encountered in working towards a range of democratic reforms to educational administration outlined in a set of Ministerial Papers issued by the Victorian Government in 1983. More comprehensive discussions of the methodology and the findings of the studies can be found in Deakin Institute for Studies in Education (1984), Bates (1986) and Watkins, Rizvi and Angus (1988).

Weber on Bureaucratic Rationality

Max Weber is widely regarded as the theorist who most clearly articulated the structure of modern bureaucracy. Most students of management are familiar with his claim that bureaucracy is technically superior to all other forms of administration. However, special care should be taken in reading Weber, since his ideas have been interpreted in a number of different ways. Some have taken Weber to be espousing a thesis which demonstrates the destructive effects of bureaucracy, while others have accommodated Weber's writings within Parsonian structural-functionalism. This latter, and more influential, group has claimed that Weber's writings on bureaucracy should properly be seen as a description of how an effective and efficient modern organization functions. Weber's ideal-type of bureaucracy is thus presented as a *model* for the effective functioning of organizations (see Hoy and Miskel, 1982). In contrast to this reading Weiss (1983) has argued that Weber's writings on bureaucracy should be understood more appropriately as an examination of the characteristics of a system of domination employing rational-legal legitimation.

To understand Weber's account of bureaucracy, we need to place it in the context of his view of rationality because, for Weber, bureaucracy, in contrast to traditional forms of administration, represents the most 'rational' arrangement of authority yet devised to achieve technical efficiency — in Weber's (1984, p. 214) words, 'technically the most perfectly adapted for achieving the highest level of performance'. Weber was writing in the heyday of positivism; so it is not surprising that his view of rationality assumed some of the central tenets of positivist epistemology. He implicitly accepted the positivist understanding of science, and constructed his theory of society in line with the prevailing views concerning the limits of scientific reason. The key assumption underpinning Weber's view of rationality is the claim that statements of fact and judgments of value are logically distinct, and that only the sphere of facts is the subject-matter of science, whether physical or social; for only facts are ascertainable by the observational methods of science (Weber, 1949, pp. 18–25). Science consists of statements of fact, not statements of value. Science can provide us with answers to such questions as what phenomena exist in the world, what law-like relations hold between them and what explains them. In contrast, value-judgments are judgments of the satisfactory and the unsatisfactory character of phenomena, of desirability and undesirability. Issues of value include all problems as to what should be done in a given situation, and what state of affairs one should try to bring about — that is, the moral and political problems of rightness and wrongness.

Weber sees values as 'choices and decisions' made by the 'acting willing person' on the basis of his 'conscience and his personal view of the world' (Weber, 1949, p. 55). He insists that the validity of such judgments is a matter of faith and that empirical science *cannot* establish norms, since no normative conclusions can be deduced or derived from factual assertions. He maintains, however, that science *can* perform a variety of functions relative to practical decisions. Science can specify means to ends; it can tell what one is able to do in certain circumstances; it can provide information that might be relevant for the acceptance or rejection of values; it can estimate the costs and consequences (intended or unintended) of holding certain values; and it can analyze the relationships between value positions. Now while science is capable of helping us make decisions in all these ways, the Weberian view of rationality, and science, remains dominated by the assumption that values, including moral and political judgments, cannot be rationally evaluated, since they are, in the final analysis, attitudes, feelings, preferences and individual choices of one's own. Practical rationality is always 'bounded' and instrumental; the rationality of matching means to ends economically and efficiently.

Modern administrative theory is fundamentally embedded within the framework of this Weberian view of rationality. It systematically eschews making judgments on the morality of organizational ends, for it rests on the assumption that ends cannot be subjected to the scrutiny of reason. In rational decision-making, organizational ends are accepted as *given*. The task of administrative theory is viewed as being concerned with formulating rationally designed *means* for the explicit realization of the given *ends*. Organization itself is seen as an instrument of efficiency and effectiveness, *neutral* with respect to the goals it has been created to serve.

For Weber, his view of rationality implies that it is in principle possible to determine empirically (scientifically) the most efficient and effective model of an organization, a model which is applicable to all administrative contexts, regardless of the purpose any particular organization might serve. It is this assumption which leads mainstream theorists in educational administration (for example, Hoy and Miskel, 1982) to believe that management technology applicable to industrial sites is also applicable to an educational institution. For organizational structures and operations are considered to be *neutral* with respect to particular purposes.

This stress on the importance of scientific neutrality is also evident in the other complementary element essential for an understanding of Weber's account of the structure of bureaucracy: the nature of authority in modern industrial society. According to Weber, the world in which we live, and will continue to live in the future, is characterized by and is subject to a process of increasing rationalization. He sees the process of rationalization as resulting from a 'disenchantment' with the present. Modern society, he notes, is increasingly distrustful of traditional authority, and there is a widely held belief that things can only be improved with increasing scientific specialization, technical differentiation and rationalization. 'The degree of advance towards bureaucracy...', writes Weber (1948, p. 218), 'provides the decisive yardstick for the modernisation of the state.' He presents bureaucracy in an explicit contrast with traditional systems of administration which were based on patriarchal or patrimonial authority. Bureaucracy, he believes, is grounded in rational-legal authority.

Weber argues that authority must be clearly distinguished from simple coercive power. The exercise of authority is legitimate, the exercise of coercive power is not. But the notion of legitimacy here must not be confused with the notion of rationality. Charismatic and traditional authorities, though legitimate in some contexts, are inherently irrational because they derive their legitimacy from matters of personality, mystique, grace and favour and, therefore, involve inconsistency and impartiality in particular applications. For Weber, the only system of administration that is rational *and* is based on authority that does not derive its legitimacy from tradition or charisma is bureaucracy.

Not only is bureaucracy based on rational-legal authority but it is also the most rationally efficient means of improving organizational effectiveness. It involves purposive-rational action, the explicit definition of goals, and the increasingly precise calculation of the most effective means to achieve them, in contrast to action arising from habit or traditionalism as a principle. As such, it is most conducive to organizational efficiency because its procedural correctness rests on neutral and rational criteria. For Weber, it is these criteria that a system of administration must satisfy if it is to count as an ideal-type bureaucracy.

For Weber, the structure of ideal-type bureaucracy exemplifies 'rationality' in a number of ways. In it a division of labour clearly defines authority relationships and responsibilities. Its offices are organized into hierarchy or chains of command. In a bureaucracy, managerial officials are selected and promoted on the basis of qualifications determined by education and examination: nepotism is ruled out. A bureaucracy places great emphasis on formally prescribed rules and regulations governing the conduct of work. It requires impersonality between management and employees. Its career-oriented officials receive fixed salaries, and its officials are administrative appointments rather than elected to office.

Schools as Bureaucracies

Similarities between Weber's ideal-type bureaucratic structure and modern schools are not difficult to find. Schools have a functional division of labour in that the principal, senior teachers, teachers and other personnel have fixed and specialized tasks which are ordered by formal rules, laws and administrative regulations. Tasks have been broken down into less unwieldy units so that complex tasks can be performed in a rational and efficient manner. The structure of schools is strictly hierarchical and there are levels of graded authority which devolve from the top downwards so that each position is under the control of a superior in the organizational hierarchy. There are, moreover, written documents, specifying rules and regulations, available in each school, some of which have been negotiated and formulated at the central level and communicated downwards to the local schools. These rules and regulations exist to ensure formalistic impersonality of relations at schools. The principal's relationship with teachers is a purely formal one and is mediated by codified rules which define the bounds of acceptable conduct. Positions in a school are, moreover, assigned on the basis of formal qualifications and credentials. In the USA, for example, all educational administrators have to be formally registered.

However, while at a superficial level many features of schools meet the criteria for identifying a bureaucracy set out by Weber, research on the subject shows diverse and conflicting findings. Thomas (1968) has identified features of educational bureaucracy which closely parallel the Weberian model. Walker's (1970) research also seems to support Thomas' findings. Walker has suggested that, in line with the Weberian postulates, along with the growth in complexity in our society has come increasing dominance of bureaucratic forms of educational governance. Against the view of Thomas and Walker, Pusey (1976) points to the limitation of the Weberian model. He argues that 'Weber's model mistakenly took organisational rationality for granted because it assumed that, in principle, it is possible and expedient to devise *general rules which will fit all the particular cases*' (Pusey, 1976, p. 18). Pusey argues that schools, more than any other organization, are characterized by 'eruption of uncertainty from within'. This is because teaching, and the organization of education, is not a mechanical activity. It cannot be assessed on strictly impersonal criteria without regard to personality factors or to social and moral values. Pusey rejects the Weberian model on 'the grounds that it does not admit of any legitimate tension between the authority structure and the "psycho-social" realm' (Pusey, 1976, p. 18). Nor does the model allow the possibility of any conflict between the officially prescribed order of the formal structure and professional judgment which is often called upon in education. In schools, moreover, there is seldom a congruence between the formal structure, the rank and the technical expertise a particular official has. Indeed, it is often the case that principals do not possess the expertise that many teachers, their 'subordinates', have (Blackmore, 1989).

The view that few, if any, schools correspond to the Weberian model of bureaucracy does seem highly plausible. Schools do not always have the formal hierarchical authority structures of the type Weber stipulated. Empirical findings by a range of researchers (see, for example, Punch, 1972; Grassie, 1973) have demonstrated that schools do not generally correspond to all the features of Weberian bureaucracy. It would be a mistake to think that these findings contradict Weber's insights, since his account of bureaucracy is meant to be descriptive: it is a rationally devised model, an ideal-type, intended to provide the normative standards against which effective and efficient organizations could be judged. The structure of the ideal-type bureaucracy is posited as the best possible organizational arrangement for accomplishing pre-determined goals. Weber's analysis is a theoretical one, applicable only to a varying degree to particular organizations. Indeed, in his political writings Weber himself argues that in practice bureaucracy seldom fulfils the ideal-type criteria: it has an inherent tendency to exceed its function.

While it may be correct to state that not all the features of the structure of contemporary schools correspond with the Weberian bureaucracy, it is also true that bureaucratic rationality remains all-pervasive in contemporary educational thinking and practice. Indeed, my research in Victoria indicates that it continues to be widely assumed by practising administrators as well as those who theorize about administration. Most educational administrators continue to believe that hierarchical authority is indispensable and to have faith in a rationalist model of organizational thinking which emphasizes a fundamental distinction between the conception and implementation of objectives. Most remain committed to the ideas of functional division of labour and levels of graded authority. In schools, social relationships mostly continue to be defined and mediated by role definitions. Most principals continue to believe that in undertaking administrative tasks they are, or at least should be, neutral with respect to any particular set of goals that school councils might have established.

Considerable support for these findings can be found in diverse areas of educational research. In his influential writings in the sociology of teaching, Apple (1979, p. 111) has, for example, argued that 'our common-sense thought in education, however, tends to move in a direction quite the opposite from moral and political considerations. Instead spheres of decision making are perceived as *technical problems* that only necessitate instrumental strategies and information produced by technical experts, hence both effectively removing the decisions from the realm of political and ethical debate and covering the relationship between the status of technical knowledge and economic and cultural reproduction.' In the policy field Wise (1979) has identified a trend towards an increasing bureaucratization of American classrooms. He has called this trend 'the hyperrationalisation of education' and has suggested that it is at least partly 'responsible for the failure to lead to real school reform'. Bates (1983) has also explored the bureaucratization of schools. He has suggested that in education it has been the technical bureaucratization requirements, rather than ethical or political concerns, that have served to define how knowledge is structured and transmitted. Similarly Wake (1983) has analyzed the way institutionalized knowledge is interpreted by school administrators imbued with what Berger, Berger and Kellner (1973) have referred to as the 'bureaucratic consciousness'.

The insights of these researchers make it clear that the modern bureaucracy needs to be understood both as a structure and as a way of comprehending the world. Although its structure admits wide variations, as a system of rationality it is widely accepted: it serves to provide the criteria against which administrative activities are judged and it defines the way emerging practical problems should be interpreted and resolved. Indeed, as a mode of thinking, bureaucratic rationality has, as MacIntyre (1981) points out, become so ingrained in our consciousness that we find it difficult to employ alternative modes of thought. As Lefort (1975) has observed, though we dislike the presence of bureaucracy in our society, we continue to *think* bureaucratically. We accept implicitly that rationality demands that activities be fragmented, services diversified, specialized and partitioned and routinized. Since all this requires more numerous structural levels and delegations of authority at each level to coordinate and control dispersed sectors, bureaucracy prospers. Urban (1982) suggests that so long as we continue to employ an organizational paradigm which stresses 'rational-efficiency' above all other goals, we will continue to view bureaucracy as a reflection of 'objective' needs in human organizations.

Bureaucratic Rationality as a Barrier to Democratic Schooling

The debate over exactly what democratic schooling consists in is extensive (see Wringe, 1984). A review of this debate shows that while there is a considerable diversity of views over the nature and extent of political power over decision-making that should be accorded to pupils, parents, teachers and principals, there is convergence of views over the main defining characteristics of a democratic community. In broad formal terms a democratic school is one in which the decision-making structures enable and encourage meaningful participation by all its members. Taylor (1982) has argued that for a community to be called democratic it should at least possess, in some degree, three characteristics. The first is that persons who make up the community share and are able to negotiate the beliefs and values by which they live together. The second is that the relations among its members are non-manipulative, direct and many-sided, 'unmediated by representatives, leaders, institutions such as those of the state, or by codes, abstractions and reifications' (Taylor, 1982, p. 28). Finally, relationships in a democratic community must be reciprocal, characterized by, among other values, care, mutual aid and some forms of cooperation and sharing. The notion of reciprocity also implies some degree of equality in power relations.

Given these characteristics of a democratic community, the ways in which they conflict with the requirements of bureaucratic rationality can be readily recognized. To begin with, relationships in a bureaucracy are mostly manipulative and always hierarchical and mediated by roles, codes and abstractions. As a process, bureaucracy defines a certain way of viewing social relationships. Bureaucratic rationality, MacIntyre (1981) has argued, consists essentially in viewing human relationships in terms of institutional roles. This requirement of depersonalization in institutional relations means that individuals are isolated from one another, and spontaneous meaningful interaction is replaced by formal associations. MacIntyre claims that bureaucratic rationality entails an 'obliteration of any genuine distinction between manipulative and non-manipulative social relations'. In an organization where moral language is given no legitimate place, human relationships come to involve persons treating each other as a means to either their own or the organization's ends. In such contexts, no criteria are available for moral debate about goodness or badness of human conduct. When relationships are viewed in technical terms, MacIntyre argues, the distinction between manipulative and non-manipulative social interaction becomes unintelligible.

As we have already noted, bureaucratic rationality defines what is subject to rational assessment and what is not. Ferguson (1984, p. 79) has observed that bureaucratic discourse is guilty of a 'radical deafness' towards any non-approved questions, and 'thus is hostile to many, perhaps most, of the usual concerns of political and social theory'. We may add normative educational concerns to this list. The debates that are internal to bureaucratic rationality often centre on relatively routine concerns; concerns that beg the larger issues of coercion and control. Bureaucracy rules out opportunities for the negotiation of substantive issues of moral and political values. Katz (1971) has shown how, in the history of American education, bureaucratic rationality has resulted in the subversion of educational concerns, for those immersed in bureaucratic processes have been consumed by *technical administrative* matters, unable to engage in debates about *educational values*.

Far from being politically and structurally neutral, bureaucracy can thus be shown to represent a range of values which are hostile to the ideal of a democratic community. Bureaucracy is, moreover, an ongoing process that is constantly reproducing its modes of domination and control. It aims at arranging individuals and tasks to secure continuity, predictability and stability by removing ambiguity in relations among participants. Bureaucratic processes thus prescribe rules of conduct which are anything but neutral. Moreover, as Hannah Arendt (1958, p. 40) has argued, bureaucracy 'expects from each of its members a certain kind of behaviour, imposing innumerable and various rules, all of which tend to "normalise" its members, to make them behave.' It thus makes sense to speak of bureaucracy as 'a type of social system, one in which certain social acts are established and maintained, certain social objects are valued, certain languages are spoken, certain types of behaviour are required, and certain motivations are encouraged' (Ferguson, 1984, p. 9).

The contention that bureaucratic rationality is inimical to democracy is borne out by the empirical data we have collected at Deakin University in Victoria. Over the past decade, there has been a sustained effort in Victoria to make school administration more democratic, 'more responsive to the wishes of the community'. A set of Ministerial Papers has set out the democratic sentiments behind the reforms, which have included giving school councils wide-ranging powers to determine their own curricular and organizational policies. The Victorian Government (Education Department of Victoria, 1983) has maintained that it is committed to 'genuine devolution of authority', meaning that 'parents, teachers, students, principals, administrators and others closely involved in the work of education will all have the right to participate in the decision-making processes.'

The Deakin research has shown that in the five years since the Ministerial Papers were introduced, there has been little progress towards the realization of the goal of democratic school administration in Victoria. The rhetoric contained in the Ministerial Papers is widely recited, but the changes have been mostly superficial. Indeed, there would be something very odd about imagining that a central bureaucracy would happily and readily devolve powers it presently enjoys. There is a central dilemma for a programme of democratic reform conducted through the agency of a well entrenched bureaucracy which defines the task of democratization as purely a technical one, thus remaining trapped within the framework of bureaucratic rationality.

Perhaps the most discernible reform that has taken place in Victoria has been the establishment of the school councils, which are representative structures given extensive powers of self-government. But our research shows that while the school councils meet monthly, the meetings are consumed by discussions which mostly centre on the day-to-day instrumental concerns of school life. When more substantial items are explored, they are often issues which the central bureaucracy has asked schools to consider. Principals do most of the talking anyway. Debates about educational values are rare indeed. Most school councillors remain unaware of the extensive powers they have. The Deakin research also demonstrates that school councils are largely unrepresentative bodies. Most councillors are middle-class men of English-speaking background.

Bureaucratic thinking and processes persist in Victorian education in other ways. The following provide just a few examples. One of the key characteristics of bureaucratic rationality, as already noted, is the requirement of *depersonalization* in social interaction. In a sense the pluralist representative decision-making structure thought appropriate for school councils, which brings people together only in their capacity as members of particular interest groups, is already operating with conditions that result in depersonalization. It is reasonable to assume that spontaneity and reciprocity in relationships are unlikely to be present in formal bargaining situations where members are required to fight for their association's pre-determined claims. In meetings, particular bureaucrats find themselves with the task of defending views which may not be their own. Such a depersonalized approach to decision-making is exemplified in the statement of a senior member of the Education Department who maintained, 'I am only a servant of the educational bureaucracy. I cannot give you my frank opinion on this issue.'

Another defining element of relations inside a bureaucracy is *hierarchy*. Hierarchical relationships within the Education Department do not appear to have changed to any great extent. Changes have been made to the names of some positions (for example, the Inspectors are now referred to as Senior Education Officers), but this has not altered the overall pattern of power distribution. In fact there is a great deal of confusion about the new responsibilities of officers. Given the philosophical orientation of the Ministerial Papers, officers had expected their tasks to be different, but in practice these have remained the same.

In Victoria, the policy of educational devolution has been promoted at precisely the same time as the Victorian Government has been preoccupied with promoting efficiency of government services through a number of new bureaucratic accountability measures. Through the system-wide application of programme budgeting, administrative tasks, both within schools and more widely in the educational system, have been *routinized*, broken into uniform manageable parts and performed in an incremental manner. Efficiency and effectiveness of the administrative processes have become the overriding concerns of not only the central bureaucrats but also the school councils. Some bureaucratic initiatives designed to secure efficiency, such as the central computerization of bank accounts and the auditing of student attendance, have also had the consequence of enabling the centre to acquire greater and more extensive powers. The *one-directional language* in which the bureaucracy expresses its need for information has generated an ever increasing number of memoranda and notices, subverting further the possibilities of dialogue which is so essential for democratic reforms.

Weber was, of course, fully aware of the dangers that bureaucratic rationality posed for democratic institutions. In his political writings Weber (1948) brilliantly traces both the liberalizing and dominating aspects of bureaucracy. Bureaucracy operates according to deliberately constructed rules which lay down a framework of hierarchical authority, defining the scope of the responsibilities of each of its members. This is meant to ensure fairness, impersonality and impartiality, but, as Weber recognized, bureaucratic administration is always in danger of becoming an instrument of élite hegemony, since it permits efficient centralized organization of power. Against what he sees as the dangers of bureaucratic domination over individuals, Weber emphasizes the need for political authority. Bureaucracy, he believes, could very easily obtain a dominant position in society by means of its organization of information and the 'efficiency' of its executive hierarchy unless it were balanced by a powerful body of responsible elected political leaders. Strong political leadership is needed to keep bureaucracy 'in check', to ensure that it remains answerable to the public and that in offering people enlightened paternalism it does not treat people as some kind of unthinking objects, only to be administered.

Bureaucratic Rationality as neither Irresistible nor Inevitable

Weber acknowledges that the increasing bureaucratization of society is undesirable: it involves the manipulation of people and leads to the subversion of democratic goals. At the same time, however, he insists that the advance of bureaucratic rationality is inevitable and irresistible. It is irresistible because mass society requires impersonal and rational organization. The development of bureaucracy is thus linked to the efforts of industrial society to establish an efficient structure, to realize technical objectivity and to assimilate human beings into a mechanized system. In both the capitalist and socialist economies, Weber notes, there is a trend towards the rationalization of authority and the separation of the worker from the means of production. This trend is a consequence of two factors: the sophistication of technology and the spread of bureaucratic operations.

For Weber, the advance of bureaucratic administration is not only irresistible but it is also inevitable. It is inevitable because rationality demands it: its technical superiority to any other system is beyond question. Weber believes that a fully developed bureaucratic system compares with other types of organizations as does a machine with other simpler 'cottage' methods of production. Just as human beings continue to invent more complex machines, there is no reason to believe that they would want to organize their lives in an analogous manner. Weber's theory of rationality thus contains the metaphysical assumption that human beings are inevitably committed to the pursuit of a mastery over the physical and social environment.

Given the world-view of bureaucratic rationality, administrative hierarchy manifests itself as a technical necessity, as the most rational organizational arrangement for the achievement of collective ends. But if hierarchy is a technical necessity, then the goals of democracy in education seem implausible, for democracy, unlike management, presupposes greater equality of power: it requires decision-making structures which enable all members of an organization, such as a school, to deliberate over educational ends *as well as* the administrative means. A reassertion of democracy in education is only feasible if we can show that bureaucratic administration can be resisted and that the Weberian view of rationality is mistaken. What needs to be demonstrated is that there is nothing necessary or essentially 'rational' about the idea of administrative hierarchy, and that other forms of organizational life which are not filled with the substance of administration and bureaucracy are possible and, indeed, essential if we are to replace the prevailing industrial mode of existence with another form of life informed by democratic values.

Bureaucratic rationality can be criticized at two levels: moral and epistemological. At the epistemological level it can be argued that the alleged distinction between facts and values, means and ends, lacks coherence, and that it is just as possible to have rational discourse about ends as it is about means. Bureaucracy cannot be justified on the grounds of its supposed neutrality since rationality has been shown not to be confined to instrumental and technical concerns. At the moral level it can be argued that bureaucratic rationality implies a number of morally objectionable consequences, the recognition of which should lead us to explore other ways of arranging organizational life.

To begin with, the notion of rationality Weber assumes is located in a foundationalist epistemology. Foundationalism accords a privileged epistemological status to certain categories of thought which are themselves determined in an a priori manner and are not subject to any revision. Weber accepts the empiricist assumptions underlying his view of rationality as foundational truths. Thus he presents his account of values and the means-ends distinction without any further justification. But recent philosophers have argued that such foundationalism is fundamentally mistaken. Rorty (1979), for example, has suggested that knowledge does not require the foundations both empiricists and rationalists thought necessary. All knowledge is contingent, subject to revision in the light of new information and interests. Just as our everyday concepts are subject to historical changes, so is the form of rationality that binds them together.

Foucault (1977) has suggested that there is no absolute form of rationality against which reality might be compared or evaluated. Rather, it is a matter, for Foucault, of investigating the rationalities inscribed within different social practices, of determining how a particular form of rationality simultaneously constitutes rules and procedures for making statements about reality and engaging in other social activities and provides the criteria with which to assess the intelligibility and the reasonableness of those discourses and practices. The consequences of Weber's and Foucault's differing views of rationality should be clear. Working with an absolutist view of rationality, Weber presents the process of rationalization as inevitable and irreversible. Foucault, on the other hand, discusses power and the views of rationality within which it is embedded as historically contingent, and therefore in perpetual presence of resistance. Weber assumes rationality to be monolithic; Foucault rejects the idea of a single, uniform and integrated process affecting all forms of human existence.

Once bureaucratic rationality has been recognized as a historically contingent doctrine, Weber's claim to its inevitability can be challenged. Indeed, as Katz (1971) has correctly argued, bureaucracy is only inevitable if social complexity is approached with certain values and attitudes. We cannot envisage alternative forms of life because we continue to value order, efficiency and uniformity ahead of the ideals of spontaneity, reciprocity, variety and flexibility. Weber's view of rationality denies that there are any truths about moral values: the only value questions that can be rationally debated are *instrumental*. This is not to say that there are no such things as moral values, since individuals do live by them, but they are no longer to be taken to have impersonal validity. Morality becomes something of which an individual is the ultimate arbiter. As MacIntyre (1981, p. 24) puts it, the unifying preoccupation of the Weberian tradition is the 'condition of those who see in the social world nothing but a meeting place for individual wills, each with its own set of attitudes and preferences and who understand the world solely as an end for the achievement of their own satisfaction, who interpret reality as a series of opportunities for their own enjoyment.'

There is something very odd about this view of moral life. It is both *ahistorical* and *asocial*. People are not like the existential Robinson Crusoe: they are *social beings* with a network of relationships, and it is within the framework of these relationships that they first learn their moral concepts, and later modify them. They do not develop their 'individual wills' in the solipsistic fashion that the Weberian view seems to imply: both the application of moral rules and the attempt to change them are public acts governed by established epistemological canons. Moreover, like all other concepts, moral concepts have histories. As Kovesi (1969) has pointed out, people construct moral notions collectively in order to understand and solve the problems they confront. In this way moral judgments are made in the same manner as judgments of all other kinds — intersubjectively and rationally. As far as the question of ultimate ends is concerned, the Weberian rationality is, as Wright Mills once put it, 'rationality without reason' (Wright Mills, 1959, p. 170). But reason is no less applicable to questions of moral ends, since they, like questions of technique, are also grounded in various traditions, are learned and are subject to historical revision.

The Weberian approach involves a gross oversimplification of how means and ends can be separated. It implies that practical decision-making always involves two distinct stages: first, when specific goals or ends are chosen for action; and second, when specific means are rationally found to achieve those ends. But separating means from ends in this way is both epistemologically troublesome and practically unachievable. The rationality of clear ends and distinct means is really an ex post facto rationality; it is the result of a construct we have placed upon completed actions as a simplification of what we would have liked those actions to be. There is in such a construct all the presumption of a simple and idealized structure which is a long way removed from the reality of social situations. In those situations, means and ends are never as easily separable as the model suggests. The ends achieved are not always preconceived by the actors in the field, but are often reflected upon in retrospect rather than prospect. Frequently the nature of ends is understood only in the context of a practice. When teachers consider their activities, for example, they do so in the hurly-burly of day-to-day activities rather than in terms of a rationality that dictates that they separate the specification of objectives from the specification of means. There is thus no dichotomy between means and ends, for in the conduct of an activity we are continually grouping and re-grouping these elements, viewing them afresh as new circumstances present themselves.

An assumption implicit in the Weberian approach is that if the organization of the goals is done by one individual for others, then somehow the psychological organization of the activity is more efficient. But this assumption overlooks the fact that the very nature of an activity requires that individuals do their own organizing — their own interpreting of the goals — to fit these into the context in which they find themselves, the same context in which they have to devise the means.

In *Human Nature and Conduct* Dewey (1957, p. 207) expressed the complex nature of the relationship between ends and means in the following way:

> Our problem now concerns the nature of ends, that is ends-in-view or aims. The essential elements in the problem have already been stated. It has been pointed out that the ends, objectives, of conduct are those foreseen consequences which influence present deliberation and which finally bring it to rest by furnishing an adequate stimulus to overt action. Consequently ends arise and function within action. They are not, as current theories too often imply, things lying beyond activity at which the latter is directed. They are not strictly speaking ends or termini of action at all. They are acts of deliberation, and so turning points in activity.

Dewey thus denies that ends exist outside activity. His idea of ends as turning points in activity places them integrally within the continuum of human experience. Ends in this Deweyan sense are best seen as arising out of natural effects or consequences: they are the result of acts which at first are just hit or stumbled upon, but which upon reflection are desired for themselves. Even when a clear definition of ends is provided, it also has to be actualized in practice. It has to be understood within a broader system of beliefs and practices. For, as Wittgenstein (1973, para. 85) points out, no rule, no matter how specific, ever dictates its own application, since we understand a particular prescription only when a place for it is already prepared in our system of beliefs and practices. Thus ends become contextualized and projected; not removed from the activity in question but turning points in that activity. They are continuously negotiated, modified, challenged and acted upon in specific circumstances. What follows from this is that, in contrast to the traditional Weberian model which sees ends as existing outside activity, the idea of ends is better seen as turning points integrally linked within the continuum of human experience.

The bureaucratization of our discourse about practical questions is a consequence of the Weberian means-ends rationality. MacIntyre (1981) has shown how it has led to the language of morals and politics being transformed into a language of management techniques through which the organization is able to exercise authority, the use of *legitimate* power. But in treating administrative language as *neutral*, bureaucratic rationality has in effect implied an obliteration of any genuine distinction between manipulative and non-manipulative social relationships. Lacking any uniform or even intersubjective criteria for the judgment of moral ends, human relationships have become a matter of persons treating each other as a means to their ends. But, as MacIntyre (1981, p. 23) argues, 'to treat someone else as a means is to seek to make him or her an instrument of my purposes by adducing whatever influences or considerations will in fact be effective in this or that occasion.' What does this observation tell us about contemporary administrative practice?

Administrative practice is, according to bureaucratic rationality, neutral with respect to any moral criteria. Administrators acting neutrally claim to be acting rationally; they regard their relationships with subordinates as neutral. In a bureaucracy it is believed that administrators have a responsibility to direct and redirect *impartially* their organization's available resources, both human and non-human, as effectively and efficiently as possible towards the attainment of organizational goals. Such management of 'resources' is carried out on behalf of the organization and is given legitimacy and authority on the grounds of the alleged neutrality of the administrator's relationship with his or her subordinates.

Bureaucratic rationality dictates that effective and efficient means be found that match predetermined ends. But in pursuit of effectiveness and efficiency the administrators need to influence the motives of their subordinates, and control and direct them in such ways as to produce maximum benefits to the organization. MacIntyre argues that a rationality based on these premises necessarily obliterates the contrast between power and authority, thereby making meaningless any intelligible distinction between manipulative and non-manipulative social relations. For MacIntyre what this reveals is that bureaucratic authority, and administrative practice, is nothing other than *successful* power.

> The Manager represents in his *character* the obliteration of the distinction between manipulative and non-manipulative social relations....The manager treats ends as given, as outside his scope; his concern is with technique, with effectiveness in transforming raw material into final products, unskilled labour into skilled labour, investments into profits. (MacIntyre, 1981, p. 29)

Finding manipulative social relations to be neither inevitable nor morally desirable, MacIntyre (1981, p. 66) concludes that 'the incoherence of our attitudes and our experience arises from the incoherence of the conceptual scheme which we have inherited.' This conceptual scheme is bureaucratic rationality, which, MacIntyre suggests, can only be overcome if we reassert forms of democratic life and begin to make judgments, moral and political as well as administrative, collectively.

We may conclude that bureaucracy is neither neutral nor impartial: it is necessarily implicated in the political process. The distinction between political and administrative matters is a spurious one. The administrator can no longer hide behind the cloak of bureaucratic rationality, claiming to be only concerned with procedural and not substantive decisions. For procedural and substantive matters, ends and means, have been shown to be inextricably linked. In determining some administrative procedures to be more appropriate than others, one makes significant value decisions. The exclusive emphasis on organizational efficiency, however interpreted, is a goal, the preference for which over other goals such as widespread public participation has to be argued in specifically political terms. Efficiency is not an ideal which is self-evidently worth pursuing — especially when it conflicts with other human interests — and it cannot be interpreted without reference to more fundamental criteria in terms of which efficiency might be measured. In assessing efficiency we need to ask such questions as, 'efficient in terms of what — monetary cost?, human labour?, suffering?, the consumption of natural fuels?, time?, or what?' (Fay, 1975, p. 50). Fay argues:

> For until this question is answered there is literally no way of choosing between alternative courses in terms of efficiency. And the point here is that *whatever* answer one gives will reflect a judgement as to that set of factors which the policy scientist thinks the most important in situations of this type, a judgement that cannot be scientifically made for it involves reference to the *values* of the scientist.

The notion of effectiveness is equally unhelpful to the Weberian theorist wishing to insist upon the means-end distinction. For, as MacIntyre (1981, p. 71) argues: '...there are strong grounds for rejecting the claim that effectiveness is a morally neutral value. For the whole concept of effective is... inseparable from a mode of human existence in which the contrivance of means is in central part the manipulation of human beings into compliant patterns of behaviour....' To emphasize effectiveness ahead of other values is to embrace a norm which represents a certain preferred mode of human existence. But this preference has to be argued for in specifically moral and political terms against other claims which might represent alternative ways of organizing social existence.

To claim that notions of efficiency and effectiveness are value-laden is not to say that they are arbitrary and can be given any meaning one likes. To do so would be to subscribe to the very theory of value discourse upon which bureaucratic rationality is based. MacIntyre (1981) shows clearly how values are not subjective and arbitrary and that they can be rationally assessed, refuted and modified. They are located in traditions which provide historically contingent criteria against which both morality and education can be judged.

Conclusion

In this chapter it has been argued that the promise of democratic schooling is constrained by the persistence of bureaucratic rationality, which is not only assumed in much of the contemporary theory and practice of educational administration but also informs the manner in which we analyze educational problems, and even formulate programmes of democratic reforms. It has been suggested that it is this view of rationality that leads Weber to make his pessimistic prognosis about the irresistibility and inevitability of the advance of bureaucratic administration in modern industrial society. In contrast, bureaucratic administration is only inevitable under certain conditions, and under certain regimes of rationalities; but these conditions are historically contingent, and rationalities are always subject to revision. To believe that they are not would be to commit the fallacy of historicism. An attempt has been made here to undercut the claims of bureaucratic rationality by showing that the crucial means-end distinction around which it revolves is both epistemologically dubious and morally objectionable.

Like all conceptual schemes, bureaucratic rationality persists in the perpetual presence of resistance. If it is to be challenged, then certain programmes of administrative and political reform are necessary. But given Weber's prognosis, how realistic is it to suppose that bureaucracy can be, or even should be, done away with? In mass societies some form of bureaucracy seems essential for coordinating disparate activities. Exactly what form that should be is a political question to be negotiated in specific circumstances.

While it has to be admitted that the task of creating and sustaining new democratic patterns of social organization in our schools is a daunting one, it is nevertheless important to work towards minimizing the impact of bureaucracy on the way schools are presently administered. Resistance to the pernicious effects of bureaucracy can be intensified. The democratic practices and institutions that exist already can be extended. It should not be beyond our imagination to think of democratic forms not yet envisaged. But all this will only be possible if we recognize bureaucratic rationality to be fundamentally ideological and anti-democratic, and begin to employ other approaches to educational problem-solving.

Democratic administration in education cannot become a reality unless we can rescue ourselves from the clutches of bureaucratic rationality, and recognize that forms of social organization that are dominated by the ideas of hierarchy, absolute division of labour and instrumentalism are historically constructed, and that they represent an ideology that has prevented the realization of human potential for a caring, collective and democratic life.

References

APPLE, M. (1979) *Ideology and Curriculum*, London, Routledge and Kegan Paul.

ARENDT, H. (1958) *The Human Condition*, Chicago, Ill., University of Chicago Press.

BATES, R.J. (1983) *Educational Administration and the Management of Knowledge*, Geelong, Deakin University Press.

BATES, R.J. (1986) 'The Socio-Political Context of Administrative Change,' in Frazer, M., Dunstun, J. and Creed, P. (eds), *Perspectives on Organizational Change*, Melbourne, Longman-Cheshire, pp. 283–300.

BERGER, P., BERGER, B. and KELLNER, H. (1973) *The Homeless Mind*, New York, Random House.

BLACKMORE, J. (1989) 'Educational Leadership: A Feminist Critique and Reconstruction', in Smyth, W.J. (ed.), *Critical Perspectives in Educational Leadership*, Lewes, Falmer Press, pp. 93–130.

DEAKIN INSTITUTE FOR STUDIES IN EDUCATION (1984) *Restructuring Victorian Education: Current Issues*, Geelong, School of Education, Deakin University.

DEWEY, J. (1957) *Human Nature and Conduct*, New York, The Modern Library.

EDUCATION DEPARTMENT OF VICTORIA (1983) *Ministerial Papers 1–4*, Melbourne, Government Printer.

FAY, B. (1975) *Social Theory and Political Practice*, London, George Allen and Unwin.

FERGUSON, K. (1984) *The Feminist Case against Bureaucracy*, Philadelphia, Pa., Temple University Press.

FOUCAULT, M. (1977) *The Archaeology of Knowledge*, London, Tavistock.

GRASSIE, M.C. (1973) 'High Schools as Staff Perceive Them', *Journal of Educational Administration*, 11, 2, pp. 179–88.

HOY, W. and MISKEL, C. (1982) *Educational Administration: Theory, Research and Practice*, New York, Random House.

KATZ, M. (1971) *Class, Bureaucracy and Schools*, New York, Praeger.

KOVESI, J. (1969) *Moral Notions*, London, Routledge and Kegan Paul.

LEFORT, C. (1975) 'What Is Bureaucracy?' *Telos*, 22, pp. 56–81.

MacINTYRE, A. (1981) *After Virtue*, London, Duckworth.

NODDINGS, N. (1984) *Caring: A Feminine Approach to Ethics and Moral Education*, Berkeley, Calif., University of California Press.

PUNCH, K. (1972) 'The Study of Bureaucracy in Schools', *Australian Journal of Education*, 16, 3, pp. 254–61.

PUSEY, M. (1976) *Dynamics of Bureaucracy*, Brisbane, John Wiley and Son.

RORTY, R. (1979) *Philosophy and the Mirror of Nature*, Princeton, N.J., Princeton University Press.

SHARP, R. and GREEN, A. (1975) *Education and Social Control*, London, Routledge and Kegan Paul.

TAYLOR, M. (1982) *Community Anarchy and Liberty*, Cambridge, Cambridge University Press.

THOMAS, A. (1968) 'Innovation within a Bureaucratic Education System', *Journal of Educational Administration*, 6, 2, pp. 116–131.

WAKE, A. (1983) 'School Knowledge and the Structure of Bureaucracy', in Bates, R.J., *Educational Administration and the Management of Knowledge*, Geelong, Deakin University Press, pp. 83–99.

URBAN, M.E. (1982) *The Ideology of Administration: American and Society Cases*, Albany, N.Y., State University of New York Press.

WALKER, W.F. (1970) 'The Governance of Education in Australia: Centralization and Politics', *Journal of Educational Administration*, 8, 1, pp. 1–18.

WATKINS, P. (1989) 'Leadership, Power and Symbols in Educational Administration', in Smyth, W.J. (ed.), *Critical Perspectives in Educational Leadership*, Lewes, Falmer Press, pp. 9–38.

WATKINS, P., RIZVI, F. and ANGUS, L. (1988) 'The Formation of Regional Boards and the Devolution of Victorian State Education', *Australian Journal of Education*, 31, 3, pp. 252–72.

WEBER, M. (1948) *From Max Weber*, ed. by G. Gerth and C. Wright Mills, London, Routledge and Kegan Paul.

WEBER, M. (1949) *The Methodology of Social Sciences*, Glencoe, Ill., Free Press.

WEISS, R.M. (1983) 'Weber on Bureaucracy: Management Consultant or Political Theorist?', *Academy of Management Review*, 8, 2, pp. 242–8.

WISE, A.E. (1979) *Legislated Learning: The Bureaucratisation of the American Classroom*, Berkeley, Calif., University of California Press.

WITTGENSTEIN, L. (1973) *Philosophical Investigations*, London, Blackwell.

WOOD, G.H. (1984) 'Schooling in a Democracy: Transformation or Reproduction?' *Educational Theory*, 34, 3, pp. 219–34.

WRIGHT-MILLS, C. (1959) *The Sociological Imagination*, New York, Oxford University Press.

WRINGE, C. (1984) *Democracy, Schooling and Political Education*, London, George Allen and Unwin.

Part Two
Teaching as a Profession

Chapter 4

Beyond Professionalism

Shirley Grundy

Many discussions about the professionalism of teachers are conducted as an argument about whether teaching has the status of 'a profession'. Often the action agenda of such discourse is that of devising more effective means of improving the professional profile of teachers. There are some fundamental problems with such discussions of professionalism, and the project of improving the work of teachers through a 'carrot and stick' appeal to professional status will ultimately fail to bring about real changes in education. In many ways 'professionalism' is a tired old concept which could well be left behind. What is needed is a fresh way of looking at teachers' work and human action through which educators can move 'beyond professionalism'.[1] This chapter will contribute to this reconceptualization by proposing a form of educational practice informed by a disposition of 'practique',[2] rather than professionalism.

Increasingly in our society, there is an emphasis upon efficient production as an indicator of success. Efficient production, it is believed, depends upon concise specification of objectifiable goals, the effective application of skills and rigorous systems of appraisal which will provide a guarantee of excellence. The production process is, therefore, dependent upon sophisticated management systems for its operation and is justified in terms of 'economic imperatives'. This dominant form of organization supports, and is supported by, the technologization of society. However, it is not just material production processes, such as manufacturing or even farming, which are regarded as being appropriate for this sort of efficiency programme; so also are social institutions and organizations such as education 'systems' and health agencies. Technological consciousness has become the dominant ideology of our time.

The temptation to justify educational work through the application of criteria relating to economic production is strong. Pleas for excellence in education are inevitably interpreted by bureaucracies as requiring quanti-fiable results of the teaching process and high quality products of the schooling system. This pressure is keenly felt by educators. It is a pressure which appears to value the product of teaching more than the process of learning, to emphasize skill rather than creativity, and replace interaction with receptivity. Hattie *et al.* identify 'skills, technology and management' as key themes in the educational discourse of our time: 'One of the catch-words in educational politics in Australia today is skills. While most educators are horrified at narrow conceptions of education, many are realising that the hand that feeds is preaching the necessity of skills.'[3]

This dominant ideology presents a direct threat to professional practice. In the light of the dominance of this technocratic consciousness, the defence of professionalism might be seen as the only reasonable form of resistance. It will be argued that defending the professional status of teachers is not a viable response because of some inherent problems with the concept of professionalism. It will also be argued that resistance to the technologization of educational work lies in social critique and not in cries for the preservation of professionalism.

In the first half of this chapter forms of human occupational activity are examined and professional and technical practice contrasted.[4] It is argued that the reduction of professionalism to technical processes will not work, since social interaction, which is fundamental to professional practice, cannot be reduced to the certainties which technology promises. In the second half, the idea of 'practique' as a guiding disposition for occu-pational action is explored. Practique is described as a critical disposition through which the fundamental assumptions underpinning a practice may be examined. While it is argued that practique cannot, any more than pro-fessionalism, provide guarantees about the outcome of social action, it does provide the possibility of exposing the problematical nature of the ethical values which ostensibly guide professional practice. This disposition provokes critical questioning of the extent to which professionalism actually serves the interests of those for whom the practice presumably exists. Is it not perhaps some other set of interests, perhaps those of the pro-fession itself, which professional practice supports? Through this process of critique the possibility arises for professional practice to serve more directly the interests of those towards whom the practice is directed.

Categories of Human Activity

Let us begin the critique of professionalism by considering a range of income generating activities in which people engage. The Australian Bureau of Statistics provides a classificatory system for occupations which furnish paid employment within Australian society.[5] Occupations are classified hierarchically on the basis of entrance qualifications. These categories are:

1   Managers and Administrators (including legislators, judges, finance managers, farmers, shop managers, etc.)
2   Professionals (including natural scientists, building professionals such as engineers, health diagnosis and treatment practitioners, teachers, lawyers, accountants, etc.)
3   Para-professionals (including medical technicians, engineering and building technicians, air and sea transport technical workers such as pilots, registered nurses and police officers)
4   Tradespersons (including metal, electrical, building, printing, vehicle and food tradespersons)
5   Clerks (including office secretaries, data processing machine operators, accounting clerks, etc.)
6   Salespersons (including sales representatives and assistants, real estate agents, tellers, etc.)
7   Plant and Machine Operators and Drivers (including transport drivers, mobile and stationary plant operators and machine operators)
8   Labourers and Related Workers (including factory workers, agricultural labourers and cleaners).

Rather than separate and disparate categories, this system can be interpreted as representing a continuum of human occupations. When regarded in this way, certain interesting trends are discernible which correspond to various conceptual analyses of human activity. Specifically it appears that as an occupation tends towards the '1' category it will involve greater opportunities for autonomy and decision-making. The action outcome is proactive and the style dynamic. On the other hand, as an occupation tends towards the '8' category, much less decision-making power is available and autonomy is prescriptive (meaning that instances where freedom of choice is possible are clearly explicated). The action outcome of occupations at this end of the continuum is reactive, while the style of the occupations is energetic.[6] Between these two extremes, tending towards the '4' category, are groups of occupations which involve decision-making within rule systems, and proscriptive forms of autonomy (that is, only the limits upon choice are explicated). The action outcome of these occupations is productive, and the style is both dynamic and energetic.

Regarded in this way, this continuum of human activity corresponds to Hannah Arendt's analysis of the human condition as manifesting itself in labour, work and action.[7] Arendt likens labour to the ceaseless round of human existence: 'unlike working, whose end has come when the object is finished... labouring always moves in the same circle... and the end of its "toil and trouble" comes only with the death of this organism.'[8] Work, according to Arendt, differs from labour in that it is an act of 'fabrication' or production which has a definite beginning and a definite end. While the products of this form of human activity are finite, work has its own reproductive character:

> The actual work of fabrication is performed under the guidance of a model in accordance with which the object is constructed.... [T]he image or model whose shape guides the fabrication process... does not disappear with the finished product... it survives... as it were, to lend itself to an infinite continuation of fabrication. This potential multiplication, inherent in work, is different in principle from the repetition which is the mark of labor.[9]

What Arendt here identifies as work is that form of human activity which the Greeks, as exemplified by Aristotle, called *poiesis* or *poietike* (making action). When this form of activity is in operation, a product results as an idea (*eidos*) is transformed into making action (*poietike*) through the human disposition of skill (*techne*).[10] In terms of the occupational listings given above this description of a form of human activity fits the category of 'Tradespersons' very well. In general these are people engaged in production whereby plans or specifications are transformed into products through the application of skill.

For Arendt and for Aristotle, this form of activity differs from another form of human activity, that of 'action' (in the Greek, *praxis*). This is the form of human activity which Carr identifies as 'practice'.[11] Arendt states that whereas 'work provides an "artificial" world of things, distinctly different from all natural surroundings,... action... goes on directly between men without the intermediary of things or matter.'[12] Since action (*praxis*) takes place between persons, 'interaction' (specifically speech) is a vital part of this way of operating in the world.

When looked at in this way, the occupations represented in the earlier categories of our listing are more forms of 'action' (*praxis*) than forms of work (*poietike*) or labour (*energeia*). These are just the sorts of occupations which are usually designated as 'professions', to which the attribute of 'professionalism' is deemed to be important.

What Is Professional Practice?

Carr provides a contrast between practice and making action which succinctly summarizes distinctions implicit both in the original Greek and in modern expression, which I have explored at length elsewhere.[13]

> Although 'practice' (*praxis*) is also action directed towards the achievement of some end, it differs from *poiesis* in several crucial respects. In the first place, the end of a practice is not to produce an object or artifact but to realise some morally worthwhile 'good'. But, secondly, practice is not a neutral instrument by means of which this 'good' can be produced. The 'good' for the sake of which a practice is pursued cannot be 'made', it can only be 'done'.... [T]hirdly, practice can never be understood as a form of technical expertise designed to achieve some externally related end.... [P]raxis is different from *poiesis* precisely because discernment of the 'good' which constitutes its end is inseparable from a discernment of its mode of expression.

When an occupation is engaged in as a form of practice, rather than as a form of production, ethical notions of 'the Good' come into play. This reminds us of the importance of 'professional ethics' and suggests that the sort of occupations which we today regard as 'practices' embody the form of human activity encapsulated in the Greek term *praxis*. This would mean that, whereas considerations of efficiency and effectiveness will provide criteria for judging the outcome of productive action, for the professional person, ethical considerations will be predominant.

Once we acknowledge, however, that professionalism is a normative rather than simply an empirical characteristic, we also must acknowledge that it exists in a realm in which evaluation of action becomes problematic, for decisions about 'the Good' must always be subjective and partial. So it is that another crucial aspect of professional practice becomes evident; that of 'practical judgment' (to Aristotle: *phronesis*). Unlike *techne*, which is the guiding disposition of the artisan, *phronesis* is not a method of determining what skills to apply to get something done. Rather it is concerned with what it is that ought to be done.

Yet another crucial difference is discernible between professionalism, as it is manifest through the operation of 'practical judgment', and workmanship, which has its outworking in skill. Skills can be individually learned and applied in isolation by a solitary worker upon the material with which she/he is working. Practical judgment can never have this solitary connotation. Not only is *praxis* a social action, always taking place between people, but *phronesis* also manifests itself communally. For the Greeks it was in the arena of judgment-making with respect to the affairs of the pupils in which *phronesis* operated. Practical judgment-making was synonymous with democratic deliberation, that is, deliberation by the *demos* (the people). In Book 3 of the *Ethics*, Aristotle emphasizes the inter-subjective and mediatory nature of deliberation, and hence of *phronesis*: 'Deliberation . . . operates in matters that hold good as a general rule, but whose outcome is unpredictable . . . .When great issues are at stake, we . . . call on others to join us in our deliberations.'[14] More recently this communal aspect of practical judgment has been explored by Gadamer who identifies it with a *'sensus communis'* (a sense of the common):

> Judgement is not so much a faculty as a demand that has to be made of all. Everyone has enough 'sense of the common' . . . i.e. judgement, that he [sic] can be expected to show a 'sense of the community' . . . genuine moral and civic solidarity, but that means a judgement of right and wrong, and a concern for the common good.[15]

But what does this mean for the professional practitioner? Does it mean that every decision must be made through communal deliberation? Although there is undoubtedly a strong tendency towards deliberation as it manifests itself in professional associations, conferences and consultative processes, practitioners do operate independently and exercise independent judgment. Yet there is a very real sense in which every professional judg-ment is a reflection of a corporate understanding of 'the Good'. The teacher, for instance, who makes the professional decision to abandon spelling 'lists' in preference for a more holistic approach to the development of a spelling consciousness in the students, is reflecting a consensual under-standing of 'the Good' in relation to the acquisition of language compet-ences by children.

This communal aspect of *phronesis* is crucial to our understanding of the meaning of professionalism, for it is at once its greatest strength, a chal-lenge to the individualization and depersonalization of technology, and its greatest weakness. It is through a new sense of communal understanding that practique will emerge. To understand the importance of this communal aspect of *phronesis*, we need first to look at the threat to pro-fessionalism which the technologization of education poses.

The Lure of Technologized Practice

Since the realm of professional practice is the realm of intersubjective action and understanding, unpredictability and uncertainty are its hallmarks. The magistrate prescribing a sentence for misdeeds can never be entirely sure that the penalty will be just; hence our appeals mechanisms in the judicial system. The teacher introducing the writing process to children can never be entirely sure that writing will be a meaningful and rich experience for every child. The social worker dealing with a client in crisis can never be entirely sure that all the factors impinging upon the client's life have been identified and their implications ascertained correctly.

Hannah Arendt accepts such unpredictability as part of the *activa vita* (the active life):

> The remedy against the irreversibility and unpredictability of the process started by acting . . . is one of the potentialities of action itself. The possible redemption from the predicament of irreversibility — of being unable to undo what one has done though one did not, and could not, have known what he was doing — is the faculty for forgiving. The remedy for unpredictability, for the chaotic uncertainty of the future, is contained in the faculty to make and keep promises.[16]

Such is not, however, how the ideology of our age would deal with the unpredictability of *praxis*. In an age where subjectivity and unpredictability are unacceptable, certainty (or at least high levels of probability) is prized. If practice cannot provide the certitude that is demanded, then action must be reduced to work, judgment to skill and deliberation replaced by rule following. Thus, more and more, rather than education being regarded as an ongoing human 'Good', we hear the education process described as a system which produces 'products'. This process is accompanied by the demand that the products be readily and regularly tested and measured to determine their quality. Moreover, teaching is regarded as the application of sets of skills in this production process.

Freire's 'banking' metaphor is a powerful portrayal of the technologization of education through which objectified knowledge is 'deposited' in passively receptive students.[17] (At least, that would be close to many teachers' fantasies about teaching in the perfect classroom.) In this age of electronic banking, the metaphor becomes somewhat chilling, for it speaks of the dehumanizing implications of the reduction of professionalism to a technical process. Thus professional practice, although continuing to operate in the arena of social interaction, is transformed into 'work' in

Arendt's sense of action *upon* rather than *within* the natural world.[18] For this to happen the world of social interaction must be transformed into a world of objects which can be acted upon. Knowledge must also be transformed from something that exists within and between persons to something that exists between the covers of books and journals.

The respect, verging on reverence, which the principle of objectivity elicits within our culture is a mere symptom of this tendency towards objectification of the social world and the technologization of action within it. The quest to discover objective knowledge which will provide a basis for social interaction has led to the transformation of social knowledge into a commodity. This commodification process is a hallmark of positivistic research methodology. The following example of a typical positivistic research project illustrates how the methodology transforms knowledge acquisition into a production process. This particular study aimed to provide knowledge which general medical practitioners could use to improve their health care practices with respect to mothers and children.[19]

The knowledge production process which this study entailed reminded me startlingly of an industrial mining and processing system. After subjects for the research were identified and recruited (in line with very strict statistical sampling procedures) they were interviewed by trained interviewers (using 'instruments' carefully designed and tested elsewhere for the purpose). The information gained from these subjects (whose confidentiality was, of course, protected by the application of numbering systems to their identities) was converted, by another set of people, into a series of numbers and entered into a computer for processing. The processed data were then taken from the computer, analyzed and interpreted by yet another set of people who then deposited the knowledge generated by this process in a journal from where it was assumed that general practitioners would pick it up for application to their patients for improved health and welfare.

The commodification process involved in the production of such knowledge for use by members of a profession is startling. Yet this was an exemplary study of its kind which had attracted large amounts of funding from a very prestigious source and had been subjected to rigorous review by a university ethics and human rights committee. Even so, the view of knowledge implicit in the project was that it is something which can be produced by the application of strict rule systems and the objectification of the subjects of the research. Moreover, there was a complete separation of research and action. Although the motivation to embark upon the research was a concern for improved practice, the link between knowledge and practice was not forged. Indeed the possibility that the researching process could actually affect the practice of those involved in the study was studiously avoided by keeping the participants ignorant of the real hypotheses being investigated, lest the data become 'contaminated'.

The implicit assumption that this is the way that knowledge which will enhance the practice of professionals should be produced, is all part of the process of reducing professionalism to technical processes. The implicit argument seems to be that, in order to enhance professional practice, more technical knowledge needs to be produced. The technologizing of practice is evident, not only in the area of knowledge production, but also in the application of professional knowledge to practice. A technological consciousness places prime importance upon the outcome of action, that is, upon what is produced. Professional practice (*praxis*), however, values action itself above the outcome of the action; that is, to act wisely is more important than meticulously following a set of rules to achieve a predetermined outcome.

This emphasis upon action rather than outcome, relates to the unpredictability of the human condition and the diversity which follows from the individuality and plurality of human agents. True professional practice would perhaps be in evidence when a teacher might, for example, say to the parents of a child experiencing reading difficulties: 'I do not know precisely what course of action will assist your child to become a fluent reader, but in my professional judgment we should act in such and such a way. Many other children have experienced improvement through this approach, it may or may not "work" for Sally, but in any event her life will be enriched in these ways . . . by this experience.' However, the response of the parent to such proposed action may well be one of outrage. 'You, as the teacher, are supposed to have the skills to produce a literate student. We'll look after her welfare and provide her with good experiences, you teach her to read.'

What is this teacher to do? No longer is this a child with a complex array of needs, only one of which is the need to read. The teacher's task is to produce a 'reader'. Thus the child becomes an object to which various procedures are skilfully applied in order to produce the desired outcome. Within reason, the means of achieving the end are not important, as long as they are successful. In this way, professionalism is reduced to technique, *praxis* to production.

It is not only in education that this objectification of the client is in evidence. Throssell has provided an interesting analysis of the objectification process in the practice of social work.[20] He argues that this tendency towards objectification is related to the predominance of positivistic approaches to the production of knowledge. Practice becomes objectified in just the same way:

> In the [positivist] approach . . . the behaviour of the person out there is 'objectively' measured against a given standard of normality defined by the observer . . . . The observer has a conception of what the norms are . . . . The most commonly accepted norms — which also carry labels like 'healthy', 'mature' [etc.] . . . are functional to society. They produce the kind of person the society needs. In this context, 'problem' means behaviour which needs changing back towards the normal. This kind of change has traditionally constituted social work 'treatment'.

Here we see the objectification of persons so that they conform to certain 'types'. The patients thus become 'objects' which can then be altered to fit ideal models through the application of the social worker's skill. Such an approach admits no possibility that problems may be interactively generated between the person and his/her situation.

The lure of technological practice is thus the fantasy of certainty in the realm of human affairs. It is also to be found in the illusion that the social world corresponds to the natural world and can be 'acted upon' in the same way. Arendt reminds us that this is not simply a characteristic of our age but has been a feature of all human history as persons attempt to escape the haphazardness 'inherent in a plurality of agents . . . . Generally speaking, they always amount to seeking shelter from action's calamities in an activity where one man, isolated from all others, remains master of his doings from beginning to end.'[21] Thus technologized practice means that individual teachers can assimilate knowledge provided for their use, hone their skills through practice and instruction so that they can generate desirable outcomes in their students. The (technically) proficient one is again someone who possesses individual knowledge which can be applied to clients with (all things being equal) guaranteed results.

If we accept that the realm of social affairs cannot ultimately be objectified in that way, then the portrayal of human activity as a technical process is seen to be only a partial representation. What is needed in the realm of social action is not so much predictability as prudence, not so much skill as judgment, not so much objectification as deliberation and interaction. And these are just the attributes associated with professionalism. Herein lies an irony, however. Even though true professionalism re-establishes respect for persons, and re-enshrines human judgment as a legitimate basis for action, there are still problems with the exercising of that attribute. Specifically these problems revolve around conceptions of the 'Good'.

As we saw above, deliberation, which is a characteristic of *praxis*, was, for Aristotle, concerned with the means of achieving the 'Good'. Human 'Good' was not of itself considered problematic. This unproblematic approach to 'the Good' is characteristic of many professional groups. Health is regarded as a 'Good'. Education is 'Good'. Justice is 'Good'. It is assumed that professional practitioners will be concerned with the promotion of the particular 'Good' through their practice.

We should not, however, be so ready to assume that the meaning of 'the Good' is unproblematic. All too often we find that what is accepted as being 'Good' reflects the interests of some powerful group in society. So it is with professionalism. It is usually the profession's own understandings of 'the Good', reflectively developed through time and imbibed by the novice during induction into the profession, which are the basis for the professional's action. In the process of professional formation and development, these conceptions become concretized into the traditional practice of the practitioners. It is not simply that such understandings may remain unexamined over time which causes problems with professionalism. The problem is that such understandings over time may have been transformed into an assumption that the 'Good' of the client corresponds to the interests of the profession or, for that matter, other sectors of society. Such may not, in fact, be the case.

Thus it is that the problem with professionalism turns out to be very similar to the problem with technologized practice; that is, a problem with the *eidos* which guides action and the relationship between that *eidos* and the action. For technical action the *eidos* is fixed and finite; it is represented by the plan, model or specifications of that which is to be produced. Knowledge required by the technical worker is knowledge about efficient and effective ways of putting plans into practice. It is not up to the technician to question or alter the plans in response to his/her own judgment about their appropriateness. His/her work consists of putting plans into action.

Professional practice, although theoretically guided by a transcendental rather than a finite *eidos* ['the Good'], turns out to be similar to technical action in this respect. The meaning of the guiding *eidos* of 'the Good' often becomes concretized into the traditional meanings attributed by the profession.[22] Although the professional practitioner theoretically has autonomy to interpret what is 'Good' for an individual or group of clients, that autonomy is limited by the accepted meanings and understandings of the profession. So professional practice turns out to be the operationalization of a static and fixed *eidos*. Once the *eidos* becomes concretized in this way, it is a small step to the technologization of practice.

It is clear, then, that whenever the meaning of that fundamental *eidos* becomes fixed by consensual agreement, professionalism is in danger of being reduced to technical processes. For 'the Good' to remain problematic and *praxis* retain its dynamism, a new disposition must emerge; that is, the disposition of *practique*.

Practique: A Critical Approach to Occupational Action

Practique is essentially a form of critical praxis. It is a form of deliberative, prudent action which refuses to accept unquestioningly embedded, static or consensually agreed ideas of what constitutes 'the Good'. This suspicion of common agreement and uncontested meanings is a consequence of an appreciation of the way in which hegemonic power relations operate.

It is not possible here to enter into an extended discussion of ideology and hegemony.[23] Rather, the focus is on ideology as the production and control of meaning, and hegemony as the meaning systems which come to have such uncritical acceptance that they become woven into the fabric of our consciousness. Professional practice is always in danger of operating within such an ideological framework when fundamental meanings, such as that of 'the Good', remain unexamined.

Hall provides a succinct account of the way in which ideology can be understood as a process of meaning production.[24] Thought of in this way, ideology involves the regular production of a single meaning which 'wins a kind of credibility, legitimacy or taken-for-grantedness for itself'. Ideology understood in this way is 'a system of coding reality'.[25] These systems, sedimented over time, form the deep structure of our interpretation of reality, which Gramsci has called 'common sense'.[26] Thus it is possible by the process of signification to represent the material conditions of life, not as historically contingent, but as 'unchangeable, inevitable and natural'.[27]

The ideological meaning systems which become hegemonic are those which gain common and consensual acceptance. Apple has described this operation in the following way:[28]

> Hegemony acts to 'saturate' our very consciousness, so that the educational, economic and social world we see and interact with, and the commonsense interpretations we put on it, becomes the world *tout court*, the only world. Hence, hegemony refers . . . to an organized assemblage of meanings and practices, the central, effective and dominant system of meanings, values and actions which are lived.

Another crucial aspect of the operation of hegemony and ideology is that these meaning systems are not simply benign systems of agreement among people. Rather they represent systems of meanings which are advantageous to certain groups. The groups that are able to make the meanings are dominant groups; dominant because they are the people who are able to have their meanings accepted and they retain their dominance because their meanings prevail. This is not to imply, however, that hegemonic meanings are uncontested. Hegemony is never a static state of intellectual or practical domination and acquiescence. It is always in a state of contestation because of the 'complex contradictory and discordant ensemble which constitutes the superstructure'[29] and the ability of subordinate groups to produce their own interpretations and meanings.

The way in which these notions relate to this discussion of professional practice becomes clear when we ask the question: 'Which are the groups that are able to determine what will count as the various forms of "Good" in our society?' Professional groups have an important role here. It is the medical profession which largely determines what we mean by 'health', it is professionals engaged in education who have a strong influence upon what is meant in our society by 'education' and it is the legal profession which controls the meaning of 'justice'. Of course, these meanings are not uncontested either outside or within the profession. However, part of what it means to be a professional in any field is to be a protector of the meaning of the particular human 'Good' with which the profession is concerned.

We must ask, however: 'Whose interests do these meanings serve?' While the answer should surely be those individuals and groups which are recipients of the services offered by the various professions, it becomes quickly apparent that the beneficiaries of the operation of these various meaning systems are often advantaged sections of the wider society and the profession itself, rather than the recipients of the services. If the actions of practitioners may not advantage the recipients of the service as much as they advantage other sectors of the society, this does not mean that practitioners are guilty of dereliction of duty or misconduct in any way. It is not that professional practitioners are stupid, bad or uncaring; it is that the meaning systems which are informing their practice are unexamined.

Thus it is important for practitioners to move beyond professionalism into a critical mode of action. The starting point for this process must be a re-examination of the knowledge and meaning basis of the occupation. A useful framework for conceptualizing this process has been provided by Habermas, who has advocated a process of theory/practice mediation grounded in processes of 'enlightenment' and the 'organization of action'.[30]

Critical Self-Reflection

The process of enlightenment is a reflective and communal process. We saw above that a sense of community was important to processes of deliberation which provide the hallmark of professionalism. So also is a critical community important for processes of critical self-reflection. Through such processes groups are able to re-examine their practice and jointly decide upon aspects of that practice which are susceptible of change or improvement.

Enlightenment in this critical sense is different from the process of reflection which has been the subject of much discussion in educational literature recently.[31] As a reaction against the pressure towards technologization of educational work, professional educators have become interested in regaining control of practice, and reflective deliberation has been identified as being crucial to that process. One of the features of this developing concern with professional deliberation and reflection is the reappraisal of the role of the outside expert. This is a form of hermeneutical reflection such as that analyzed by Gadamer:[32]

> Hermeneutical reflection fulfills the function that is accomplished in all bringing of something to a conscious awareness... reflection on a given pre-understanding brings before me something that otherwise happens behind my back....Thus only through hermeneutical reflection... can [I] deem freely what in my pre-understanding may be justifiable and what unjustifiable....This is something that hermeneutical reflection teaches us: that social community, with all its tensions and disruptions, ever and ever again leads back to a common area of social understanding through which it exists.

But while this 'leading back' to shared understandings and values may be empowering for a professional group seeking to re-establish control over its knowledge and practice, it does not deal with the problem of hegemony and the interested construction of a shared understanding of the meaning of 'the Good'. This is where Habermas' notions of 'critical theorems' and 'critical self-reflection' become important.

Critical self-reflection is not atheoretical in the way that deliberative reflection can become. It involves the consideration of critical theorems developed within the discourse of critical social science. Habermas explains the agenda of critical social science as being:[33]

> concerned with going beyond [the] goal [of producing nomo-

logical knowledge] to determine when theoretical statements grasp invariant regularities of social action as such and when they express ideologically frozen relations of dependence that can in principle be transformed. To the extent that this is the case, the critique of ideology . . . [takes] into account that information about lawlike connections sets off a process of reflection in the consciousness of those whom the laws are about.

This quotation highlights an important dual function in this theoretical process. First, there is the development of critical social theorems by theoreticians working within a critical social science discourse. These theorems develop out of a rigorous critique of ideology and ideological social relationships. Their aim is to provide a basis for distinguishing between the ideological and the natural. For instance, critical theorems which have emerged from feminist critique are aimed at distinguishing between those elements of gender relations which are natural and those which have to do with power relations. Critical social science discourse is situated in the interaction between cognitive rationality and personal understanding, for information about these 'connections sets off a process of reflection in the consciousness of those whom the laws are about'.

However, work on the theoretical plane is not sufficient of itself. Indeed the development of critical theorems (which Habermas also calls 'reconstructions'[34]) has no practical consequences. It cannot be assumed that critical theorems can be 'applied' to practice in the way that it is assumed that positivistic generalizations can. Practical consequences can only ensue if the group about whom the theorems have developed gains some enlightenment through critical self-reflection upon these theorems in relation to their own situation. In this way the theorems will be authenticated for the actors. But this also differs from the reliance simply upon deliberation and reflection which hermeneutic approaches encourage. Only critical self-reflection provides the possibility of a challenge to the otherwise taken-for-granted shared understandings.

Critical self-reflection is not, however, a solitary process.[35] It is carried on within critical communities, and it will be these critical professional communities within which the disposition of 'practique' will be developed. The critical professional community will not revere the 'expert' as providing unquestionable guidance and advice, nor will the critical theorist be denigrated as having nothing to offer. This relationship between the critical theorist and the professional group is similar to that proposed by Gramsci as being the relationship between 'organic intellectuals' and the people:[36]

Critical self-consciousness means, historically and politically, the creation of an *elite*[37] of intellectuals. A human mass does not 'distinguish' itself, does not become independent in its own right without, in the widest sense, organising itself; and there is no organisation without intellectuals, that is . . . without the theoretical aspect of the theory-practice nexus being distinguished concretely by the existence of a group of people 'specialised' in conceptual and philosophical elaboration of ideas.

Gramsci's 'intellectual *elite*' are 'organic' in that they arise out of a particular class or group with whom their interests are congruent. It is the organic intellectual, as opposed to the traditional intellectual, who is capable and responsible for 'the foundation of a new and integral conception of the world'.[38] These critical theorists do not exist in a world separated from practice, but are mediators of the process of enlightenment of others. Gramsci sees this as an important project:

to work incessantly to raise the intellectual level of an ever-growing strata of the populace. . . .This means working to produce elites of intellectuals of a new type which arise directly out of the masses, but remain in contact with them to become, as it were, the whalebone in the corset.[39]

This concept of the organic intellectual makes 'good sense' (to borrow another Gramscian term) with regard to the creation and mediation of critical theorems in communities of practitioners. Critical theoretic work is intellectually demanding, 'full of contradictions, advances and retreats, dispersals and regroupings',[40] and it is not conceivable that each practitioner would have the inclination, time or mental energy to engage in the scientific discourse which is part of this quest for understanding. If the insights upon which decisions are to be taken about what constitutes ideas of 'the Good' are to be constituted by more than the sharing of common traditional understanding, a critical theory base is necessary. It follows that, if such theory is to avoid the 'otherness' of a technical relationship to practice, critical theorems must be developed from within the practitioner community, not outside it.

The Organization of Enlightenment and Action

It must be stressed continuously, however, that this process of critical reflection in the light of critical theorems is not a hierarchical theory-practice relationship. Critical theorems provide a basis for reflection only. Of themselves they have no power to determine action. Enlightenment is dependent, not upon acceptance of theory, but upon critique. Critique entails not only the identification of what is wrong, but the probing of current practice to discover the 'cracks and crevices' which offer toeholds for possible change and improvement.

Such an approach presupposes a receptive and open organization in which participants have the opportunity and are, moreover, encouraged to challenge freely all theories, all interpretations and all practices. McCarthy has expressed this practical condition in the following way:[41]

> All participants must have the same chance . . . to put forward or call into question, to ground or refute statements, explanations, interpretations and justifications, so that in the long run no opinion remains exempt from consideration and criticism.

It is only within an organization which respects and practises freedom in concrete terms that the possibility exists for a challenge to traditional meaning systems. For the practitioner this means that freedom to engage in critical discourse and to critique that discourse in the light of personal experience is essential. The most important question that accompanies the engagement in critical reflection is not 'is this true?' but 'is this true for me and for our group?' This means that not only must theory become problematic, but the practice of the practitioners must become problematic also. The bringing together of theory and practice in this sense can only be retrospective. Habermas argues that:[42]

> The theory that creates consciousness can bring about the conditions under which the systematic distortions of communication are dissolved and a practical discourse can then be conducted: but it does not contain any information which prejudices the future action of those concerned.

It is still the practitioner who must decide, in the light of critical self-reflection upon critical theorems and past practice, what action will constitute 'the Good'. Technological consciousness seeks to avoid questions about 'the Good' by reducing action to predefined behaviour, substituting finite goals for transcendental aspirations and replacing judgment with skill. Professionalism continues to embrace the idea of the moral imperative for action, but then accepts the definitions of its own traditions as determining 'the Good' and as guides to action. Practique, however, acknowledges that the moral imperative to action is essential, but problematical. To find a prudent, rational basis for action, theoretical considerations are important, as is critical reflection upon practice. But such theory can only provide an aspiration for action. Action following upon critical self-reflection will be more likely to serve the real interests of those to whom the practice is directed rather than inadvertently serving self-interest or dominant interests in society. This will always be a risky business. Therefore, action arising from practique will always contain an element of experimentation. Experimentation, in a rational sense, is not haphazard or irresponsible. It does, however, admit to uncertainty.

I have argued elsewhere that action research provides a way of operating that is consistent with this form of critical practice.[43] However, it is essential to recognize that not all forms of activity designating themselves 'action research' have this critical perspective. But forms of action research which are most consistent with its epistemological and political foundations do provide an organizational framework for the development of the critical practice discussed here.

It should not be thought, however, that this call for the end to professionalism only has consequences for how practitioners act in the interests of their clients. The political ramifications are far wider. As the process of critical self-reflection develops, it becomes clear that it is not only the practitioners' interpretations of the meaning of the critical theorems or of past action that become important. The critical community will expand to encompass all those affected by the practice. This will include the clients as well as an ever increasing number of practitioners. Through the process of making practice problematical, it will no longer be possible to regard the clients merely as the *recipients* of practice. They will become joint participants in the quest to realize 'the Good' in relation to their lives. Thus the critical educator will see him/herself as a co-worker with students in pursuit of education rather than a provider of knowledge for passive recipients.

This change in existing professional relationships will not be without consequences for the professional or lay community. The challenge to taken-for-granted meanings is a challenge to hegemony, an affront to existing power relations. Once it is acknowledged that participants in the action have a right and a responsibility to challenge the hegemony of traditional meanings within the profession, it also becomes clear that for practitioners to continue to make all decisions on behalf of their clients is to perpetuate another form of hegemonic control. A concern for a critical reappraisal of the meaning of 'the Good' must involve a concern to embrace the client as a joint participant in action with the practitioner. In this way the adoption of the disposition of practique means the demise of professionalism not only in a theoretical sense, but in the practical sense as well. Practitioners who are serious about adopting a critical consciousness with respect to their practice will no longer be satisfied to work within the organized power relationships which characterize professional practice today.

This does not mean, however, that power is lost to the practitioner. Such a radical reconstruction of the meaning of practice will mean empowerment and a new potential for practitioner and participant. As Hannah Arendt reminds us:[44]

> Power is actualised only where work and deed have not parted company, . . . where works are not used to veil intentions but to disclose realities, and deeds are not used to violate and destroy but to establish relations and create new realities.

In this chapter a vision of the construction of new educational realities has been presented. This vision can only be actualized through risk-taking and action. Arendt again reminds us that 'action can be judged only by the criterion of greatness because it is in its nature to break through the commonly accepted and reach into the extraordinary' . . . [and] greatness . . . can lie only in the performance itself and neither in its motivation nor its achievement.'[45]

Notes

1　My thanks to Stewart Bonser for discussion and critique of drafts of this paper
2　S. Grundy, *Beyond Professionalism: Action Research as Critical Pedagogy*, PhD Thesis, Murdoch University, 1984.
3　J. Hattie, R. Kefford and P. Porter, *Skills, Technology and Management in Education*, Deakin, ACT, The Australian College of Education, 1988, p. 5.
4　A detailed conceptual analysis will not be provided here, for I have discussed these ideas at length elsewhere: S. Grundy, 'Critical Pedagogy and the Control of Professional Knowledge', *Discourse*, 7, 2, 1987a, pp. 21–36; *Curriculum: Product or Praxis?* Lewes, Falmer Press, 1987b; 'Teachers' Work: Making or Doing?', *Education News*, 10, 1988.
5　I. Castles, *Australian Standard Classification of Occupations*, Canberra, Australian Bureau of Statistics, 1986.
6　I am using the terms 'dynamic' and 'energetic' in their Aristotelian sense of *dynamis*, meaning a capacity of potentiality, and *energens*, meaning activity or active exercise. For example, 'a man [sic] who knows the art of building possesses the *dynamis*, capacity or potentiality of building a house; but this capacity is only something latent in him until he actively exercises it (*energeia*) by actually building a house.' M. Ostwald (trans), *Aristotle: Nicomachean Ethics*, Indianapolis, Ind., Bobbs-Merrill, 1962.
7　H. Arendt, *The Human Condition*, Chicago, Ill., University of Chicago Press, 1958.
8　*Ibid.*, p. 98.
9　*Ibid.*, pp. 140–2.

10 For a more detailed discussion of the Aristotelian concept of 'making action' see Grundy, 1987a (*op. cit.*) and 1987b (*op. cit.*), pp. 2–27.

11 W. Carr, 'What Is an Educational Practice?', *Journal of Philosophy of Education*, 21, 2, 1987, pp. 163–75.

12 Arendt, *op. cit.*, p. 7. Arendt, consistent with her era, uses masculine nouns and pronouns as generic terms for human persons.

13 Carr, *op. cit.*, p. 169; S. Grundy, 'Three Modes of Action Research', *Curriculum Perspectives*, 2, 3, 1982, pp. 22–34; *op. cit.*, 1987b, 1988.

14 Aristotle, *Nicomachaen Ethics*, 3, 1121a, 5–15.

15 H-G. Gadamer, *Truth and Method*, 2nd ed., London, Sheed and Ward, 1979, p. 31.

16 Arendt, *op. cit.*, pp. 236, 237.

17 P. Freire, *Pedagogy of the Oppressed*, Harmondsworth, Penguin, 1972.

18 For a discussion of this distinction between action upon and within the world see the chapter entitled 'Three Fundamental Human Interests' in Grundy, *op. cit.*, 1987b.

19 The results of this study have not yet been published.

20 H. Throssell, 'A Critical Appraisal of Social Work', in P. Boreham *et. al.*, *The Professions in Australia*, St Lucia, Queensland University Press, 1976, pp. 132f.

21 Arendt, *op. cit.*, p. 220.

22 I explore this notion of the relationship between traditional professional practice in a paper entitled 'Teachers Work: Making or Doing?', Grundy, *op. cit.*, 1988.

23 Some of the references that I have found useful in coming to an understanding of complexities of the concepts of ideology and hegemony are: Birmingham Centre for Cultural Studies, *On Ideology*, London, Hutchinson, 1978; J. Larrain, *The Concept of Ideology*, London, Hutchinson, 1979; A. Gramsci, *Selections from the Prison Notebooks*, ed. and trans. Q. Hoare and G.N. Smith, New York, International Publishers, 1971; L. Althusser, 'Ideological State Apparatuses: Notes towards an Investigation', in B.R. Cosin (ed.), *Education: Structure and Society*, Harmondsworth, Penguin, 1972; C. Sumner, *Reading Ideologies: An Investigation into the Marxist Theory of Ideology and Law*, London, Academic Press, 1979; M. Apple, *Ideology and Curriculum*, London, Routledge and Kegan Paul, 1979.

24 S. Hall, 'The Rediscovery of Ideology: Return of the Repressed in Media Studies', in M. Gurevitch *et al.* (eds), *Culture, Society and the Media*, London, Methuen, 1982, p. 67.

25 *Ibid.*, p. 71.

26 Gramsci, *op. cit.*, p. 328.

27 Hall, *op. cit.*, p. 76.

28 Apple, *op. cit.*, p. 5.

29 C. Mouffe, 'Hegemony and Ideology in Gramsci', in C. Mouffe (ed.), *Gramsci and Marxist Theory*, London, Routledge and Kegan Paul, 1979, p. 333.

30 J. Habermas, *Theory and Practice*, London, Heinemann, 1974.

31 See, for example, J. Schwab, 'The Practical: A Language for Curriculum', *School Review*, 78, 1969, pp. 1–23; W. Reid, 'The Deliberative Approach to the Study of the Curriculum and Its Relation to Critical Pluralism', in M. Lawn and L. Barton (eds), *Rethinking Curriculum Studies*, London, Croom Helm, 1981; G.W.F. Orpwood, 'The Reflective Deliberator: A Case Study of Curriculum Policy-making', *Journal of Curriculum Studies*, 17, 1985, pp. 293–304; T.W. Roby, 'Habits Impeding Deliberation', *Journal of Curriculum Studies*, 17, 1985, pp. 17–35; S. Bonser and S. Grundy, 'Reflective Deliberation in the Formulation of a School Curriculum Policy', *Journal of Curriculum Studies*, 20, 1988, pp. 35–45; P.P. Grimmett and G.L. Erickson (eds), *Reflection in Teacher Education*, New York, Teachers' College Press, in press.

32 H-G. Gadamer, *Philosophical Hermeneutics*, Berkeley, Calif., University of California Press, 1977, pp. 38, 42.
33 J. Habermas, *Knowledge and Human Interests*, London, Heinemann, 1972, p. 310.
34 Habermas, *op. cit.*, 1974, p. 23.
35 See S. Grundy and S. Kemmis, 'Social Theory, Group Dynamics and Action Research', Paper presented at the 11th Annual Meeting of the South Pacific Association of Teacher Educators, Adelaide, 1981, for a discussion of the importance of group interaction to critical reflection.
36 Gramsci, *op. cit.*, pp. 5f., 334.
37 Hoare and Smith, the editors and translators of the *Prison Notebooks*, *op. cit.*, p. 334, n. 18 add a note: 'The *elite* in Gramsci is the revolutionary vanguard of a social class in constant contact with its political and intellectual base.'
38 *Ibid.*, p. 9
39 *Ibid.*, p. 340.
40 *Ibid.*, p. 334.
41 T. McCarthy, 'A Theory of Communicative Competence', *Philosophy of Social Science*, 3, 1973, p. 145.
42 Habermas, *op, cit.*, 1974, p. 39.
43 Grundy, *op. cit.*, 1987b.
44 Arendt, *op, cit.*, p. 200.
45 *Ibid.*, pp. 205, 206.

Chapter 5

Professional Knowledge and the Beginning Teacher

Peter Gilroy

Experience is a method of endorsing prejudices.

(Deighton, 1966, p. 197)

Some two years ago I was invited to take part in a research project, 'Knowledge, Books and the Initial Training of Teachers', funded by the British Library Research Department (Squirrell *et al.*, 1989). The project was intended to build on work previously carried out by Jean Rudduck which, amongst other things, showed that teachers of sixth-form students made unjustified assumptions about the ability of their students to make use of library books, with the result that their sixth-form students had particular views of study and knowledge which did not necessarily include extensive library work (Rudduck and Hopkins, 1984). We were interested in discovering whether similar assumptions concerning library use, books and knowledge were being made in the initial training of teachers. If such assumptions were paralleled in initial teacher training courses, we wanted to see whether we could make any positive suggestions for breaking what would be a worrying and self-perpetuating cycle of library deprivation (in which sixth-formers who found that library skills did not seem to have a high priority for their own teachers then had this experience reinforced during their initial teacher training courses and so returned to schools to continue giving the same low priority to book-based skills as their own teachers had done).

During the course of interviewing student teachers it became obvious that they had little or no conception of the meaning of 'professional knowledge', although most accepted that they were being introduced to knowledge of some sort in preparation for a profession. This led me to wonder whether epistemological considerations might be relevant to those concerned with teacher education, especially as recent work analyzing 'professional knowledge' was concentrated primarily on the concept of 'profession', with little being offered which related philosophical advances made in our understanding of the concept of knowledge to the related context of teacher education.

This chapter moves beyond the immediate concerns of the research project which generated it. It begins by analyzing the recent literature on professional knowledge and continues by examining philosophical work on the concept of knowledge to enable a clearer understanding of the nature of 'professional knowledge'. The implications of such a view of knowledge for the so-called 'theory-practice gap' are described. Finally, the alternative analysis of 'professional knowledge' proposed here is used to highlight and offer a way of resolving an important tension that beginning teachers face during the one-year PGCE course in particular and their professional lives in general.

'Profession' and 'Professional Knowledge'

The literature on 'professional knowledge' mirrors the student teacher's uncertainty in that it accepts that there is such a thing as teachers' 'professional knowledge', but recognizes that there is some difficulty in identifying quite what that knowledge might be. This is well summarized by Calderhead:

> The nature of teachers' knowledge is not well understood but its complexity, and the ways in which different types of knowledge are developed, are clearly crucial in our efforts to understand and improve teacher education. (Calderhead, 1988, pp. 8–9)

It was claimed in the early 1970s that a central problem for teacher education was its 'inability to construct a unified body of knowledge from which educational practice evolves' (Roth, 1972, p. 9). A decade later the 'absence of a universally accepted body of practitioner knowledge' is still bemoaned (Watts, 1982, p. 37). It is significant that neither of these authors felt able to identify such knowledge. In addition it is clear that many teachers, enmeshed as they are in the immediate demands of their classrooms, are likely to endorse the view that 'experience is . . . what counts most' (Hargreaves, 1984, p. 253). This, of course, raises the question whether experience alone can ever be a sufficient base for the development of professional knowledge.

If teachers' professional knowledge is so poorly delineated in both universities and schools, it is unlikely that students will easily identify the 'knowledge' that is supposed to be distinctive to their so-called profession. This is not to say that teaching is not a legitimate profession and that teachers are deserving of low regard in comparison with other professionals such as doctors and lawyers (cf. Roth, 1972, p. 10). Rather it is to suggest that the focus of attention should be moved away from the question of what constitutes a 'profession' and directed instead to what constitutes 'knowledge' in the particular context of schoolteaching.

The fascination with the concept of 'profession' is a strong one. Carr and Kemmis, for example, offer three criteria that are intended to explicate the term 'professional'. They conclude that teaching, because it does not fit their criteria, cannot, except in a very limited way, 'be regarded as a professional activity' (Carr and Kemmis, 1986, p. 8). They continue by suggesting ways in which teaching can be developed to meet their criteria and so be recognized as a profession.

However, although there is much of interest in what they say (especially in what they see as constituting teachers' knowledge, pp. 41–2), the search for criteria to identify particular concepts is fraught with difficulty. Elsewhere I have criticized what I termed the 'criterial approach' to understanding meaning (Gilroy, 1982), and it would seem best to abandon the search for hard and fast logical criteria which purport uniquely to identify 'the' concept of 'professional' and instead to accept that the relationship between criteria and what they are criteria for is conventional and context-dependent. Langford, for example, argues that a 'profession is a social phenomenon' (Langford, 1978, p. 45) and that both members of the professions and the general community must recognize them as such in order that the group might actually *be* a profession. Thus whether or not teaching is a profession is simply a question of whether teachers and the community as a whole accept that teaching is a profession and not merely a matter of identifying appropriate criteria through some sort of spurious philosophical analysis (*ibid* p. 51).

Other writers have suggested that the application of the term 'professional' should be withheld from the activity of teaching because teachers are 'a-theoretical at the level of their day-to-day teaching' (Hoyle, 1974, p. 17). This argument requires that the term 'profession' refers to practice informed by theory and research, which is to assume the point at issue. Others, especially student teachers, would want to argue that 'professionalism arises from the actual job . . . in the school' (Morris *et al.*, 1974, p. 7). Yet others would see the term 'profession' as a convenient way of distinguishing teachers from amateurs (*ibid.*). Given this multiplicity of uses, it is no surprise to find the term becoming little more than a piece of meaningless rhetoric (HMI, 1988, p. 13). However, once the emphasis is shifted onto examining the nature of the *knowledges* involved in becoming a teacher then, provided there is no attempt to identify knowledge by means of logically necessary and sufficient criteria, the shackles of the criterial approach to the problem of identifying professional knowledge fall away.

'Knowledge' and 'Professional Knowledge'

Until quite recently most philosophical work in epistemology could be categorized into one of two traditional positions. The first, often termed objectivism, holds that by its very nature knowledge is in some sense fixed, objective and absolute. The task of the philosopher is to find some means of identifying such knowledge, these means varying from Plato's attempt through metaphysics to identify a 'world' of objective knowledge separate from but related to our own (see, for example, his *Republic*) to more recent attempts to identify logical criteria for the use of the term 'knowledge' (Ayer, 1956).

The paradigm example of objective knowledge would seem to be that of science, with its empirical search for timeless truths matching the metaphysical and logical searches of the philosophers. This layman's view of science is still a dominant and influential one, especially in education (see, for example, Peters, 1975, p. 105), although it has come to be seen by many scientists as identifying nothing more than pseudo-science (Chalmers, 1978, p. 33). In the context of education it can with some justice be identified as an autocratic view of knowledge, in that students, teachers and teacher educators who consciously or subconsciously adopt such a viewpoint are likely to interpret their role as that of either imparting or passively receiving what they would see as the 'correct' body of knowledge, with any alternative being seen as at best derived from the correct body of knowledge or, at worst, simply false.

In the context of teacher education such autocracy lends support to the view that there is a fixed body of knowledge that can be imparted to student teachers and which, together with certain so-called behavioural performance indicators, could provide the basis for accrediting students as teachers (see McLeish, 1978). As it is difficult to identify any uncontentious body of shared knowledge in education, it becomes natural to concentrate instead on behavioural norms, where it is assumed that there is some set of objective practices which, if all teachers were trained in them, would dramatically improve the standard of education. It also produces an essentially imperial relationship between those who have such knowledge and those who do not.

There are many problems with this viewpoint, the most debilitating being the difficulty of identifying a body of knowledge which is 'objective' in the required sense, without simply producing a list which is little more than a set of particular prejudices. To put this point in a different way, Plato's attempt to locate objective knowledge in a 'world' other than our own founders on the impossibility of using our world's apparently non-objective language to refer to the objective world. Having used his metaphysics to create two worlds, he has nothing with which to bridge them. Those who wish to use logically necessary and sufficient criteria to identify objective knowledge have a similar problem in bridging from the formal, empty realm of criteria to the substantive reality of meanings in actual use. The layperson's view of science follows this pattern, for how can particular empirical enquiries properly justify non-particular, objective statements of knowledge?

The problem is produced by creating two exclusive, yet in some sense related, categories, one referring to objective knowledge and one to knowledge which is not objective. As these two categories are mutually exclusive, it follows that there is no other category which can be used to relate them to each other; yet paradoxically it is claimed that there has to be some sort of connection between them.

The problem of bridging the unbridgeable finds expression in a different form in education, namely that of explaining the way in which the theory and the practice of teaching can be connected. It has been suggested, for example, that bringing schoolteachers and teacher educators together (the current 'partnership' ideal) would on its own explain how to connect the theory and the practice of education (Hatfield, 1984, p. 60). As it stands, however, such an apparent resolution would leave untouched the theory-practice dichotomy that the autocratic view of knowledge creates. The reality would be either that theoreticians would have to become practitioners, and practitioners would have to become theoreticians (as indeed has happened — see McNamara, 1976; Medway, 1976), for nothing has been offered as a way of bridging the theory-practice gap that the autocratic view of knowledge creates.

From the perspective advanced here it can be seen that when PGCE students criticize their university-based, non-method work as being inappropriate to their needs (HMI, 1982, p. 112), one interpretation of their criticism would be that it is a result of accepting the autocratic view of knowledge. PGCE tutors are not schoolteachers, and so an autocratic view

view of what they are doing on their methods course could well be that they are attempting to pass on what they see as teacher-knowledge, but which students, using the criterion given by their new-found, post-teaching-practice experience, reject. Given the all-or-nothing viewpoint of the autocrat, one of these knowledges must be wrong or, still worse, out of touch with the new reality of teaching. In the immediate and urgent context of teaching practice the obvious candidate for rejection is the PGCE tutor's conception of knowledge.

The alternative traditional position concentrates on the personal, subjective nature of knowledge, hence its title of subjectivism. If all knowledge is 'my knowledge' (Rowland, 1987, p. 81), then it would appear that the objectivist's problem of bridging the unbridgeable disappears, for there is only one type of knowledge, that of the individual. In philosophy the two-world theory of Plato is replaced by the one-world theory of Epicurus and in science by the subjectivist account of Feyerabend (1975). In education the objectivism of curriculum theorists such as Phenix (1964) and Hirst (1965) is opposed by the subjectivism of the deschoolers. Thus autocracy can be seen as being replaced by the absolute autonomy of the individual.

In addition the theory-practice gap has been neatly removed as a problem, for there now exists only the individual's knowledge of his or her own practice, with external theory being seen as irrelevant at worst, and at best as a mere formalizing of that particular practice. This position justifies direct experience over alternative forms of knowledge, for without it individuals cannot properly produce their own knowledge and so cannot be said *really* to know.

In so radically 'resolving' the objectivist's problem of bridging two mutually exclusive categories of knowledge by positing only one category, the subjectivist effectively denies the existence (or at least the usefulness) of knowledge which is not 'personal'. Such a viewpoint has many difficulties but, in the context of this chapter, it could be seen as condemning students and teachers to the ghettoes of their own practice, making higher education tutors and even other schoolteachers largely irrelevant to the individual's development of his or her 'own' knowledge.

A thoroughgoing subjectivist would not find this a problem, insisting that 'each man *is* an island' (Postman and Weingartner, 1969, p. 100) and arguing that simply to assert that there is other non-personal knowledge is merely to assume the point at issue. The standard rebuttal to the subjectivist is not so easily parried, however. If the language in which their position is expressed were indeed constructed by every individual (as they would have to accept, to be consistent with their own subjectivism), then they could not even communicate their subjectivism through a shared language, as there would be as many different forms of language as people attempting to communicate. Yet the subjectivists *do* communicate and so the very statement of their position can be seen as an example of its failure (and this is to leave aside the question whether there could be unstructured experience — see Inglis, 1985, p. 40; Chalmers, 1978, Ch. 3).

In the context of teacher education the notion of uninformed experience providing the only basis for a teacher's professional knowledge so savagely narrows the vision of the individual concerned that they would be little more than an island in the educational sea, blind and deaf to all around, unable directly to communicate their situation, except perhaps to themselves through some sort of unstructured reflection. Of course, this nightmare of autonomous autism is precisely the situation that teacher trainers and their students are at pains to avoid and so cannot be seen as representing the reality of teacher education (although the forthcoming category of unlicensed teachers might well find themselves in something like the subjectivist's situation).

Because of the difficulties outlined above it is clear that an alternative account of knowledge is required. Such an account has to avoid the major problems that the objectivist and the subjectivist face (an unbridgeable dualism and a too extreme monism respectively) without rejecting the positive aspects of their theses. In particular, an alternative account of knowledge has to allow for some sort of objectivity, to avoid the accusation that the account is nothing more than subjectivism in disguise, while at the same time accepting that individuals do have a crucial part to play in creating and in some sense 'owning' knowledge, so as to avoid the complementary charge of being nothing more than objectivism in disguise. In effect, an alternative account of knowledge has adequately to describe our perception of knowledge as having both objective and subjective aspects without making one of these aspects dominate the other.

Such an account was first advanced by certain of the classical Greek sophists as an alternative to the objectivism and subjectivism they faced (see Kerferd, 1981) and more recently by the philosopher Wittgenstein (see also Popper, 1972). The key to what is in effect a major paradigm shift in philosophy is the move away from accounts of knowledge which overemphasize approaches which are logical or personal (objectivism and subjectivism repectively) towards an account which lays great stress upon the *social* dimension of knowledge, recognizing in particular that neither objectivism nor subjectivism can on its own properly reflect the complexities of knowledge provided by our social world with its concomitant 'type of rationality that is historically situated and practical, involving choice, deliberation, and judgment' (Bernstein, 1983, p. xiv).

The introduction of the social world as a phenomenon to which an account of knowledge must accommodate points up the problems that the two alternatives face. The objectivist is claiming that there is some kind of certain knowledge which is not contaminated by the uncertainties that contact with the social world generates, whereas the subjectivist is claiming that the social world has no significance for the individual. If, however, the social world is seen as the starting point for an enquiry into the nature of knowledge (the 'given'), as opposed to the 'given' of the objectivist (absolute knowledge) or of the subjectivist (the individual), then the objectivist has to accept that contamination with uncertainty becomes inevitable, and the subjectivist has to accept that individual autonomy can only be expressed within the context of the social world.

Even a cursory examination of the social dimension of knowledge reveals that there is not simply one sort of knowledge (that of the objectivist) or as many knowledges as there are individuals (as the subjectivist would argue) except, perhaps, in a closed and very homogeneous society. Rather, there appear to be many knowledges which interconnect and which are relative to the particular social situations in which they are located. These knowledges find their expression in groupings of people and come into existence, or disappear, as these groupings coagulate or dissolve. They are as objective as the groupings demand, as variable as the contexts and individuals that make up those groupings. Thus the acceptance of the centrality of the social aspect of knowledge for informing philosophical considerations of the nature of knowledge has the crucial effect of making the search for absolutely certain knowledge otiose. Knowledge, because of its social nature, is inevitably uncertain (although there appear to be degrees of uncertainty), and this is a feature of the concept which should be accepted as a 'given', rather than avoided as some sort of a failing. Again because of its social nature, knowledge cannot be individual-dependent, because individuals' understanding of 'their' knowledges are provided with their structure by the social contexts within which they operate. To rephrase a Kantian maxim: knowledge without a context is empty; the individual without a context is blind (cf. Kant, 1787, B76, p. 93).

This alternative account of knowledge is merely a description of how we actually use the term, as opposed to a prescription for its proposed use. We seem to apply the term 'knowledge' to a very wide range of contexts. In some there appear to be relative certainties (for example, that the sun will rise tomorrow), in others relative uncertainty (for example, that there exist 'black holes'), but the criterion for their appropriate use is provided by the context within which they are used, not their objective or subjective certainty, whatever that might be. It would seem to follow that many statements could be both true and false, depending upon the context within which they are used, and that we as social creatures live in a sea of knowledge whose uncertain currents we, in the main without conscious effort, adjust to. However, it has to be accepted that we sometimes are made aware of the uncertain nature of knowledge when we are faced with new and unfamiliar social contexts, especially when we are flung into such contexts with little or no understanding of what they involve.

Uncertain Knowledge and the Student Teacher

If this account of knowledge is acceptable as an adequate description of a social phenomenon with which we are all familiar, its relevance to initial teacher education remains to be shown. A key problem would be that of helping students to understand and appreciate the values of the different knowledges that a course of training will introduce them to. This problem is compounded by a further difficulty, namely that many undergraduates enter university having experienced only an autocratic conception of knowledge, an experience more often than not confirmed by their undergraduate experiences of the standard autocratic mode of transmitting knowledge, the formal lecture.

With this background it is only natural that student teachers should expect their teacher training course to consist of a series of certainties, often referred to as a teacher's 'survival kit'. One mature student I interviewed, for example, thought that his PGCE course should be organized along the same lines as those provided for double-glazing salesmen, with a list of clear-cut objectives laid out for students to acquire. If, however, the context within which a teacher operates is seen as being far too complex for such simplistic certainties, many student teachers can be seen as being in the very situation described earlier, in that they are having to face the difficulties inherent in attempting to apply one context's conception of knowledge to radically different contexts. It is not too much of an exaggeration to say that the experience of knowledge that most student teachers bring with them to their PGCE courses is generated by a context which is a *prima facie* example of the simple homogeneous grouping referred to earlier, relying as it does upon simple unstated certainties concerning the value of acquiring objective knowledge in an autocratic way (through lecture and testing).

There can be few solid certainties in the fluid contexts that make up the teaching situation. The first encounter with this disturbing feature of the teaching profession is usually a little way into the academic year, as courses tend to begin with the comforting features of objective knowledge familiar to students from their past (the distribution of booklists and the description of objective elements of the course given within formal or semi-formal teaching situations), and is often a result of having to reflect upon their pre-course experiences. This is because their previous autocratic experience of knowledge makes alien the conception of self-reflection as being another form of knowledge. Similarly, if their first experiences of schoolteaching are not similar to those with which they were once familiar as pupils, the loss of a common, shared context of knowledge strikes them all the more forcefully. The natural autocratic reaction is to dismiss much of what they are experiencing as not being knowledge *per se* rather than, as the arguments here make clear, as representing different *types* of knowledge. Despite the fact that they have been catapulted from one social context to another (with the concomitant shift in what is acceptable as 'knowledge'), the autocracy with which they are familiar prevents them recognizing the implications for their understanding of knowledge that such a shift provides. In this way an opportunity for using their own experience as the basis for understanding the way in which contexts define knowledge can be lost.

The experienced mismatch between a search for certainty in an uncertain world is rarely highlighted and analyzed by tutors for their students. Moreover, once students are on teaching practice and away from the direct influence of their tutors it becomes very difficult for students to look beyond their need for immediate practical solutions to pressing practical problems. The stage has been set for student teachers' easy acceptance of the view that the teaching profession has no 'real' (that is, objective) knowledge base, for such knowledge is not provided by the tutors on the course and is seen as being in the main irrelevant to the practical concerns of the classroom.

Langford's view of teaching is useful here. For Langford (1978), teachers' professional knowledge can be seen as consisting of a web of appropriate practices which are specific to the particular contexts within which these practices have life, as representing a particular social phenomenon among many. Such a context-specific view of professional knowledge would allow students (and teachers) to welcome the diversity of their experiences in education, rather than to reject some out of hand as irrelevant. It also suggests that tutors should provide their students with as many diverse experiences as possible and the opportunity to analyze them, as many tutors do now, although it must be accepted that this will be no easy task, as students are bound to find the pressures of teaching practice a simple way of identifying what is and is not immediately relevant. This is merely another aspect of the contextualization of knowledge, for as long as students are aware that what they see as relevant for their teaching practice is not necessarily relevant in other contexts, then no harm is done. The danger arises when students believe that what they find as relevant for one context is relevant for all. One student I interviewed, for example, claimed that reading had not informed her teaching practice and that reading was therefore irrelevant to both her PGCE course and to teaching itself. Such contextual blindness represents an acceptance of a crude autocratic conception of knowledge, with all that it implies for students' later teaching and the conception of knowledge that they in turn transmit to their pupils.

Another useful aspect of approaching professional knowledge in this way is that the theory-practice gap disappears, without at the same time creating the problems that the subjectivist's similar resolution of the problem creates. The gap only exists when knowledge which is appropriate in one context is imported into another, apparently inappropriate, context without its relevance being adequately explained. Once the context-specific nature of knowledge is grasped, there is no longer the need to accept the simplistic viewpoint that knowledge is necessarily split between the theoretical and the practical, for the complexities of context override such an autocratic approach to the concept of knowledge (cf. Eraut, 1985, pp. 127–8). In this way so-called 'theoretical' and 'practical' knowledges interact in various contexts, and it is the appropriate *context*, rather than knowledge itself (whatever that might be), that defines which is to be termed 'theory' and 'practice'. As Carr has pointed out, in trying to bridge the theory-practice gap the 'transition is not . . . from theory to practice as such, but rather from irrationality to rationality' (Carr, 1980, p. 66), and the criteria for rationality are as certain, or uncertain, as the contexts allow.

Conclusions

It has been argued here that one way of coming to understand the meanings inherent in the term 'professional knowledge' is to concentrate on a modern conception of knowledge which avoids the weaknesses of the traditional objectivist and subjectivist approaches, while taking account of their strengths. Moreover, the modern contextual conception of knowledge has important implications for those concerned with teacher education. On a very personal level student teachers experience the difficult problems produced by having to shift rapidly from one social context to another; on another level their profession provides a paradigm example of the contextualization of knowledge. For both of these reasons it is important that they be given the opportunity to come to terms with the implications of such a radically different conception of knowledge from that with which they are familiar.

The contextualization of knowledge seems not to be a problem for doctors, lawyers and other such 'professionals' (perhaps because autocracy reigns supreme in these disciplines), whereas for teachers it is the medium within which their working lives find expression. As such it is a particularly interesting aspect of the phenomenon of initial teacher education, for student teachers have to learn to move *within* this new medium to be recognized as effective teachers. In doing so, students have to find ways of accommodating to the unnerving, context-based relativities of building professional knowledges during their training year, and tutors need to devise ways of encouraging them to accept the diversity of their profession's knowledges. To do otherwise is to allow beginning teachers to accept a simplistic, autocratic view of knowledge with the concomitant danger that they, in their turn, will pass on the same limited and limiting viewpoint to their own pupils.

Acknowledgment

I am indebted to Wilf Carr, Jean Rudduck and Gillian Squirrell for their comments on earlier drafts of this chapter.

References

AYER, A.J. (1956) *The Problem of Knowledge*, London, Macmillan.

BERNSTEIN, R.J. (1983) *Beyond Objectivism and Relativism: Science, Hermeneutics and Praxis*, Oxford, Blackwell.

CALDERHEAD, J. (1988) 'Introduction' to his (ed.) *Teachers' Professional Learning*, Lewes, Falmer Press, pp. 1–11.

CARR, W. (1980) 'The Gap between Theory and Practice', *Journal of Further and Higher Education*, 4, 2, pp. 60–9.

CARR, W. and KEMMIS, S. (1986) *Becoming Critical*, Lewes, Falmer Press.

CHALMERS, A.F. (1978) *What Is This Thing Called Science?*, Milton Keynes, Open University Press.

DEIGHTON, L. (1966) *Billion Dollar Brain*, Harmondsworth, Penguin.

ERAUT, M. (1985) 'Knowledge Creation and Knowledge Use in Professional Contexts', *Studies in Higher Education*, 10, 2, pp. 117–33.

FEYERABEND, P.K. (1975) *Against Method: Outline of an Anarchist Theory of Knowledge*, London, New Left Books.

GILROY, D.P. (1982) 'The Revolutions in English Philosophy and Philosophy of Education', *Educational Analysis*, 4, 1, pp. 75–91.

HARGREAVES, A. (1984) 'Experience Counts, Theory Doesn't: How Teachers Talk about Their Work', *Sociology of Education*, 57, pp. 244–54.

HATFIELD, R.C. (1984) 'A Role for Teacher Educators in Developing Professional Knowledge', *Action in Teacher Education*, 6, 1–2, pp. 57–62.

HIRST, P.H. (1965) 'Liberal Education and the Nature of Knowledge', in Archambault, R.D. (ed.), *Philosophical Analysis and Education*, London, Routledge and Kegan Paul, pp. 113–38.

HMI (1982) *Education Observed 7: Initial Teacher Training in Universities in England, Northern Ireland and Wales*, London, DES.

HOYLE, E. (1974) 'Professionality, Professionalism and Control in Teaching', *London Educational Review*, 3, 2, pp. 13–19.

INGLIS, F. (1985) *The Management of Ignorance: A Political Theory of the Curriculum*, Oxford, Blackwell.

KANT, I. (1787) *Critique of Pure Reason*, trans. N.K. Smith, London, Macmillan, 1929.

KERFERD, G.B. (1981) *The Sophistic Movement*, Cambridge, Cambridge University Press.

KORNER, S. (1974) *Categorial Frameworks*, 1970, Oxford, Blackwell.

LANGFORD, G. (1978) *Teaching as a Profession*, Manchester, Manchester University Press.

MCLEISH, J. (1978) 'Effective Teaching: A New Analysis', *British Journal of Teacher Education*, 4, 3, pp. 215–23.

MCNAMARA, D. (1976) 'On Returning to the Chalk Face: Theory not into Practice', *British Journal of Teacher Education*, 2, 2, pp. 147–60.

MEDWAY, P. (1976) 'Back with Nellie: Some Experiences and Opinions Arising from David McNamara's Article', *British Journal of Teacher Education*, 2, 2, pp. 161–6.

MORRIS, M., MACLURE, S., PORTER, J. and TAYLOR, W. (1974) 'Conversation', *London Educational Review*, 13, 2, pp. 6–12.

PETERS, R.S. (1966) *Ethics and Education*, London, Allen and Unwin.

PETERS, R.S. (1975) 'Subjectivity and Standards in the Humanities', in Nyberg, D. (ed.), *The Philosophy of Open Education*, London, Routledge and Kegan Paul, pp. 91–109.

PHENIX, P.H. (1964) *Realms of Meaning*, New York, McGraw-Hill.

POPPER, K. (1972) *Objective Knowledge*, Oxford, Oxford University Press.

POSTMAN, N. and WEINGARTNER, C. (1969) *Teaching as a Subversive Activity*, Harmondsworth, Penguin.

ROTH, T.C. (1972) 'Towards a Delineation of Professional Knowledge', *Kappa Delta Pi Record*, 7, 1, pp. 9–11.

ROWLAND, S. (1987) 'My Body of Knowledge', *British Journal of In-Service Education*, 13, 2, pp. 81–6.

RUDDUCK, J. and HOPKINS, D. (1984) *The Sixth Form and Libraries: Problems of Access to Knowledge*, British Library Information Research Report 24.

SQUIRRELL, G., GILROY, D.P., RUDDUCK, J. and JONES, D. (1989) *Books, Libraries, Writing and the PGCE Course*, British Library Information Research Report.

WATTS, D. (1982) 'Can Campus-Based Preservice Education Survive?', *Journal of Teacher Education*, 33, 2, pp. 37–41.

Chapter 6

Practical Professionalism

Hugh Sockett

Paul Hirst's articulation of 'Educational Theory' in 1966 began a crucial debate about the nature of educational theory and its relationship to practice (Hirst, 1966). The alternatives promoted and the issues raised in the past two decades appear throughout the chapters in this volume. The impact of Hirst's account on UK higher education institutions is acknowledged to have been in the teaching of the 'disciplines' in undergraduate and postgraduate education programmes. It matched the Robbins Report recommendations that teaching should become an all-graduate profession with the institutional reorganization that followed in the 1970s. Since then, education degree requirements in the UK have moved away from the disciplines to incorporate more topic-focused and school-based work, as the practical model (see Carr, 1986) would suggest: but it is hard to credit that model with those changes. Yet Schools of Education in the UK and the US remain more or less where education is researched and taught: and schools remain places where teachers teach and begin to learn their art. Changes in the perceptions of educational theory and practice do not yet seem to have been reflected in institutional design.

In recent years the rhetoric of educational improvement has come to be couched in the language and lore of 'profession' (Darling-Hammond, 1988; Sockett, 1989a). In the US, the Governors' Report (*Time for Results*, 1986) lauded the ideal of profession and spelt out some ways to achieve it; in the UK the White Paper, *Better Schools* (1985), was equally enthusiastic that teaching be a profession. Eric Hoyle (1980) made the significant distinction between professionalization, where the *status* of the occupation is at stake, and professionalism, which focuses on the quality of *practice*. Views about educational theory and practice and their interrelations provide different criteria for the knowledge base of practice which yield different accounts of professionalism.

A central question is posed: what shape ought educational institutions, whether schools or Schools of Education, to have if the aspiration for increased professionalism is well founded and in the light of changing understandings about the nature of theory and practice? If it is true that educational institutions imply a particular epistemology, presumably institutional shifts should follow as alternatives gain ground.

This chapter does not attempt to describe the range of theoretical possibilities, of which there are no doubt many, nor to examine practical initiatives in the matching of institutional shape to changing epistemologies. Rather the task is to describe and reflect on the founding phase of an institution, namely the Center for Applied Research and Development in Education (CARD) at George Mason University, Fairfax, Virginia, which seeks to take the 'practical model' seriously and embody its epistemology in an institutional frame. If both the development of professionalism in teaching and the expansion of new understandings of an epistemology of practice are desirable, then we need to learn how to construct institutions to match these aspirations. The institution itself becomes an object for self-study, perhaps even a hypothesis about how such aspirations can be attained. Three central features of CARD are first described, followed by a discussion of five major challenges it presently confronts, as it begins to wrestle with the forbidding challenge of practical professionalism.

A Brief History of CARD

Larry Bowen, Dean of the College of Education and Human Services at George Mason University, had spent several months in 1969 working with Lawrence Stenhouse and Barry Macdonald at The Humanities Project. He had been attracted by the general notion of a Center for Applied Research (CARE) which Stenhouse and Macdonald came to found at the University of East Anglia in 1970. In his work as Dean, Bowen had been anxious to promote strong relationships between his college and the school districts (or divisions as they are called in Virginia), particularly with Fairfax County Public Schools, the tenth largest district in the US, where the University is located. This initiative took the usual forms of collaborative committees on specific projects and topics. Nationally, many such collaborations were attempted, notably by John Goodlad and others through the Center for Educational Renewal (Sirotnik and Goodlad, 1988).

Following a visit to the University of East Anglia in 1984, Bowen determined to push ahead with the idea of founding a center which would have some similarity to CARE but with a broader scope. He created interest across a number of school divisions and, after a period of discussion and consultation, received from a representative planning committee a mission statement for CARD, which focused on the significance of collaboration and on practice-based research.

The context for this initiative is particular and promising. First, George Mason University is in the process of transformation from a small outpost of the University of Virginia to a 'major player' in higher education in Virginia under the guidance of President George Johnson. Johnson believes that the University should be identified with a strong commitment to the community and should also be prepared to redefine the nature and scope of university activity. Second, the northern Virginia community is a fast developing, hi-tech area, in close proximity to Washington DC. It continues to attract such major corporate institutions as Mobil Oil and Xerox. The educational level of its population is very high — 50 per cent of the inhabitants of the largest county have a college education — as are the educational demands made by parents and business. Third, both university and community are geared to innovation. It is possible in such a context to create 'systems-busting' institutions, even though institutional conservatism and inertia are always powerful. Finally, there was an existing example of excellence in collaboration: the university and the school divisions had for ten years supported the Northern Virginia Writing Project, which itself had developed a strong emphasis on teachers as researchers (see Mohr and Maclean, 1987).

In this favourable context the Center was established as a collaborative venture involving nine northern Virginia school divisions and the University. I was hired as Director in 1987, and the Associate Director, Todd Endo, is released from Fairfax County Public Schools for a quarter of his time. As Director of Fairfax's Office of Research and Evaluation, Endo had been promoting school-based research and development by teachers and principals, and he was the author of the CARD mission statement. I had experience with institutional innovation at the (former) New University of Ulster and at East Anglia and had more than a nodding acquaintance with the work of CARE and its political and intellectual origins.

Structure, Partnership and Substance

The Center did not spring fully armed from the mission statement or the discussions between the University and the school divisions. Rather, a conscious decision was made to engage all interested education professionals across the nine school divisions in the creation of the institution 'bottom up', and frameworks had to be established to provide that opportunity. Partnership, a better term than collaboration, was therefore open to education professionals within a general climate of passive support from the nine school divisions and the University.

The budget is modest, to say the least. The CARD office is provided by Falls City Church Public Schools (one of the nine member divisions), and CARD is thus based in a junior-senior high school, partly for convenience but primarily to indicate an allegiance to practice. Arlington County Public Schools sponsors CARD's quarterly newsletter. Two other school divisions have commissioned consultancy work which provides additional financial and political support. The initial planning committee decided not to negotiate up-front financial commitments from the school divisions to avoid any possible risk that CARD might have to kowtow to their agendas.

All who come into contact with CARD as participants, do so out of professional interest, not as a result of a hierarchical allocation process. Thus in the meetings held within CARD people attend as volunteering individual professionals, although there are occasionally representatives of this or that institution, usually as a result of misunderstandings. There is no exclusive 'membership' of CARD: any professional can join in.

Three major features of the Center seem, as CARD approaches the end of its second year, to be retrospectively significant as they relate both to the development of professionalism and to the epistemology implied by the practical model.

Structure

Collaboration demands a distinctive institutional structure, not a mere partnership between existing institutions. Some lessons about educational innovations have already been learned: many curriculum projects of the 1960s and 1970s, for example, were extremely fragile, however well funded they were in their development phase. The same could be true of university centres. Equally, collaboration is often dependent on enthusiastic volunteers *within* institutions who may move to other posts, leaving behind them not so much a loss of commitment but no strong institutional framework within which activity can be promoted (Parish, Underwood and Eubanks, 1986–87).

For its structure, CARD has built a system of *networks* and *forums*. The former group education professionals broadly into roles. There is thus a Teachers' Network, a Principals' Network and a Network for

Community, Administrative, Business and Lay Educators, known as CABLENET. University faculty are invited to attend any of these, although some have recently proposed that a network be created for faculty to include George Mason and universities with outposts in northern Virginia.

The agenda for the first meetings of networks was the brainstorming of appropriate topics on which CARD might work: the proposed topics were grouped into forums, twenty-seven in all. A forum thus seeks to bring together professionals interested in such areas as Minority Students' Achievement, Structuring Schools, Early Childhood Education, Gender Equity and so forth. Each network and forum determines its own agenda. This proposed structure was implemented after wide circulation for comment and criticism.

The keys to this approach were: first, education professionals, whatever their role, had to be given a sense of *ownership* of the Center; second, the structure had to allow for *change and permanence*.

Ownership. Education professionals work in very different roles: some are classroom teachers, some have become assistant principals or principals, some are in universities, some are central office administrators, supervisors and advisers and so on. Bureaucracies, within which all professionals work, can be tyrannical and exclusive: tyrannical, not in that they are run by latter-day Attilas, but in that the institutional agendas drive the exercise of the roles, to which any would-be Attilas are also subject; exclusive, in that professionals become totally preoccupied with the agenda and the politics of their own jurisdiction and exclude the learning opportunities available from their neighbours. Educational institutions are the political embodiments of epistemologies, and they dominate the lives of their personnel.

Education professionals must somehow come to own the institution if the notion of increasing practical professionalism is to take hold. This is a quite different aspiration for a collaborative venture than one in which negotiations for the new institutions are conducted top-to-top. Ownership comes from collaboration not merely across institutions, but also across professional roles.

The first step toward that goal is a structure which is flexible. That is, we cannot tell whether creating networks and forums *per se* is going to prove the best framework. We have had to revise the numbers of forums created: we have the proposal for a new network, for joint network meetings and so on. We have accepted projects initiated by school system leaders when those are compatible with the CARD philosophy. More important for ownership is flexibility of agenda. As forums and networks meet and adjust to their novel context, so there will be an instability of agenda which will gradually be negotiated and refined.

Second, the structure must celebrate professional equality. For example, it must make possible adaptation to new roles, e.g. a classroom teacher chairing a meeting including academics and administrators. That can take time: professionals invariably meet with status consciousness, finding role-cloaks difficult to shrug off.

Third, it must create the space for interaction for people from different jurisdictions, and it must begin to provide for them a focus of identity outside a workplace role. There needs to be a constant search for ways to offer ownership and for it to be accepted.

Change and Permanence. If the *flexibility* of the structure (and the agenda) is necessary to adapt to the development of ownership, how is this reconciled with the demand for permanence? In the process of giving the whole institution and its separate parts permanence, it becomes apparent that the institutional framework must have both a sense of adaptability to changing need and sufficient permanence to enable individuals to relate to its parts. It must permit flexibility, and therefore must expect to be seen as vague for those used to hierarchical patterns of work. As agendas take time to settle, activity within the structure will be seen as ambiguous, vague and slow moving, particularly in a dynamic society used to 'the quick fix'.

This is not at odds with the need for permanence. For us the notion of permanence is that the structure will provide sufficient stability with respect to access and organization to enable professionals to move in and out of CARD work, as other professional commitments allow. It will not, like the typical curriculum project, no longer be there in two years' time. CARD needs to remain open to structural change, while offering a firm pattern of organization to which individuals can relate. Above all, individuals need to share these understandings.

Our conclusion on structure is that the framework is a crucial piece in collaboration design. It must facilitate ownership and adjust to a context of change *and* permanence. This process of institutionalization of an innovatory centre needs to be carefully monitored and consistently evaluated for its effectiveness. For example, the original plan for regular central meetings of networks and forums may need to be modified by 'local', perhaps 'branch', meetings with an annual full meeting.

Partnership

Implicit in this account of the structure is a principle of equality among education professionals (principal, teacher, administrator, researcher) and institutions (schools, universities). That is not merely equal opportunity to join or to contribute to the work of CARD, but a symbol of a common professionalism. That common professionalism extends to content *and* process. The commitment to partnership includes a continuing exploration of what professionalism and its obligations are. These principles are expressed in the brochure:

CARD's Beliefs

CARD believes that

- o   practicing educators are too isolated and need opportunities to share, reflect, plan and act together;
- o   practicing educators are equally teacher and learner, leader and follower;
- o   collaboration among colleagues will increase the effectiveness of each participant and the whole;
- o   creativity and initiative are at the core of professionalism;
- o   real life is the source of wisdom and thus theory must be grounded in practice and research must be grounded in action, and
- o   practicing educators possess an unlimited reservoir of good ideas.

The most obvious way in which partnership is realized is through the development of the agenda for each network and forum. Each professional is a source of differential knowledge and understanding about the practice of teaching. Yet a common assumption among many educational researchers in search of objective knowledge is that teachers are simple technicians. It is no accident that the major publication by the US Department of Education on the application of research to schools is called *What Works* (US Department of Education, 1986). (*Works*, you will notice, not challenges or intrigues, but *works*.) Teachers rapidly are socialized by situation and by the need to look for what works — the 'hunger for technique' as Lortie (1975) describes it. Researchers support that hunger. One will look for a classroom or two where teachers will practise what he or she has designed and 'test it'; another will 'market' a technique to groups across the nation. These traditional patterns of research activity, with the teacher as consumer and user of products, are familiar enough. Yet the primary weakness of these patterns is the extent to which the teacher is then *professionally* undermined, the extent to which the epistemology they encounter actually makes their experience 'worthless' even though it looks like support. It emasculates many teachers. It inhibits the opportunities for them to become developers, researchers or producers, not least because opportunities are not provided for them to test their ideas with a broad audience.

The establishment of a partnership of mutual expertise is thus much more complex than developing a structure. The differential status of people within administrative and academic hierarchies effectively 'silences the teacher's voice' (Richert, 1987). For CARD, three things are required. The first is the patient creation and development of leadership roles not determined by status. The second is a continuing validation of the teacher's experience and the quest to involve university faculty in that enterprise. The third is a mutual responsibility for building the partnership and for exploring the obstacles to it. All who wish to practise professionalism have to find out how to do it, and how to create a discourse about it.

Substance

The third key factor in the development of CARD is the commitment to a substantive idea of what would constitute practical professionalism. This commitment shifts CARD away from being simply a mechanism of cooperation. For CARD, the twin notions of reflective practice and teacher research constitute the substance. This is not the place to examine the work of Donald Schon (1983) or Lawrence Stenhouse (1983). The question is in what ways might the force of their ideas be critiqued and expanded *institutionally*.

First, as I wrote in 1985, the debate about what constitutes educational theory and practice is not simply an arcane encounter among academics (Sockett, 1988). It is reflected in hotblooded controversy within universities, though with less heat as it spreads across the profession. The title 'applied research' is consistently misunderstood by people with a traditional conception of research. With that goes a disdain for the very idea that mere teachers could do research: some of this is boundary-building, but it is more commonly a profound belief that teachers ought to be technicians as they are incapable of research. Whole institutional structures in education are built around views of research. A pervasive theme throughout CARD discussions has to be an examination of what educational 'talk and action' ought to be. Professionals rarely address the question of the nature of the enquiry they are engaged in: rather they take the assumptions of positivism in educational theory as a kind of common sense (see Schon, 1983). Yet as they try to work out, say, how very different schools, each wanting to promote the teaching of higher-order thinking skills to low-ability minority children, can get sufficiently similar activity going, so they are entering a quite new realm of thought about educational thought and practice.

Second, the power of technical rationality in educational research is such that the development of an institution devoted to an alternative view, at the very least, takes time and care. Our first stage has been like the opening of a conversation, in the networks and forums. That is trivially a form of teacher empowerment: it is 'unsilencing the teacher's voice' in the educational enterprise and creating a mutually supportive climate. So teachers begin to talk evenly with principals or administrators, to university people and to their colleagues in other jurisdictions. It is a conversation unfettered by any form of 'assessment'; it is serious and it is free, cut off too from the politics of individual institutions.

Yet that conversation has to be in a language. Sometimes teachers do speak a proto-research language (the kind of common sense referred to) and they need to see the descriptive and explanatory power of other languages, drawn from Schon and Stenhouse. So while they may couch their discussion in the language of Maslow, Skinner, 4MAT or whatever as they talk, it is critical for that to become self-conscious and for all professionals to explore the language of others. Stenhouse, for example, writes with great passion about emancipation, not empowerment, about vernacular humanism (as a contemporary context for the humanities), while Schon presents portraits, of Quist and his student, which introduce a language of design.

The second stage is the development of ways of thinking with intellectual rigour which match the conversation. That is a process which, for any constituency of people, is one of exploration and uncertainty. That means beginning to relax in a context of tolerable ambiguity. CARD is about to begin the second stage, though the two stages will always overlap. The crucial feature here is the notion of an educational idea being at the heart of the collaboration: it is not collaboration for collaboration's sake, but a collaboration moved by a concern for reflective practice and teacher research.

Eighteen months after the foundation of CARD these three features — structure, partnership and substance — seem critical aspects of institutional design. The task is monumental and its ambitions may outrun its spirit. As yet, it is too early to be thoroughly confident, except in the way that education professionals from very different roles respond.

Practical Professionalism: The Emerging Challenges

There are five major challenges CARD has to respond to at this early stage of its development: the challenges of the agenda, ownership, professional career conflict, innovation and leadership. No doubt, after twelve months these challenges will be construed differently.

To be a profession, teaching must get hold of its *accountability* and its *research* (see Sockett, 1989b). The accountability of teachers is broadly bureaucratized through the various mechanisms that the phenomenon of mass education has thrown up: it is not a system which teachers designed. Yet both in school-based management systems in the US and in moves to weaken local authority control in the UK, there are opportunities for the professionals to pick up the challenge.

The Challenge of the Agenda

Getting hold of research and development is a different matter. Research and development agenda on education are rarely constructed by teachers (or other school-based educators). They spin out of the heads of academic researchers with ideas to explore, or dead horses to flog, often progressively within the limitations of a particular research canon. Alternatively problems are defined from the top, wherever that happens to be. Governments and foundations focus on needs they define. Of course, such agenda are political — as they always will be — but teachers in the classrooms have no say in their development.

First, need teachers always be left out of the establishment and execution of research and development agenda except as it appears through their unions? Across the profession practitioners must become a major engine for taking our understanding of teaching and teaching excellence forward (see Shulman, 1987). Some can and will become teacher researchers, examining their own practice and sharing that enterprise with others. They can become part of the attempt to ensure that schools do become places where teachers learn, and learn through rigorous research on practice. This is a development which seems conspicuously part of teaching professionalism. The challenge is to invent ways to facilitate teacher participation in the definition and execution of the agenda for research and development. Presently the agenda is defined elsewhere.

Second, existing sources of research agenda are sources of power: and there is a marketplace competition for funds. That is a market teachers will have to enter qua teachers. They will need to construct a research and development agenda with other education professionals from their practical deliberations: and that will constitute a threat to those bureaucrats (in education offices?) or professionals (in universities?) who wish to limit the competition. Even though teachers see that they can define the agenda for the research they want to participate in, that very attempt begins to undermine existing sources of the agenda, whether in the school division or in the university. Teachers are, of course, making a claim for resources which, if allocated, will not be allocated elsewhere. Moreover, they are also claiming opportunities of time (which have resource implications) for activities which may be regarded as outside contractual limits. Teachers are not employed to undertake research and development. As teachers, or collaborative institutions of which they are a part, seek resources to develop an agenda, they encounter power-blocs.

CARD has some experience over the past two years of these problems of the agenda for research and development. First, in bringing together different school divisions and the university there are substantial demarcation problems. On any given area in which teachers see research as needed, there may be nine different sets of interests as there are nine school divisions. Some divisions already have a research and development programme internally funded and designed by an 'administrator/researcher' who may have little interest in, and even hostility toward, a coordinated programme of work across divisions. Others give low priority, administratively, to problems which teachers rate as very important.

Second, university staff may have their own clear perceptions of 'what needs doing' in an area and lack any commitment to working with teachers except as tools of their own work. It is thus possible to find a group of teachers with a clearly articulated sense of direction for research and development related to practice but without anyone experienced in proposal writing or prepared to volunteer their time and with little support from either university or school division. Moreover, education faculty correctly perceive it to be much easier to negotiate an agenda privately with administrators than to seek it with groups of teachers. If they are productive researchers, they will also have existing agenda of their own.

Third, there is a distinction made between research and development in the academic world which is reflected in federal, state and foundation funding. 'Development' money by the bucketful may pour out of the federal coffers on politically sensitive educational areas, e.g. special education, bilingual education, 'at-risk' children; but 'development' means a focus on new curricula, institutional changes and immediately useful products which can be marketed. 'Research' funds, on the other hand, seem to focus on usable, generalizable conclusions on 'what works'. Teacher research in an 'applied research' mode seems to fall between the two stools of research and development, and its horizons are too long and its focus is not generalizable in the sense that sponsors seem to think valuable. That distinction between 'research' and 'development' is fallacious for an epistemology of practice, as described, for example, by Schon (1983). It is drawn precisely from the model which the epistemology seeks to replace. As seen in this chapter, we are having difficulty using terminology other than research and development. The term 'applied research' does not help much. Perhaps Schon's 'reflective practitioner' come closest to what we intend.

CARD's response to the three aspects of the challenge of the agenda is not yet fully fledged. First, we seek to develop proposals through forums with mutual responsibility for the design and proposed participation. That represents an effort to ensure that 'authorities' become accustomed to teacher involvement in research and development design. That may mean the creation of opportunities in a familiar style out of which negotiations for teacher involvement can be developed, e.g. by the negotiation of a traditional contract with a school division out of which a different kind of contract can be negotiated. Second, the autonomy of university faculty is such that opportunities can only be offered and participation invited since faculty members may perceive little pay-off (given existing criteria) in the time consuming process of building a different culture. The catch-22 is that university investment in a collaborative venture will not, from that point of view, be seen as delivering the goods: that is, the presentation of a clear context for a researcher to move in and exercise his or her talents. Third, proposals for funding may best be couched in the broader framework of professional development.

In sum, this challenge of the agenda reaches far into issues of the government of education. En passant, the second largest school division participating in CARD, Prince William County, is moving to a system of site-based management which will have the eventual effect of enabling the schools to use central office specialists as advisers and consultants rather than working under their direction. As that substantial reform gets under way, the schools may be more effectively placed to ensure that they have a major say in the definition of the agenda for research and development.

The Challenge of Ownership

Networks and forums in CARD provide opportunities for education professionals, from different roles, to hold office and carry responsibility as part of the pattern of developing professional ownership of the Center. Working in CARD gives a professional a new and active role to learn in an institution exploring its own definition. Becoming an owner is a major learning experience with dimensions which are not yet clear. It is easy to say 'you own it', but more difficult to ensure that it happens. The challenge of ownership is to create professional identity as owners of an exploratory professional institution.

The dimensions of this challenge are at different levels. First, learning new roles is complex. Chairpersons need to learn the skills of chairmanship which are both executive and enabling. Some have experience of executive chairmanship where the task is a given; few have experience of managing other adults in a learning experience. The fact that CARD is in an early stage of growth and that time is at a premium means that the composition of different networks and forums changes; new members require induction. Moreover, with a University and nine school divisions, individuals will be rooted in a range of different cultures with differences of style. Professionals have to learn how to occupy roles with these diverse parameters.

Second, most professionals come to those CARD activities which are of particular interest to their main role. Committed to innovation and development, professionals find themselves critiquing their own institutional (division or school) policies, and in some cases learning to do so with some distance. Equally, those policies can be subject to critique by others from different divisions. While the positive aspect of focused discussion is the opportunity to learn from others and use their ideas, the critique too must come to be valued as a major aspect of professional autonomy. There are some occasions when the etiquette of respect for the work of another division inhibits that critique. On others, professionals from different divisions can easily distance themselves from their formal role. Professionals are 'allowed' within university programmes or in-house meetings to criticize. In the seminar their comments are, as it were, sanctioned. The CARD professional is more exposed: he or she volunteers interest; his or her critique is independently given and is unprotected. Developing a sense of ownership implies developing an independence of an existing role. That may be easy for university faculty, but much harder for a teacher or an administrator.

Third, ownership in a research and development institution demands not merely the development of critical distance, but the engagement in different forms of critical evaluation. Few educational institutions are actually interested in process as opposed to content evaluation. Dominant evaluation modes, furthermore, are either too open or too goal-oriented. Professionals want to evaluate ideas or proposals in terms of function and applicability; they are unaccustomed to dealing with the hypothetical, in content terms, or to evaluating their own work as a learning experience. Wheels must never be reinvented; navels must be left unexamined. As the epistemology of practice is explored and new institutional relations created, so the criteria of evaluation shift to process. Embracing ownership thus anticipates a much broader perspective of evaluative enquiry.

The CARD structure begins to give professionals an alternative identity, and they can become ambassadors for its ideas. The major dimensions of that challenge appear to be the learning of new roles and relationships, particularly in the development of a critical distance and a familiarity with different perspectives of enquiry.

The Challenge of Professional Career Conflict

The criteria for career progress, both for university faculty and for teachers, are familiar and they are to some extent interlocked. For university faculty in the US working more closely with schools and teachers raises the perennial problem of rewards and promotions. With published research remaining the dominant criterion, there is a positive disincentive to many faculty, as they see it, to take the risk. Yet university teaching is also influenced by teacher-student perceptions. Faculty have also become accustomed to a pattern of teacher in-service demand which seeks 'cash' rewards: masters' degrees are worth this much salary increase, credit courses for recertification are a condition of employment and so on. The dominance of prespecified objectives in teaching at all levels leaves little room for mutual exploration of complex issues between teacher and student. Indeed the pressure from students is for clear definition of 'what is required' to make the grades, to get the award. 'What', asks the typical teacher-student of his or her professor in respect of an assignment, 'do *you* want?' The pedagogical impact of such attitudes is that courses are heavily instructional. Furthermore, in many institutions student evaluation of courses is the primary source of rating a professor's teaching ability (which in turn will influence his or her salary). The risk of seeking to create a different pedagogical environment matching a notion of professional equality is considerable. Teachers have to get credits for recertification on a regular basis. Reward systems are geared simply to classroom performance, and the priorities of time and energy do not lead to an ambiguous uncertain enterprise.

Both for the teacher and the university faculty, therefore, CARD activity cuts across well established patterns of career progress. It is unrewarded in university promotion criteria; its exploratory character makes it an uncertain 'subject' for a 'course'. Both for classroom teacher and for academic faculty, the challenge of professionalism and an epistemology of practice conflicts with established norms. These factors in career structure are rooted in the traditional epistemology of theory and practice, in shared perceptions of the purposes of a university, and in the fractured profession of which educators are members. The traditional epistemology supposes that research and development ideas are theories which can be applied to practice if they can be learned in the university by practitioners who then go forth and implement them. Both student and faculty, as we have seen, are locked into a relationship driven by their different career structures. Both of these factors indicate how the profession of teaching is split between theory and practice, *and* between researcher, administrator and practitioner (Sockett, 1989a). They also indicate the split between teacher and learner, creator and implementor, degrees and learning.

The challenge for an institution seeking to alter them is to create a culture, not a cult, within which the framework of a professional's identity is understood as something that might be otherwise (see Leiberman, 1988). CARD seeks to create different conceptions of 'career', to expand and to reshape conventional expectations.

CARD is beginning to engage with these complex issues, first, by undertaking experimental masters' level programmes which celebrate its educational principles; for example, by promoting a course (called an Internship in Education) which will allow a teacher-student to study an aspect of his or her own work in schools, and by offering an individualized programme (called Origins and Horizons) which will enable teacher-students to begin the process of reflection on their educational practice by examining it in the light of their educational ideology and constructing from that a perspective on that individual's career future in the classroom. CARD is also seeking to establish summer programmes with graduate credit. CARD would like to find some way in which the work done in CARD by its members who need it can also be recognized for credit. The urgency is demonstrable: one teacher has recently told us that, while she values the CARD work very much, she needs to limit her work in it so that she can get an MA. We need to find institutional ways to remove that tension. Yet that will still contain problems: for instance, the balance may be difficult to strike between supporting a system of legitimate rewards and becoming merely a convenient source of credit. Finally, CARD is seeking to develop formal roles that combine school-based teaching, university teaching and research. Roles and ideas embodied in the concept of a professional development school are appealing.

For university faculty the problem is well expressed by Clifford and Guthrie in their demand that Schools of Education turn their focus away from the university to the schools (Clifford and Guthrie, 1989). With that comes the large problem of shifting the criteria of promotion and tenure to support those faculty who wish to discover and work in new patterns of relationships with other education professionals. The difficulty for a fragile new centre is to resist the power of existing arrangements. If the tension between CARD activities and existing career demands can be resolved, that will only be part of the answer: the Center's activities need to become a priority for education professionals.

The Challenge of Innovation

Education is manifestly a political matter. In both the UK and the US it has become increasingly politicized. The central problem of change in mass education is this: political horizons are very short; educational horizons are very long. For the politician, if there is something wrong, then it can (or must) be 'fixed'. Results have to be there within two to five years: and, if it has not 'worked', the political opponent will engineer other manifestos and slogans. The parents with a 10-year-old child wants changes now — or it is too late. In northern Virginia, as elsewhere, the systems have to respond to these kinds of political imperatives.

The length of educational horizons is assumed by politicians to be an excuse for incompetence. But the implementation of, say, a different mathematics curriculum may require a generation of schooling to establish success or failure. CARD experiences, as education professionals of creativity and initiative come together, the development of radical diagnoses of institutions and policies such that the horizon of change is out of sight. For example, how might the school curriculum be changed to counter the appallingly high 25 per cent dropout of American secondary students? What has to be done to offset the fact that most American children do not study any mathematics beyond Grade 9? That kind of agenda, even if resources were available and variables could be controlled, is not to be realized within a one-term presidency.

This mismatch of the political 'quick fix' and the reality of the problems as perceived by education professionals is compounded in CARD. For the differences between a positivist and a political model, as they find embodiment in conceptions of professionalism and in institutions, are profound. The traditional model, coupled with political myopia, is geared to the 'quick fix'. The real danger for CARD is that it will be seen as a *potential* 'quick fix' (albeit of a funny kind) which, if it 'delivers' few 'results', will be trashed.

That unfortunate possibility has to be guarded against. One minor protection, as far as operating circumstances allow, is to keep institutional baseline funding low to avoid the attraction of a cut and seek to live off soft money with ground-level, small-sum grants for specific tasks matching the ideals of CARD. That way, a constituency of support can be built offering the best opportunity of preserving the institution and allowing its reputation and the quality of its work to grow. The challenge of innovation is how CARD can sustain a long-term horizon within a political and social context of short-term change.

The Challenge of Leadership

Professionalism, it has been claimed, demands a context of equality. Manifestly that implies rejecting any general view of hierarchy in which the classroom teacher is at the bottom. It does not mean that there will be equality of contribution, insight or experience among education professionals. But it does mean that teachers make the largest contribution.

The challenge of leadership within this kind of institution is to create a 'community of leaders' who contribute to the articulation and implementation of its vision. Roland Barth sees schools as places where professionals can each have the opportunity to exercise leadership, not in the sense that leadership responsibilities are seen as 'just part of the job', but in the search for those enthusiasms and skills which individuals have which can be set in a leadership context (Barth, 1988). Forums and networks have to be challenged by the belief that 'educators are equally teacher and learner, leader and follower'. Moreover, understanding this as a challenge is something those who participate in CARD must accept.

It would be disingenuous to suggest that the vision is clear and coherent to everyone in CARD, or to suppose that it has arisen or has been articulated by large cross-role groups of professionals. It has come from the basic mission statement and been developed by us. Yet we have merely been initiators, as forum and network chairs and others have picked up the challenge. Through particular kinds of work and meetings, conversations and workshops, the ideas gradually gain currency within the CARD constituency. The crux for us has been not how to share the vision but how to get professionals to see that they can develop and reshape its rough-hewn state.

Practically this implies the testing of as many ideas for development as can reasonably be handled: to support a 'forum of one (where a determined person pursues an interest); to be prepared to plan workshops or conferences which fail to attract; to be acutely sensitive to the articulation of ideas or phrases which catch the sense (The Teachers' Network was called 'a professional library of people' by Phyllis Porter, a Prince William County teacher); or to promote ideas which then lie dormant waiting for money or an enthusiast. Above all, it is to build through the feeling of ownership a sense that CARD is a vision to be portrayed.

Conclusion

CARD is at a beginning. It differs from most consortia in that we have not been constructed with a clear agenda agreed by the hierarchies of collaborating institutions. It has to make its way. It is interpreting the notion of 'collaboration' as *both* across institutions and school divisions *and* between the levels of education professionals. It is focusing on the development of a culture and a constituency which does not quickly yield the kind of research results which universities instantly recognize. Its mission has shifted, in part, as the development of the Restructuring Schools Movement, the work of the Center for Institutional Renewal, and the movement to teacher professionalism have gained pace. Collaboration is not a fixed goal, but a principle of procedure constantly to be interpreted. The Center stands for professional equality and for that different epistemology, roughly characterized as reflective practice.

George Mason University proclaims its mission as one to the northern Virginia community, a fast paced, fast growing, hi-tech society. It is too early to judge whether CARD's flexible design is an ideal, except in its focus on the education professional as an individual rather than as a role-player. From the university perspective, it is an exploration of ways in which the 'interactive' university can find its place in the education community.

Acknowledgment

I am grateful to Todd Endo for his critical comments on an earlier version of this chapter.

References

BARTH, R.S. (1988) 'School: A Community of Leaders', in Leiberman, Ann, *Building a Professional Culture in Schools*, New York, Teachers College Press, pp. 129–48.

Better Schools (1985) London, HMSO.

CARR, W. (1986) 'Theories of Theory and Practice', *Journal of Philosophy of Education*, 20, 2, pp. 177–86.

CLIFFORD, J.W. and GUTHRIE, G.J. (1989) 'A Brief for Professional Education', *Kappan*, 70, 5, pp. 380–6.

DARLING-HAMMOND, L. (1988) 'Policy and Professionalism', in Leiberman, Ann, *Building a Professional Culture in Schools*, New York, Teachers College Press, pp. 55–78.

HIRST, P.H. (1966) 'Educational Theory', in Tibble, J.W. (ed.), *The Study of Education*, London, Routledge and Kegan Paul, pp. 29–58.

HOYLE, E. (1980) 'Professionalization and Deprofessionalization in Education', in *The Professional Development of Teachers*, World Year Book of Education, London, Kogan Page, pp. 42–57.

LEIBERMAN, A. (ed.) (1988) *Building a Professional Culture in Schools*, New York, Teachers College Press.

LORTIE, D. (1975) *Schoolteacher*, Chicago, Ill., University of Chicago Press.

MOHR, M. and MACLEAN, M. (1987) *Working Together*, Urbana, Ill., National Council of Teachers of English.

PARISH, R., UNDERWOOD, E. and EUBANKS, E.E. (1986–87) 'School-University Education', *Metropolitan Education*, 3, pp. 44–55.

RICHERT, Anna E. (1987) *Reflection and Pedagogical Caring: Unsilencing the Teacher's Voice*, AERA.

SCHON, D. (1983) *The Reflective Practitioner*, London, Temple Smith.

SHULMAN, L. (1987) 'Knowledge and Teaching: Foundations of the New Reform', *Harvard Educational Review*, 57, 1, pp. 1–22.

SIROTNIK, K.A. and GOODLAD, J.I. (eds) (1988) *School–University Partnerships in Action*, New York, Teachers College Press.

SOCKETT, H.T. (1988) 'What Is a School of Education?' in Gordon, P. (ed.), *The Study of Education: The Changing Scene*, London, Woburn Press, pp. 300–18.

SOCKETT, H.T. (1989a) 'Research, Practice and Professional Aspiration within Teaching', *Journal of Curriculum Studies*, 21, 2, forthcoming.

SOCKETT, H.T. (1989b, forthcoming) 'Accountability, Trust and Professional Codes of Ethics', in Goodlad, J. *et al.*, *The Moral Dimensions of Schooling*.

STENHOUSE, L. (1983) *Authority, Emancipation and Education*, London, Heinemann.

Time for Results: The Governor's 1991 Report on Education (1986) Washington, D.C., National Governors' Association.

US DEPARTMENT OF EDUCATION (1986) *What Works: Research about Teaching and Learning*, Washington, D.C., US Government Printing Office.

Chapter 7

Accountability and Teacher Professionalism

Maurice Kogan

In the search for new paradigms in educational studies, the meaning and present state of teacher professionalism will surely be a central theme. The problems of establishing its meaning and boundaries are obvious. Many of the statements made about it provoke recollection of the Shavian jibe about conspiracies against the laity. Yet experience is that when asked, clients prefer to trust professionals (for example, Munn *et al.*, 1982), and believe that teachers should be strong and right.

Any analysis of accountability and teacher professionalism treads on steep ground, all the more so since the received definitions of professionalism and some of the most potent contemporary discussions contain explicitly normative programmes for action rather than detached analyses. For that reason it will be desirable, if tedious, to begin with a definition that might clarify some of the assumptions underlying this chapter. In so doing, I will follow a schema established elsewhere (Kogan, 1986) which analyzes models of teacher professionalism on the dimensions of values, authority or institutional characteristics and epistemology. These models will then be deployed within present experience as the government's schema for a national core curriculum, for pupil testing and for combinations of national and consumer control come into play.

The Professional Model of Accountability

Professionalism, and its assumptions of power, duty and autonomy, have several linking connotations. In education it is assumed to be justified on technological grounds because practitioners are required to make individual judgments about individual clients. It is further assumed that the working essentials of education demand that its professionals possess a stock of esoteric knowledge and skills not available to the layman, not to be promiscuously shared with him, and to be conducted within relatively autonomous boundaries. This has effects on the institutional arrangements. Professionals are expected to have an altruistic regard for their individual clients. Accountability assumes the requirement to answer to the broader social community. I have remarked elsewhere that professionalism is individualistic, whereas accountability, at least in its more traditional senses, is collectivist (Kogan, 1975). These technological justifications are reinforced by those characteristics of education deriving from its rules of knowledge or epistemology; if knowledge is in its essence bounded and exclusive rather than permeable and demotic, professional power is the more justified.

A related set of characteristics is social or institutional. Education is here a mixed case. The social aspects of its individualism offer protection for practitioners from managerial control. However, the majority of professionals, teachers, doctors, social workers, engineers and architects work within the managerial systems of public services. Of these, only doctors working with individual patients in hospitals and family practice are almost wholly free of managerial control. However, in the past public sector professionals have had varying degrees of the characteristics of élite groups; there is delegated to them the authority to decide and act by those who inhabit the political system and who are themselves mandated by public election or appointment.

It should be readily seen that there are connections between the three sets of characteristics. The technology of education, the ways in which teachers work, derives from the extent to which knowledge components are protected or permeable. If they are protected, accountability will be largely about defined outcomes. If they are permeable, it is more possible for non-professionals or managers to interest themselves in the style and process of what is on offer. The organization of the curriculum, and the knowledge assumptions underlying it, thus affect the institutional frames and prescriptions within which education is conducted.

Against this background of definable characteristics of professionalism we can do no better than consider Hugh Sockett's professional model of accountability (1980), lately elaborated further in his thinking about professional codes which links practice and research and practice and professional aspirations (1988). It directs itself to teacher anxieties about the contemporary demands for 'results' and hypothesizes instead the professional as a freestanding entity contractually committed to ethical practice rather than for the production of results embodied in pupil performance. It explicitly eschews deference to managerialism because accountability 'would be rendered to diverse constituencies rather than to the agglomerate constituency of the public alone' (Sockett, 1980). The 'how' of accountability would not entail evaluations through measurement of pupil performance but through the provision of information for constituents allied to a system of proper redress through a professional body. On this view of accountability, the professionals would create a covenant committing them to discuss with interested parties what the schools and teachers do, and to deliver an account which would justify and explain that which is relevant to the concerns of these different parties.

Sockett's model is consistent with the standard definitions of the professional. It assumes a body of knowledge and skills, a prolonged period of training, a social acceptance that the expertise is legitimate 'and a professional culture containing ideas relating to organisational modes and ethics and standards' (Greenwood, 1966).

Sockett's model is consistent, too, with that of many other authorities in the field who write of the condition governing the creation of 'responsive' schools (Elliott *et al.*, 1981; James, 1980) and 'the democratic approach to evaluation' (Simons, 1979). The epistemological contents of these professional accountability models are implied rather than stated, but they seem to contain the assumption that educational knowledge and the skills for its acquisition derive from the operation of free minds on the subject material in a largely self-determined process. The kind of relationship with clients they envisage no doubt adds to the quality of the knowledge generation and selection.

These models of teacher accountability and professionalism have been largely consistent with much of the received wisdom of British education, at least until the drastic changes in assumption and policy which have culminated in the Education Reform Act of 1988. Teachers are formally within managerial hierarchies. Their contracts and their legitimacy derive from the election of councillors who constitute local education authorities. Legally speaking, local education authorities have delegated control over the curriculum and conduct of schools to governing bodies who, in their turn, delegate them to schools and teachers. Within the protection of that political and legal legitimacy, schools and teachers have developed the characteristics of nearly autonomous professional groups. They are indeed socially legitimated élites who could 'make a selction from the culture' in creating the curriculum, and administer it in terms of their perception of what would most benefit their clients.

Of course, this picture of high professional freedom must be seriously modified by the existence of important constraints: external examinations which have thrown a shadow over the last two or three years of compulsory schooling; the power of inspectors and advisers and, indeed, of the local authority at large to apply sanctions through promotions, appointments and the award of resources and other statuses; and the growing power of client groups. Nor have teachers fully secured the positively responsive stance some of them might have expected, and the covenant of full report and explanation has not been achieved, except in a small minority of schools.

A further problem is that the exponents of professional models of accountability seem curiously unconcerned about the truisms of British democratic life. The coexistence of professionalism and local elections is not an easy one. But any effective or legitimate model of teacher professionalism would surely have to find ways of negotiating between the power of collegia of teachers and the need for democratic control over public institutions — Sockett's 'diffuse constituents'. Hugh Sockett is the only commentator in this vein to even acknowledge the issue.

Epistemological Assumptions Underlying the Professional Model

The professional models are explicit on only a limited range of epistemological issues which need to be faced. Sockett and the leading authorities from our two principal East Anglian Centres (Universities of East Anglia and Cambridge) argue that the professional model is desirable because it will protect the schools from a requirement to concentrate on 'product', in the form of quantitative learning outcomes, in the interests of emphasizing the importance of 'process', in the form of qualitative learning experiences. The merits of that educational preference need not concern us here, except that we must note that there is no unbreakable logical link between teacher control and an emphasis on process rather than product. Historically, strong teacher professionalism often allowed product to reign supreme and the nature of that product to be determined by the teacher rather than by the clients. It is romantic to assume that all teachers are liberals fighting the dour instrumentalism of the laity.

A somewhat different view is that the accountability of a teacher or school might be defined in terms of their success in enabling pupils to master disciplines or fields of knowledge (Taylor, 1978). This view lays emphasis upon the quality of the teacher's information and knowledge as a subject specialist and, in particular, on the ability to communicate a respect for the 'truth criteria as well as the disputes surrounding the nature of truth' which are academic to his discipline. Taylor assumes that there is a stock of knowledge to which truth criteria can be professionally applied so that the teacher will know whether the known is truth or not. This derives from J.S. Mill's perspective that knowledge is derived, inductively and empirically, from experience.

Yet a further perspective is that the classification and framing of educational knowledge is not a product of its inherent content (Bernstein, 1975); instead society's selection, classification, distribution and evaluation of knowledge reflect how power is distributed and the nature of social control. Knowledge is, therefore, a product of power and institutional arrangements as much as of its substantive content. If curriculum defines what counts as valid knowledge, knowledge is simply that which is agreed upon according to the values of interested parties. Pedagogy defines what counts as a valid transmission of knowledge, while evaluation defines accounts of the learning achieved.

Bernstein's celebrated account of the curriculum needs to be summarized in only the briefest terms here. Curriculum entails a hierarchy of time and content according to the value systems of those deciding the hierarchy. The contents of the curriculum are within boundaries which are either closed or open. Thus allocations of time and the degree of autonomy or closedness allocated to subjects determine their status. In a similar vein collections are distinguished from integrated types of curriculum.

Taylor and Bernstein start from different epistemological perspectives, but the institutional or social consequences need not be different. Thus Taylor endorses the nature of the inherent truth criterion which helps us to sort out, verify and order knowledge for its authoritative transmission by teachers. On such a model of the generation of knowledge, the accountability of teachers becomes crystal clear. The good teacher can demonstrate what he says to be true and can show pupils how to learn what is true and to demonstrate that it is so. The teacher's professional authority stems from the fact that he is 'an authority' in the particular knowledge discipline he or she teaches. Professionalism is thus the antithesis of any mere repetition of received truths. The hallmark of the professional is that he or she can demonstrate truthfulness and also encourage the development of the kind of curiosity and critical ability which is required to challenge concepts and facts.

The Bernsteinian account is more concerned with social morphology or structures of knowledge than with whether knowledge responds to truth criteria. Paradoxically, however, his analysis might lead to a stronger and more determined model of teacher professionalism than William Taylor's. If there is a hierarchy of social endorsement, the determined professional will have control over the hierarchy. It will be the curriculum experts and teachers who decide which elements of the curriculum might be integrated or connected and which are permeable or not. That is, in effect, what happens in the generation of knowledge. At the research and higher education level, come and, presumably, soon go the Enterprise Initiative; it is not external forces but the academics themselves who decide what are the boundaries between disciplines, which subjects are most prestigiously ordered within disciplinary hierarchies and who search, somewhat more meekly, and sometimes separately, for paradigms which will make their disciplinary timber good and lead them away from the connotation of a problem-related 'domain' (Trist, 1972).

It seems, therefore, that professional models of accountability might themselves vary according to assumptions about the nature of knowledge (epistemology), or just as easily according to levels of teacher aspiration for power. A professional model could indeed be positivistic (pace Carr in his 'Introduction'). If it is assumed that meaningful propositions are independent of value and derived from demonstrable scientific process, the invitation is to create relatively unresponsive isolated centres of authority: in fact, a traditional and pre-progressive view of teacher professionalism. Epistemological relativism would pay little heed to proof but would regard knowledge and understanding as bound by the context within which they are formed and therefore potentially negotiable. Sockett suggests a more open and multi-level of authority responsive to competing value imputs. In this model teacher professionalism offers all kinds of capacities for shared 'ownership' of the curriculum, social learning as opposed to teacher-led instruction. Both Sockett's model of teacher professionalism and Sallis' model of partnership (Sallis, 1979) point in this direction.

Before turning to the implications of recent policy developments, a further assertion must be lodged. Some claim to have seen a visible connection between social macro-policies and models of education accountability (for example, Elliott *et al.*, 1981). Thus public accountability systems have been linked with the productivity managerialist order, while concepts of professional accountability have been associated with the supremacy of the individual pupil in good relationship with the supportive teacher. The highly ambiguous policies implicit in the Education Reform Act of 1988 seem to reinforce the notion that professional accountability is to be diminished in favour of training for the economically productive and socially disciplined society. But that connection is not logically essential. Managerial control over teachers could as well be used to endorse tough regimes based upon positive concepts of equality, as is well witnessed in some local education authorities, let alone the USSR or Iran.

Present Concerns

The Education Reform Act of 1988 directly challenges and seeks to displace the received assumptions of British education as they have grown up since 1945. It imposes a national core curriculum which flatly contradicts the assumption underlying the professional accountability model — that teachers develop the curriculum not to produce discernible and measurable outcomes, but rather to provide a negotiated order of knowledge to be explained and discussed with client groups. The public contractual model of accountability, too, is drastically changed. The local authority, as mediator of the electorate's wishes, is to be greatly weakened; powers and finance will be delegated to the schools. Schools may opt out from local authority control altogether.

Yet the provisions are shot through with ambiguity. One reading of the Act seems to reinforce the management and contractual model of accountability by giving such enormous powers to the centre. The curriculum is to be framed nationally rather than to arise from interactive processes at the school level. At the same time, however, curriculum, financial and other provisions are to be in the hands of the governors and the heads. The consumer is to have the power of exit (Hirschman, 1970) over the schools and thus influence their 'delivery' of the curriculum. Three levels of power will thus bring three assumptive worlds into play. The only definite loser will be the local education authority which must now move from the role of the benign manager, leader and provider towards a second-order role of monitor and adviser.

What constructs of accountability arise from these new dispensations? And what might be the outturns in terms of the professionalism of teachers? Will they lead to an epistemic shift? As far as accountability is concerned, the economically stated categories of the Education Reform Act of 1988 have been elaborated by Circular 7/88, and guidance on curriculum in the different subject areas begins to flow. The ambiguity of these proposals lies in the fact that the centre states that it will relieve local authorities of much of the business of tedious control and emancipate them so that they can better evaluate, monitor and guide schools within a general planning framework. The Circular promises LEAs a lot without making it plain how monitoring can be converted into planning, given open enrolment and the prohibition on Local Management Scheme (LMS) formulae which do not follow traditional age-related funding.

At the schools it is plain that the governors and head will take on enormous new powers. The governors will authorize the curriculum within the National Curriculum and the head will 'deliver' it. The governors and head will also be able to reward and sanction teachers through the conditions of the Pay and Conditions Act, 1986. The schools under Local Management Schemes will have the bulk of the budget, excluding capital works, within their control. These provisions potentially bring great freedom to the schools. They should be able to emancipate themselves from local authority control over the balances to be struck between expenditures on teacher and non-teacher salaries, teachers of different grades, on equipment or books or on keeping a warm school or a well staffed one. But the burden of managing resources and fabric might well mean that leadership roles in schools change from those of leading professionals to those of resource managers, a position becoming increasingly familiar in the universities where vice-chancellors are supposed to become chief executives and deans and heads of departments 'middle managers'. The need to cope with open enrolment might also set in motion a new mode of leadership — more entrepreneurial, more public and managerial than that of a leading professional educator brooding over the curriculum.

Such changes might colour the environment within which professionalism works. The first-order changes are those associated with the nationally imposed curricula and testing, the enhanced powers of governors, the constant bombardment of centrally determined initiatives through Section 11, statementing and other bits of Warnockry, education support grants and GRIST, the succession of Training Agency initiatives. All of these add up to prescriptive frameworks, some carrying legal prescription and some carrying monetary inducements, within which the schools will move the more constrictedly. Some believe that with these provisions the curriculum development movement has lived out its brief summer.

The epistemological connotations of the Education Reform Act are not too difficult to discern. The curriculum will certainly not be the result of artistic interaction between the teacher and the individual pupil who, in Plowden's words (borrowed from Hadow), is the agent of his own learning. There is to be a selection from the culture, and that selection will be made in the first instance by national experts appointed by the Secretary of State, under the guidance of a retired, very senior DES administrator. The Secretary of State himself has no inhibitions about stating his own view on the place of grammar in the curriculum.

Equally, while the testing system will not be as traditional and as grinding as might have been feared, there can be no doubt that national normative frames will be established. The teacher is certainly to be accountable for products, although it may well be that the processes will still contrive to be reasonably liberal. The epistemological assumptions will be idealist, that is concerned with the transmission of tested and accepted knowledge, rather than progressive (Evetts, 1973), and the idea that the truth shall be demonstrated and known is thus brought into operation.

While these prescriptions will be the firm base upon which teachers' accountability must be rendered, the processes of securing accountability will surely change too. Governors will have a say on how the National Curriculum is rendered locally; teachers who fail to meet consumer wishes might find their trade taken away through the system of open enrolments; and if they fail to keep the customers, so the governors will be able to adjust the system of rewards through the Pay and Conditions Act procedures. What has been represented as the oppressive local authority, through its inspectorial and advisory services, will thus be replaced by more immediate political pressure groups. At the same time, however, inspectors are expected to develop far stronger frames for monitoring and evaluating the work of the schools and for giving an account of them to the local authorities and to the governors. The technology of education will thus tend to be one of transmitting received knowledge, within a delivery 'system' in which there will be quality inspection and quality inspectors.

It is difficult to see whether a new kind of teacher professional will emerge from these changes. 'Meeting the market' need not mean simply pandering to parental anxiety and ambition. It could mean schools, and local authorities, making a competent and empathetic assessment of client needs and wants and embodying them in their curriculum policies. That would be quite technical work, involving expertise. Advisers and inspectors too will have to become far more expert (professional) in their evaluation of the work of teachers. The issue is whether in the end the professionals will be able to construe client needs, local authority evaluative criteria and National Curriculum perspectives in terms of their own epistemological assumptions about the generation and dissemination of educational knowledge and skills. The balance between managerial and systemic values, putatively stated on behalf of society, and individualistic and professional values, expressed altruistically in the educational interest of individual clients, will be difficult to strike within a legal frame which is so determined to impose a collective notion of the good and the true.

References

BERNSTEIN, B. (1975) *Class, Codes and Control. Vol. 3: Towards a Theory of Educational Transmission*, London, Routledge and Kegan Paul.

ELLIOTT, J., BRIDGES, D., EBBUTT, D., GIBSON, R. and NIAS, J. (1981) *School Accountability: The SSRC Accountability Project*, London, Grant McIntyre.

EVETTS, J. (1973) *The Sociology of Educational Ideas*, London, Routledge and Kegan Paul.

GREENWOOD, E. (1986) 'The Elements of Professionalism', in Volner, H.M. and Mills, D.C. (eds), *Professionalisation*, New Jersey, Prentice-Hall.

HIRSCHMAN, A.O. (1970) *Exit, Voice and Loyalty: Responses to Decline in Firms, Organisations and States*, Princeton, N.J., Harvard University Press.

JAMES, P.H. (1980) *The Reorganisation of Secondary Education*, Windsor, NFER.

KOGAN, M. (1975) *Institutional Autonomy and Public Accountability: Autonomy and Accountability in Educational Administration*, University College, Cardiff, British Educational Administration Society.

KOGAN, M. (1986) *Education Accountability: An Analytic Overview*, Hutchinson (2nd ed. 1988).

MUNN, P., HEWITT, G., MORRISON, A. and MCINTYRE, D. (1982) *Accountability and Professionalism*, Stirling Educational Monographs No. 10.

SALLIS, J. (1979) 'Beyond the Market Place: A Parents' View', in Lello, J. (ed.), *Accountability in Education*, London, Ward Lock Education.

SIMONS, H. (1979) 'Suggestions for a School Self-Evaluation Based on Democratic Evaluation', *CRN Bulletin*, No. 3, pp. 1–6.

SOCKETT, H. (1976) 'Teacher Accountability', *Proceedings of the Philosophy of Education Society of Great Britain*, Vol. 10, July, pp. 34–57.

SOCKETT, H. (1988) 'Research, Practice and Professional Aspiration', *Journal of Curriculum Studies*, 21, 2, pp. 97–112.

SOCKETT, H. (forthcoming) 'Accountability, Trust and Professional Codes of Practice', in Goodlad, J. (ed.), *The Moral Dimensions of Teaching*.

TAYLOR, W. (1978) 'Values and Accountability', in Becher, T. and Maclure, S. (eds), *Accountability in Education*, London, SSRC and NFER.

TRIST, E. (1972) 'Types of Output Mix of Research Organisations and Their Complementarity', in Cherns, A.B. *et al.*, *Social Science and Government: Policies and Problems*, London, Tavistock Publications.

Part Three
The Professional Development of
Teachers

Chapter 8

Being Caught in Schoolwork: The Possibilities of Research in Teachers' Work

Martin Lawn

People just couldn't go to him and that wouldn't have been so bad but at staff meetings he would say 'now nobody's got any problems, have they?' You sat there pretending you hadn't. (Wise, 1982)

This is a teacher talking about being a teacher and about being managed. It points the way to a critique of teacher research by focusing on the silences of schoolwork, the labour process of teachers' work. It was produced within an oral history of a school by a teacher who interviewed teachers, from each decade since the Second World War, about their work. Indeed, the very idea of work is central to it. The researcher tried to reconstruct the experience of work in the school from discussions about curriculum activities, the organization of the classroom, the production of resources, the use of spaces and relations with each other, the headteacher and parents. The teachers in the conversations were strangers to each other, but they brought a recognition to their sharing of ideas and insights that although they taught at different times, they had many similar problems of work. The research became a reclamation of the experience of work, even an expression of a combinatory culture at times, from the condescension of researchers who have ignored this aspect of teaching. A key element of their shared experience is that the school is a place in which they worked but it was not a place of their own, it 'belonged' to others.

In whatever decade was being discussed the headteacher was the employer and the superior. Although teachers determined many aspects of their classwork, and even this varied considerably from head to head, they felt powerless as individuals at the school level. They rarely acted in combination but they had many strategies for deception produced to cope with the felt power of their superior. This inequality at work, a constant feature of the discussions and lying alongside talk on innovations in reading or creativity in producing resources, was also expressed in gender terms; they were women supervised by men. The study also showed how the teachers coped with technical changes which redefined their work, such as the radio or the early portable language laboratory, and with the constant lack of 'normality' expressed in the 'making do' with low resourcing, teacher shortages and large or small pupil numbers.

This study revealed aspects of work which do not find a place in educational research. It revealed primary schooling to be open to discussions on its labour process which parallel those in industries or offices; it raised questions as to the fragmentation or loss of a collective memory of teaching in a school or in the industry; most of all the silences of work are revealed as significant in understanding its processes (Lawn, 1988). This is the point at which a review of an educational research approach as sympathetic to teachers as the teacher research (teacher as researcher) movement should be undertaken to explore why these aspects of work are not contained within it and how they could be.

There is probably more than one teacher as researcher movement, certainly a number of differences among authors writing from within it. Sometimes it is not clear why teachers were adopted as researchers: first, because they help to improve administrative policy by informing administrators about school realities (McCutcheon, 1981); or, second, because a shrinking educational research community needed cheap apprentices, a version of the amateur sociologist argument (Stebbins, 1978); or third, evaluation of 1970s education projects suggested that their ineffectiveness lay in management's ignorance of detailed, closely developed data which only teachers could give (Smetherham, 1980). Whatever the reasons for its appearance, the language and practice of teacher research in Britain have often been progressive, supportive and emancipatory for many teachers who have been involved with it. The language of emancipation, autonomy and reflection has produced powerful images in teacher discourse and although they may be addressed towards a reality of good pedagogical practice, they involve feelings about loss and value for many teachers about their place in society. The practical realism of ethnographic methodology and action research have provided clear, structured routes for many teachers in renewing their own bruised commitment to their craft. The idea of the reflective teacher is a crucial one for teacher education and stands in increasing relief to a limited vocational training which is imposed on tutors and students. As centralization and changed priorities are altering the direction of a state system of education, the 'teacher as a researcher' begins to have the appeal of an oppositional culture in teaching or at least a constant re-expression of past values.

It is not the purpose of this chapter to discuss the methodology associated with teacher research, nor will the argument be expressed in terms usually associated with this approach, such as practical theorizing or grounded theory, though there are implications in the argument expressed here for the methodology. This chapter, in drawing attention to the partial or limited version of teacher research which is operating at present, will address itself to the shibboleths which seem to surround it. In particular, the idea of professionalism needs to be rethought and the idea of teachers' work or the teacher's natural world to be limited to the classroom needs consideration. Teacher research which did not include the very place where teachers use and develop their craft skills would be strange indeed, but so is teacher research which constantly draws lines around the admissibility of what is studied, lines which always follow the walls of the classroom. If every plan or project in curriculum or teacher research includes a version of the teacher and the teacher's work, what is the dominant model present in the idea of the teacher researcher and how can we develop it (Carr, 1983)?

Improving Teaching

The main element, the thrust of the movement, is about improving practice. The practice of teaching is seen, without hesitation, as being in the classroom. Practice may be improved by systematic study and reflection. In the process of studying teachers will be developing professional judgment, taking responsibility and restoring their dignity. They will be liberating themselves.

This is a précis of the arguments used by David Hopkins, which are in turn a reflection of some of the ideas of Lawrence Stenhouse (Hopkins, 1985; Rudduck and Hopkins, 1985). A précis does not do justice to the arguments which underpin the view, but it does reveal the basic elements. It is a way of reconstructing the progressive teacher in hard times. Its intention, though not perhaps its particular vocabulary, would not be disagreed with by Sir Alec Clegg or Ronald Gould; it represents the way they saw teachers in the 1950s and 1960s. It is a contemporary reworking of the ideas of liberal humanism, ideas among teachers which grew in alliance with the process of educational reconstruction after the last war. They existed at school or local authority level, depending upon the headteachers, the education officers or teachers' associations. Alec Clegg might have talked more of the civilizing process of craft or intellectual ideas, but he saw this process as liberating teachers from their past servitude, broadening their cultural and social horizons and allowing a creative classroom practice to be developed and shared.

Like much progressive practice in Britain, the appeal is made directly to the classroom teacher. The process of emancipation appears for the teacher, first, as one of release, indeed a psychological release. It offered a new way of life which was available without change of circumstance. You did not change your classroom, your headteacher or your salary, but you could change the way you lived as a teacher. Second, there was a new language, a language of endeavour in which the usage of educational terms had to become precise or judgments had to be justified or ambiguity or difference had to be dealt with. Third, even if the employers or their managers did not disappear, being a teacher as researcher allowed you to ignore them. You were either dealing with your classroom practice or another teacher's practice. This sense of power, of a sort of collective even if not based in a school collective, is important. But the new way of life could be less than specific about outside classroom influences. While the Humanities Curriculum Project may now be described as emancipating teachers from 'heads, advisers, . . . etc.' (Hopkins, 1985, p. 3), or while the movement may be recast as 'in opposition to centralized control', this was not a call to arms so much as a call to introspection — back inside the classroom.

It is a visionary appeal not dissimilar to that offered by the young A.S. Neill or James Maxton (Lawn, 1987). It is utopian, a chance to build a new society. One of the differences from an earlier version in the 1920s is that this vision was offered to collectives of teachers and often corresponded to or overlaid their socialist purpose. When they visited Summerhill or Bedales, argued about Russian education or discussed civics in the elementary school, they too talked of emancipation, but it lay both in their classrooms, for they were *teachers*, and in their social and political project *as teachers*. Like Stenhouse, they were searching for a way to liberate 'teachers from a system of education that denies individual dignity', their own and that of children in the state schools, but when they conducted research, this was an individual *and* a collective act based not only on the study of classrooms, their own teaching roles and the curriculum, but on the nature of the education system in a class-divided Britain. If they wanted to take 'more responsibility for their actions' or 'develop more power over their professional lives' (Hopkins, 1985), which they did, that was because of the system they were in. They were servants of the state.

To a degree this critique might be trading one version of radical change against another, that is, a sense of personal renewal against that of a societal reconstruction. But the 'teacher as researcher' movement always makes reference to this non-classroom world even if it is not emphasized. It may be opposing centralization, restoring dignity to a large group of workers and building 'informal support structures', so it has to be judged on these grounds. A consequence of the privatization of the public sphere in Britain in the 1980s is that an appeal to a personal renewal, to emancipation and to increased self-worth, even among teachers, could succeed as long as it was a consumer service offered in the market. The forthcoming privatization of in-service work will no doubt include many courses, even if disguised, on 'teacher as researcher' bases. But it is in the public sphere that much of importance in this movement lies: it came out of an historical movement by teachers to share in the determination of their work; it is allied to progressive educational practice at school or local level; it was shaped (in the late 1960s and early 1970s) by teacher involvement in curriculum policy at a national level; and it was legitimated by it. It is an expression of a period and of a need. Its very expression reflects its genesis: it is about professionalism and autonomy. This has both a classroom meaning and a meaning in the national, public and collective aspects of teachers' work.

Professionalism par Excellence

Lawrence Stenhouse was influenced in his thinking by a categorization of teachers produced by Eric Hoyle. This divided teachers into two broad categories: the restricted, intuitive, classroom-bound teacher, and the extended, rational, education-bound teacher (Stenhouse, 1975). This is an unfortunate categorization which has now had a shelf life far beyond its sell-by date. A close reading of the categories suggests that the restricted category comprises women teachers and the extended category men teachers. The former appears to be an 'objective' listing of a series of complaints by male primary headteachers about their women staff, and the correspondence between the categorization and gendered management complaints about their workforce is remarkable.

However, the use of these types skewed the teacher as researcher's visionary appeal: it is rather as if the bulk of teachers cannot be capable of improved judgment and practice because of their limited functions, and only the minority of teachers (a substantial minority) was capable of developing their craft and building a professional autonomy. This unfortunately tends to tie in the teacher as researcher idea, at least in its early days, to an argument on professionalism which saw teaching as a low-status semi-profession because its membership consisted of a majority of women (Etzioni, 1969).

Loose talk about professionalism, a key idea within this visionary appeal, is common within discussions of the teacher as researcher perspective. It ranges from an argument about emancipation and self-worth (Stenhouse), a moral responsibility within a democracy (Pollard and Tann) to collective decision-making about education and social policy. It is an ahistorical appeal usually, not grounded in the debates and actions of teachers in their communities or organizations, but rather vague, an imperative applied to teachers by those who want them to do something they do not appear to be doing. This is the case even within otherwise useful accounts of research perspectives (Carr and Kemmis, 1983) or guides to reflexivity (Pollard and Tann, 1987). The urgency of the appeals to an authentic professionalism, and extended professionality or an opposition to conformist professionalism has become more focused as the trend to centralization, low resourcing and a vocational education has grown. It is suggested that the teacher as a researcher in its authentic professional version will oppose these trends. For Pollard and Tann, this is expressed by means of an argument about democratic rights and duties. It is not only a classroom-based activity, a systematic reflection, but a public one, contributing to the formation of public policy in education and recognizing the social context in education. Reflective teachers 'have both a right and a direct responsibility to consider the school context in which they work and should not avoid it' (Pollard and Tann, 1987, p. 176).

Professionalism here involves skills, a process of reflection, making judgments and acting at the school level and in the public sphere. For Carr and Kemmis, professionalism is less a concept which divides teachers into those who have more or less of it (that is, restricted or extended), but into teachers who are conformist or not. The latter are cultural and political agents who will be able to use action research to develop a critical, practical professionalism in the classroom and the school. Professionalism is a collaborative exercise, within and outside teaching. It is seen as a protection against 'bureaucratic management', a management that controls teachers ideologically, by predetermined curriculum packages and by allowing a local consumerist 'market' to develop around the school, keeping teachers in line. Although Carr and Kemmis distract themselves with a discussion of whether teaching *is* a profession, they do offer a critique of teachers' working conditions which is more grounded than that of Pollard and Tann:

Teachers operate within hierarchically arranged institutions and the part they play in making decisions about such things as overall educational policy, the selection and training of new members, accountability procedures, and the general structures of the organisations in which they work is negligible. (Carr and Kemmis, 1983, p. 13)

Professionalism has a number of meanings, some of them contradictory, and it operates at a number of different levels in an explanation of teachers and their work. It may be seen as certain inherent qualities which denote a profession (trait theory), as a process of external persuasion or élite support in gaining professional status or as a form of state licensing or control over teachers' work. In relation to the form and genesis of the teacher as researcher movement in Britain, it is worthwhile moving beyond appeals to professionalism to explore it further (see Lawn and Ozga, 1981).

The post-war period saw great changes in the education services. The war had seen elementary education falter, boys and girls mix, town and rural teachers work together and the curriculum move out of the school. The post-war reconstruction involved new buildings and new ideas. If there was a political and social consensus post-war, it was based on community and collectivism. In education the teachers who had kept the service alive in the war appeared to be taken as partners in the work of the education service. The post-war idea of professionalism was significantly different from that of the pre-war years: it was used by the local and national government to imply responsibility and autonomy. Teachers' work was seen as being more influenced by teachers than by other groups, a sore point previously. The ideas of progressive education grew within this settlement and involved education officers, HMIs and teachers. The formation of the Schools Council in 1964, in a period of acute teacher shortage, appeared to confirm the particular strengths and responsibilities of an English professionalism, a professionalism which was a direct expression of a system described as devolved or shared, distinguishing our democratic society from others.

Professionalism was taken to imply a particular responsibility for the curriculum and for pedagogy, at the level of the classroom, but with a significant expression of this responsibility in local and national policies and their negotiation. It is not surprising that when the state moved in a radical direction away from the ideology of a post-war consensus and the policies associated with it, the resistance to this change should affect the rhetoric of the teacher as researcher. Its justification altered or expanded into a declaration of human rights (Pollard and Tann, 1987) once perhaps implicit in the consensus but now overtaken, or into a critique of educational researchers and a conformist professionalism. But the new policy direction has not led into a critique of the possibilities and practices of the teacher as researcher but only to fulmination against centralization and a call for emancipation.

Schoolwork

How could a 'critique of renewal' in the idea of the teacher as researcher be developed? This could develop, first, from a close look at the nature of teachers' work — the labour process of teaching; and second, from a re-definition of professionalism associated with teachers' work.

What is teachers' work? There is an argument today, based on trends in the USA and in Britain, that suggests that teachers' work is going to be (or already is) more clearly defined, more fragmented, more supervised and more assessed, and that teachers are losing control over it. This trend exists within the implementation of new educational policies on teacher training, the curriculum, the provision of state schooling and with the new management of teachers, emphasizing control, productivity and local labour markets.

The analysis of these trends taking place within labour process theorizing (Apple, 1983; Lawn and Ozga, 1981; Connell, 1985) has drawn attention to the possibility of the deskilling of teachers, their work under a line management, the franchised nature of educational work, etc. Yet although this may be expressed in a deterministic fashion, as an inexorable process, it should be recognized that it is not. It can be contested or resisted in the classroom, the school and the society. The production process, if this is what schooling is, is not just a material but a social process and involves a struggle over its control and its purpose. Professionalism is in part an expression of that struggle and involves the possibility of resistance and of the creation of alternatives. It acts to create a defensible space around teachers' work.

If professionalism is to be used, at least let it be used in its real sense, not as a vague ideal typology nor a moral imperative, but in the way teachers have used it. Professionalism contains in this particular period an ideal of public service, a defence of the quality of state education and a statement of the value of the state's employees. While the employer may wish to reinstate the pre-war distinction of grades of teacher, not dissimilar to restricted and extended professionals, unity has been a major political demand within the main teacher associations for sometime. So the teacher as researcher movement may adopt with some confidence the language of a professional discourse that has been rooted in teachers' past and present actions.

Schoolwork, or the labour process of teaching, needs analysis and policy formulation. Teachers will need support in any project that seeks to research the effect of structural changes on their work and that will promote a wider intelligence about these changes. But this implies that the movement of teacher researchers is operating in collectives and that their research agenda will be based upon the contemporary realities of teachers' work. It will be emancipatory and educational, it might improve individual dignity and it will be oppositional.

It is a truism that teachers are isolated by their classrooms. Yet the teacher reseacher movement seemed to be based on this isolation, even increasing it if the teacher was not in a strong network. Obviously the classroom was the place to start and the place to continue research, but it is not the only place. The skills of the teacher are expressed within the classroom, but they are often created or defined outside it. In the 1980s the very idea of a teacher and her skills has been redefined; for instance, in the primary school the teacher will move from being a generalist to a specialist and from being classroom-defined to being school-defined. Teaching skills are no longer defined in terms of pedagogy or curriculum but now include required managerial features — pleasantness, teamwork skills, etc. (see Lawn, 1988). Local contracts may soon incorporate tight job specifications including these skills, and appraisal will test their practice. In the 1980s the natural emphasis on a classroom pedagogy, improved within the classroom, must now be made into a contradiction: the teacher works within a limited area but the conditions which define and limit that area lie within school or local management, operating a national policy. It is no longer possible to improve teaching skills without an argument about what they are or should be, nor to improve them in isolation, nor to see emancipation as an isolated act. Skill is socially constructed in teaching, skills are somebody's version of teachers' work, increasingly the central state's version though locally supervised. The move to schoolwork implies research *on* schoolwork, its ideology and required practices, and this cannot be something that individuals do, except covertly. It needs a collective purpose and network.

Researching Schoolwork

In the early 1970s a group of young teachers in a local NUT association in a seaside town produced a pamphlet of about fourteen pages, called

Education on the Cheap, which was aimed at local teachers. It included information on the local education system culled from local publications, council minutes and national documents (on local authority spending, etc.). Its stated intention was to provide teachers with information about the underlying trends in local education provision and to help them discuss the possibilities for action. It was sold to teachers and to parents. What kind of information did it include? It compared the post-war development plan for the borough with actual provision in the early 1970s (and included the information that there was a decline in the number of nursery schools); it compared proposed spending plans for local schooling with actual spending; it contrasted social provision in areas of high deprivation in the town with areas of affluence; it recorded delays in the establishment of a comprehensive school system; it compared local spending on schoolbooks and resources with that in similar towns. The pamphlet received many hostile comments from local councillors. It was fragmented in style and not well produced or edited. Yet it is a forerunner of the possibility of a new practice in teacher research. Its authors said that it was 'not intended to be a piece of academic research. On the contrary we hope that it will be of practical use to local teachers...' (*Education on the Cheap*, p. 1). They were obviously searching for a new method. By practical, though, they did not mean class-based, a way that practical (as opposed to theoretical) is often used to deny teachers a place in the theorizing about their work. Practical meant useful in changing the conditions described. It was not reflexive nor tightly based around a considered practice. It was a squib, not a report. It was also anonymous. In summary, it was practical, political, collective, local and change-based.

A much more significant example of schoolwork research occurred in Boston (USA) several years ago. The Boston Women's Teachers' Group comprised public school teachers who wished to study their work situation, particularly their sense of isolation one from another and their changing attitudes to their work (Freedman *et al.*, 1982, 1983). Although the Group was a support network for its members and acted as a forum for the discussion of educational research, members recognized that they needed to develop a project into teacher isolation, into 'the working relationships in the school buildings and the school systems'. They decided to research the 'concrete experiences' of elementary school teachers, within the 'actual opportunities, circumstances and consequences of life in the classroom, the school and the school system', and the feelings that teachers had about their work experiences. They interviewed twenty-five teachers twice a week throughout a school year.

In brief, they were concerned with the institutional nature of school systems, the very thing which is not discussed in training nor openly in schools, yet which causes teachers great problems. Indeed the idea of teacher 'burn-out', the subject of the study, implied it was their fault not that of institutional management:

> As teachers ourselves, we had never been urged to look beyond our own classrooms, to search for similarities and differences between ourselves and others, either within the structure of the school or other institutions of society. (Freedman *et al.*, 1984)

The report has a lot to say on teacher professionalism, on isolation and on institutional management, but it never loses touch with classroom life; it is a view down the corridor.

The research did not stop with the report. The Group acts as a teacher support group for teacher-initiated change, and with a tape-slide show, its workshops always begin by emphasizing the structural barriers teachers face in schools before going on to the particularities of the teacher's own teaching situation. A teacher's personal history is compared with another's to develop a critique of institutional constraints and the possibilities of change. This form of schoolwork research is collective, practical, change-based, supportive and reflexive. It builds from life history to institutional structures. It aims to emancipate from isolation and from institution.

In the last few years I have worked with primary in-service teachers who were engaged in school-based research. Initially they would attend with rather neat research projects on curriculum content, but after discussion over several weeks their project would change. It changed because of their growing confidence about what educational research could be and with a recognition that it could be relevant to their concerns. I have never determined the nature of the research, only the method of achieving it (participant observation/interview). Although there is a range of topics studied and they do not directly overlap, they are united in one thing: they all explore an aspect of their work. It might be their relations with the head-teacher, the use (or lack of use) of computers by teachers, the relations with each other, finding a role, labour disputes in the school and mid-term career analyses, for example. A recent one was a study of the idea of a 'normal' teaching day in the primary school. This seemingly innocuous idea was chosen because of the importance of the idea of normality in a teacher's day and the interruptions, seasons, interventions, etc. which cause it to remain only an idea. There is no normality because the teachers do not control their own labour process, 'normal' was their own invention, an idea of what could be if only they could control it. It was impossible in practice, but of everyday significance, as teachers tried to control it and achieve a 'normal' day. Another example is the subject of display in the primary school. Again an innocuous subject turned out to be a significant feature of the labour process. In primary schools, since the rise of a progressivist idea that children are significant and what they produce is of significance, display of work has developed into a major way in which the teacher and the school can be assessed. Teachers spend a great deal of time having to produce displays, with or without children's work, which according to the amount of wall space, the schedules for change or the head's policy on community use, can amount in practice to a teacher's main work. There is no other form of work that is used to assess her so often and with such an effect by the head.

When the labour process of work in primary school has changed so dramatically, as it has with the rise of supervisory specialists or postholder roles, then this began to feature in the projects as well. Relations between staff have moved from a marginality in schoolwork to a centrality. Primary school supervision, based on specialist responsibility for whole school policies, has led many teachers to despair. The problem lies within inter-personal relations and the awkwardness of a hierarchical position within a culture of classroom-based equality. Primary teachers now supervise others and are in turn supervised. They are in competition with each other as to the nature and practice of the supervision undertaken. At the same time the culture of the institution remains one of nominal equality and headteacher paternalistic control. They may even be called in to assess a failing teacher, with a report that has consequences other teachers fear.

There is a labour process in teaching. It is the subject of research by teachers when opportunity arises. It is increasingly regulated by its managers and employers. Teacher research needs to recognize its effects in schools and upon teachers.

Review

Schoolwork research can encourage teachers to turn their attention to those aspects of their work which define it so closely and create the contradictions they have to deal with: management, supervision, job definition, time, intrastaff relations, resources and so on. First, teachers have to be encouraged to recognize these things as valid issues for research. They are important to their working lives, but that is not the question. They have to be seen by researchers, working with or encouraging teachers, as important so that they can be studied and acted upon.

An illuminating example of a researcher with a similar problem to overcome was that of Favret-Saada studying witchcraft in the Bocage in recent years. She had no intention of seeing her subjects as 'backward, credulous peasants' nor of reducing their knowledge to a 'body of empty recipes'. But these French people saw her as an outsider, somebody who either patronized them or was dangerous in her naivety. Anthropology was built on the notion of the primitive and of the outsider, of practice and the theorizer, and of the researched and the researcher. This is the very kind of mental/manual divide which the proponents of teacher research wish to overcome. But the subject of the research can be dangerous if let outside the classroom walls — the authors of *Education on the Cheap* were anonymous and the Boston teachers were redundant. Teachers may be uncertain whether educational researchers could not include schoolwork issues as valid for teacher research purposes because they were too gauche to be allowed in. Favret-Saada's people explained the rules to her about witchcraft: ' "You have to be caught to believe." "For those who haven't been caught, they [the spells] don't exist." "Those who haven't been caught can't even talk about it." ' (Favret-Saada, 1980).

Where does this leave teacher research? It must be recognized that it must include the study of those silences and feelings which come from the problems of dealing with schoolwork. If the researchers were caught, they would not need to ask, and because they ask, they do not believe, they do not know. Teacher research must include the possibility of dealing with schoolwork issues if it is to emancipate. If teachers are to be seen as the ones who should study their work (Stenhouse, 1975), how foolish it would be to restrict the boundaries of what we consider their work to be. This will not be emancipatory for teachers.

Second, a discussion of the argument for teacher research must move beyond borrowed elements of an outsider's descriptions of what teacher professionalism should be. This defines the nature of the subject studied as tightly as the research which lays no claim to teacher involvement, let alone teacher partnership or self-direction, would. Professionalism becomes less a question of how teachers use it or what the management of teachers intend it to be, than elegant lists of saintly requirements. The living tradition of professionalism as a set of sometimes contradictory meanings and actions for teachers has to be taken on squarely. A way of working with teachers that includes a vagueness about such a key term, and a willingness to apply it evaluatively to discriminate between teachers or to produce a required goal for their work, is inappropriate. Professionalism is a key contested term in the history of teaching. The teacher research movement grew out of a particular period when 'professional autonomy', as an ideology for explaining teacher-state relations, was dominant. The decline of that ideology will make teacher research become either oppositional, a way of holding onto or recapturing the teachers' version of themselves in work, or managerial, a way of subtly imposing on teachers school evaluations or work study which is not emancipatory. Professionalism is capable of holding both meanings. It is a contested term, not a shibboleth.

Third, teachers' work mainly occurs in classrooms, but it is influenced by aspects of school or local and national policy and politics. It is a confusion to substitute the place of this work for the subject of the study. Teachers are social, cultural and political actors. They also work in a system of production, a once-hegemonic state industry now in the process of balkanization and privatization, which has its own labour process. Management, technology, training, resources, school policy and job descriptions all affect the way a teacher works, what counts as work and who is seen as 'good' at doing it. This is schoolwork. The idea of a teacher's skill or skills is not constant, it has altered and changed; recent versions even include the personal and social characteristics of being a 'good teacher' which have been turned into technical requirements. The definition of a teacher is contested — a teacher's biography might contain critical incidents bound to the idea of equality of opportunity — yet teachers might work in a system that treats this as an irrelevance. It makes a mockery of teacher research to exclude the very being, the very definition, of the teacher as teachers define it; the alternative is to turn teacher research into a managerial upskilling movement.

It is not clear what schoolwork research will look like in the future, but the nature, provision and policy of the education system that teachers work in are in flux. Such research will be professional and collective; it will probably be oppositional and emancipatory; it will have to be reflexive; it will be classroom, school and nationally-focused; it is only likely to be accredited if it is part of another project; it is likely to be localized.

Sir Ronald Gould, a long influence on the National Union of Teachers in the post-war decades, said that if the central state lost its willingness to act with the consent of teachers or in partnership with them and became centralized and authoritarian, then it would be necessary for the teachers to develop their own alternative research base. The time to develop this base is now.

References

APPLE, M. (1983) 'Work, Class and Teaching', in Barton, L. and Walker, S., *Gender, Class and Education*, Lewes, Falmer Press.

CARR, W. (1983) Footnote in Nias, J. (ed.), *Teaching Research-based Courses: Possibilities and Problems*, Conference Report, Cambridge, Cambridge Institute of Education.

CARR, W. and KEMMIS, S. (1983) *Becoming Critical: Knowing through Action Research*, Geelong, Deakin University.

CONNELL, R.W. (1985) *Teachers' Work*, London, Allen and Unwin.

Education on the Cheap (1972).

ETZIONI, A. (1969) *The Semi-Professionals and Their Organizations: Teachers, Nurses and Social Workers*, New York, Free Press.

FAVRET-SAADA, J. (1980) *Deadly Words: Witchcraft in the Bocage*, Cambridge, Cambridge University Press.

FREEDMAN, S., JACKSON, J. and BOLES, K. (1982) *The Effects of the Institutional Structure of Schools on Teachers*, Boston, Mass, National Institute of Education.

FREEDMAN, S., JACKSON, J. and BOLES, K. (1983) 'The Other End of the Corridor: The Effect of Teaching on Teachers', *Radical Education*, 23, pp. 2–23.

FREEDMAN, S., JACKSON, J. and BOLES, K. (1984) *Establishing Teacher Support Groups to Foster Teacher Initiated Change*, Project publication.

GOULD, R. (1963) *Power in the Education Service*, London, NUT.

HOPKINS, D. (1985) *A Teacher's Guide to Classroom Research*, Milton Keynes, Open University Press.

LAWN, M.A. (1987) *Servants of the State: The Contested Management of Teaching 1900–1930*, Lewes, Falmer Press.

LAWN, M.A. (1988) 'Skill in Schoolwork: Work Relations in the Primary School', in Ozga, J.T. (ed.), *Schoolwork: Approaches to the Labour Process in Teaching*, Milton Keynes, Open University Press.

LAWN, M.A. and OZGA, J.T. (1981) *Teachers, Professionalism and Class*, Lewes, Falmer Press.

MCCUTCHEON, G. (1981) 'The Impact of the Insider', in Nixon, J. (ed.), *A Teacher's Guide to Action Research*, London, Grant McIntyre.

POLLARD, A. and TANN, S. (1987) *Reflective Teaching in the Primary School*, London, Cassell.

RUDDUCK, J. and HOPKINS, D. (eds) (1981) *Research as a Basis for Teaching*, London, Heinemann Education.

SMETHERHAM, D. (1980) *Towards a Participant Evaluation*, unpublished.

STEBBINS, R. (1978) 'Toward Amateur Sociology', *The American Sociologist*, 13, November, pp. 239–47.

STENHOUSE, L. (1975) *An Introduction to Curriculum Research and Development*, London, Heinemann.

WISE, L. (1982) *Curriculum Change in a Primary School: An Oral History*. BEd dissertation, Westhill, Birmingham.

Chapter 9

Teachers and Their Research

Michael Golby

There is a crisis in education. Who knows its ultimate source? But its manifestations for the purposes of this chapter are the reduction of teacher
education to narrow practicality, and the casting of teachers into the role of
functionaries in the delivery of prespecified and uncontestable 'goods'. The
present crisis demands of liberal educators a keeping of the faith with
teacher autonomy. By reference to continuing work with a research group
of practising teachers, I hope to show that, though we may for the present
have to take to the hills as guerillas, there is a hope that we may return to
power with renewed vision. It is most important that the connection
between teachers, and research is sustained and developed. Specifically,
teachers must exert themselves in the area of educational values. Now that
the schism between the predominantly liberal educational values of
teachers and the materialistic outlook of their political masters is complete
and ratified in a National Curriculum, to foster educational research at
sites where the contest continues is to promote a critical rather than a
technical view of education. It requires an appropriate research methodology in support of the view that the aims of education are themselves
problematic and practitioners more than delivery agents of a curriculum
conceived and approved elsewhere than in the schools and even outside the
education system itself. Research is the most effective and credible form of
counter-attack against prejudice. Educational research for teachers should
not in these circumstances be contained within the sphere of technique, but
should extend beyond the classroom and school to investigate the contexts
of power and control within which educational and social values are now
being generated. An example will be provided from the work of the Exeter
Society for Curriculum Studies and its research into school governorship.

Over the past twelve years I have taught a full-time course in curriculum studies as well as parallel part-time courses. Over 150 graduates with

Bachelor of Philosophy and Master's degrees in Education have been 'produced' (to lapse into the deplorable jargon of the day). These teachers came predominantly on secondment from full-time teaching posts. With new arrangements for INSET, such secondments have all but ceased, and we have moved to part-time modular patterns in the attempt to preserve depth, coherence and above all a critical edge to our courses. How this is to be done I shall return to as part of the challenge facing us in the 1990s, but, first, I shall describe the measures at present available and point out some of the achievements upon which a future for teachers' research might be built.

Teachers who took full-time courses faced two problems, entry and re-entry. Stripped of status and deprived of 'busywork', they at first came de-skilled into an academic environment which prized different qualities from those which had made them successful and esteemed teachers in school. Headteachers had particular problems in coming to terms with loss of identity and status and becoming one equal member of a learning group. At the other end of the full-time course came the problem of going back to school where no one was interested in the newly won academic knowledge of the returner. In some cases hostility, in most a 'don't want to know' attitude was encountered. This seemed to apply equally to colleagues, senior staff and advisory staff. Academic qualifications were looked upon as individual attainments, badges of merit in the competition for advancement. The idea that staff who had benefited from advanced study should be in a position to make important contributions to curriculum development, simple as it may seem, did not work much that way in practice. Note too that both entry and re-entry are taken as problems only because of the assumption that what happens in between is of undoubted value. In the new order of things, that assumption can and must be questioned, causing us, the providers, to reconsider our definitions of the worthwhile in teacher education.

The considerable literature on the 'theory-practice' gap is evidence that not all academics took the view that what was on offer in advanced courses was of straightforward relevance to practitioners. In particular, the view that theory could be handed down in some unproblematic way was rejected by those who advocated the idea of theory deriving from practice, as a commentary or critique (Pring and Wilson, 1972). Since higher education, particularly but not exclusively in universities, makes a claim of linking teaching to research, the place of research in advanced courses came under close inspection. The principal product was the teacher as researcher. Here the emphasis moved away from initiating teachers into professional educational research, with its mainly positivistic concerns, towards helping teachers to solve the problems of their own practice. Where traditional educational research sought generalization following upon detailed empirical and statistical work, the teacher as researcher was interested in the specific and particular features of his or her working situation. The product of the teacher's research was better practice in the local circumstance. It is a move away from universal and towards local 'knowledge'. But it brings with it considerable problems of epistemological validity and some real dangers of restricting teachers to narrow channels of research. There is enormous value in the achievements of the teacher researcher movement, yet it is time to build upon those achievements by exploring more fully its potential development as regards both method and focus. I shall consider case study methodology since it is the approach most commonly used in teachers' research. I shall argue that the epistemological rationale for case study has not been fully developed and its practice, therefore, has been less powerful than it might be. Second, I shall suggest that teachers can be brought into the centre of educational debates when their perspective is sharpened by the use of appropriate research instruments. Case study can lock the researcher into received structures. Its qualitative features are indispensible but need to be expanded by a judicious use of other methods which place the scene of the action in a system-wide context.

Case Study

Because of its popularity there has been much discussion over the past ten years or so of the epistemological basis for case study work in education (Stenhouse, 1975, 1978, 1980; Shaw, 1978; Kenny and Groteleuschen, 1984; Tripp, 1985; Adelman, Jenkins and Kemmis, 1976). The vogue in educational research for case study work requires us to clarify some fundamental conceptual matters which have a clear bearing on our present work. If conventional or traditional research consists in 'asking questions and getting answers', as Chanan (1977) has complained, then too much of case study work looks in danger of merely 'telling stories' (Chanan, 1977, p. 58). To describe a piece of research as 'anecdotal' is in almost all circumstances to condemn it. This condemnation may itself need reconsideration if anecdote is ever to be accorded significance beyond itself.

If we wish to learn more from a case than is contained within it, we must conceive case study as the exploration of an *individual* instance as an example of a *general* question. If this is so, we must establish at the outset of our work what we take the 'case' we are studying to be a case *of*. This means at an early stage of research identifying a focus which can be clearly established as an instance of some general question. It also means, in pursuing the work, doing so not only in order to establish the idiosyncrasy of the case in question but also in order to establish its typicality.

Viewed from a traditional positivist standpoint, perhaps the biggest objection to case study lies in its apparent rejection of the idea of generalization. This criticism may be met by suggesting a view of case study as the pursuit not of uniqueness — for that would be to deny the association of the case with others of its kind — but instead of particularity. The particular, though individual and specific, is to be seen as an intelligible thing or event related under a method of description to others of its kind. This may be illustrated by reference to historical enquiry. Is history in search of the unique or the particular? Elton has it thus:

> As for history's preoccupation with the particular, that must be seen in its proper light. It is often asserted that the special distinction of the historical method is to treat the fact or event as unique. But frequent assertion does not create truth, and this statement is not true. No historian really treats all facts as unique; he treats them as particular. He cannot — no one can — deal in the unique fact, because facts and events require reference to common experience, to conventional frameworks, to (in short) the general before they acquire meaning. The unique event is a freak and a frustration; if it is really unique — can never recur in meaning or implication — it lacks every measurable dimension and cannot be assessed. But to the historian, facts and events (and people) must be individual and particular: like other entities of a similar kind, but never entirely identical with them. That is to say, they are to be treated as peculiar to themselves and not as indistinguishable statistical units or elements in an equation: but they are linked and rendered comprehensible by kinship, by common possessions, by universal qualities present in differing proportions and arrangements. (Elton, 1967, p. 23)

These are no small demands on the intellectual endeavour of case study. There is rather little guidance that can be offered in advance of the pursuit of particular enquiries. Instead of clear recipes or procedures we must look for highly specific and contextualized judgments and arguments to establish what is unique and what is typical in our studies.

The idea of a single case being an instance of a more general phenomenon is one constantly to bear in mind. This is particularly difficult in educational enquiry for we lack the widely recognized traditions, institutions and techniques within which a case may be pursued. In the field of law, by contrast, a lawyer will take on a case and will study it with a view to advising a client and defending an interest. This is an adversarial situation. Now, although much educational work does consist in promoting a particular view of a case, we have little in the way of adjudication to look to, no equivalent of the judgment of a court to provide validation of enquiry.

To take another example where cases are pursued, consider medical enquiry. Here a doctor investigates a case clinically in order to determine its exact nature. Only when a presenting symptom such as skin rash is properly diagnosed can it be appropriately treated as eczema, an allergic reaction, or whatever. Here the emphasis is on the exact determination of the nature of a case with a view to treating it. The parallel with our educational work is obvious, for in this analogy the desire to improve the situation is one shared with education. There are, however, clearly defined procedures in diagnosis and in treatment; indeed, they are so clearly defined in medicine that there is a real possibility of programming a computer to diagnose and prescribe at least as well as the average GP. We lack in education a prospect of similar diagnostic and prescriptive procedures, although one should not assume that at some levels there may not be appropriate routes for problem-solving and prescription.

A third analogy, perhaps even more instructive for educational enquiry, is in journalism. Here there is a wide range of enquiries, some more respectable than others. Journalists work under imperatives to produce readable and sellable stories to tight deadlines. Nevertheless, they have responsibilities to the truth and can be held to legal account when transgression goes too far. Consider the activities of reputable 'investigative' journalists such as *The Sunday Times* former 'Insight' team or the Woodward and Bernstein partnership at *The Washington Post*. These journalists took cases and pursued them until their exact nature was revealed. What might begin as simple cases of faulty drug prescription or burglary turn out on investigation to be a major thalidomide tragedy or a political crisis leading to the resignation of the President. In these examples the approximation to educational enquiry is in some ways closer than in law and medicine. Journalism is practised at many different levels and to many different audiences. Though there is always a recourse to legal action where the truth is grossly misrepresented, there is only a loosely defined ethical code guiding journalists' activities. Moreover, there are few stable and recognized techniques available to journalists and they must choose their methods opportunistically, according to the situation they find themselves in.

What the law and medicine possess, to a degree lacking in journalism and education, are stable procedures of enquiry, clear canons of adjudication and appropriate institutions within which enquiry can be conducted and defended. For journalists and educationalists there is nothing to fall back upon of the significance of the Law Society or the General Medical Council. What education does possess, and journalism lacks, is an academic and research tradition within the universities. The present study suggests that there is a role for the universities and other institutions of higher education in developing traditions of teachers' research.

These considerations redefine the question of methodology. It is not asserted here that case study is the name of a single method or coherent set of methods of research. It is seen instead as a focus for enquiry; the case is the subject for enquiry. By what methods this enquiry is to be undertaken is an open question, not a matter of principle. Methodology is a matter of what is appropriate and possible, given the research situation and its aims.

Research Topics for Teachers

Teachers are centrally concerned with practice. Case study has enabled a great many teachers to address classroom and school problems to great personal and institutional advantage. There can be no doubt that large numbers of pupils have had a better school experience because their teachers have been engaged in classroom research. Though only a fraction of the 400,000 serving teachers have attended taught courses or enrolled in research degrees, the influence of the teacher researcher movement has been widespread. As a vehicle of INSET case study, loosely formulated though it has been, has been of great professional value. However, there has been an accompanying tendency wrongly to polarize case study and positivistic methods. Case study is not the name of a method but more a signal that a concrete instance is to be investigated by all appropriate means. I shall illustrate how, for a group of teachers, an instance was the starting point for a departure from the classroom and into the power environment of school governorship. This critical incident called for investigation by a range of methods until its significance was more fully explored.

A teacher was teaching a lesson in his school's personal, social and moral education programme when he was visited by a school governor. The governor took objection to the teacher's treatment of sex education. All of this was before the 1988 Education Act's requirement that governors decide if sex education is to be offered and in what form. There ensued an enquiry before which the teacher had to attend, together with his 'friend'.

The teacher was completely vindicated. Meanwhile, the Exeter Society for Curriculum Studies was resolving to set out upon some collaborative research.

The Exeter Society is an independent group of teachers, some 100 strong, based upon, though no official part of, the University of Exeter School of Education. Since 1978 the Society has been fostered by the author in response to a demand from teachers graduating from BPhil and MEd courses for continuing contacts with one another and for professional refreshment. Termly conferences have been held throughout this period and these have been addressed by speakers of national standing. The Society is self-financing and self-governing, being run by an elected committee. The idea of a research effort developed naturally from the conference activities of the Society. When the author called for suggestions on research topics, two clusters of ideas came in: special educational needs in the wake of the 1981 Act and the widespread discontent with LEAs' implementation policies, particularly as regards 'statementing'; and, from the teacher mentioned above and others, school governorship in view of the 1980 Act and its provision for parent governors in all schools. Both of these were strongly felt areas of anxiety for the teachers concerned. It was not difficult to gain commitment to a project which would interview teacher governors of Devon secondary schools in order to see how peers could help expand our understanding of the contemporary situation. Nearly 100 interviews were conducted by twenty practising teachers who met periodically during the two terms taken to prepare, analyze and interpret the work. The results of this enquiry were published in the School of Education's Perspectives series and gained national attention. As a result, funding was obtained from the Leverhulme Trust in aid of further research, this time on parent governors. Again this research topic reflected the temper of the times when the 1986 Act had legislated for a much increased parental constituency on school governing bodies and the 1987 Conservative Manifesto, subsequent Great Education Reform Bill (sic) and in the end the 1988 Education Act strengthened the powers of those same governing bodies.

It is not to the point here to discuss the findings of this research; they are documented elsewhere (Golby, 1985). Rather it is to record the fact that the work was completed, secured the commitment of a group of very busy, experienced teachers, working part-time, and made an impact on the climate of opinion through its media coverage. The completion of the work involved nearly 100 interviews with all the necessary preparatory work and subsequent analyses. All of this was coordinated from the School of Education by the author. Two completely incommensurable factors were at work: the practical capacity in terms of the author's research time, and

and the university facilities which were vital to the conduct of the project. Included in this are items such as the £1000 grant from the university research fund in aid of expenses and that fraction of the university's resources legitimately available to support lecturers' research, including telephones, postage, reprographics, the use of the library and university rooms for meetings. All of this, though mundane, is essential.

Equally important is the lending of the name of the university to the project. Regrettable it may be, but the credibility of any project is enormously enhanced by association with a university. Universities are excellently placed to support teachers' research. Universities have a strong commitment to research and their staff a professional responsibility to conduct research. They provide appropriate facilities, although financial support can never be provided at the levels we would all like. Most importantly there is academic freedom to defend and live up to. This can be best achieved by opening up research to a wider circle, such as to practising teachers, and by ensuring a continuous critical scrutiny of the research effort. In education this must mean again making work accessible to practitioners and then seeking ways of widening the circle. In connection with the research on school governorship, obvious audiences and potential participants are school governors themselves and the wider policy-making community.

In Exeter, the Exeter Society for Curriculum Studies serves such purposes. It bridges the gap between the academic and professional communities. Its membership is predominantly teachers, but administrators, advisers and academics also play a part. Its connection with the university helps and is not allowed to stultify its initiatives. In the new period of constriction of the curriculum, and of teachers themselves, institutions such as this bestow dignity and value upon teachers. In sustaining such nerve centres we are engaged in a battle for education itself, not merely competing for the contract to deliver teacher education. In the climate of the 1990s no political authority is going to pay for the raising of critical consciousness. Questions about the forms of control of schooling, actual and desirable, are simply not required. Yet education entails critical consciousness in pupils and *a fortiori* teachers. In keeping a vestige of this alive educational research has a grave responsibility.

Conclusion

What then are the prospects for educational research? All the signs are adverse for a view of teaching and its associated research which is other than purely technical. It is likely that the energies of the professional educational research community will be taken up with the hunt for funds and then the delivery of results which will support the introduction of the National Curriculum, above all through the machinery of testing. Initial teacher education, itself subject through CATE, to a National Curriculum that even specifies time allocations, will continue to be preoccupied with meeting centrally prescribed criteria which stress the instrumentality of the teacher's role rather than what is problematic about it. The elimination of secondments for teachers has withdrawn the main opportunity of high-level, intrinsically motivated research. The observable intensification of pressure on teachers will continue to diminish the amount of time and energy available for purposes not officially prescribed.

All of this is gloomy. For the present it remains important to keep alive the spirit of critical enquiry. This is intimately bound up with the capacity and freedom of teachers to conduct research beyond the confines of their own immediate environment. New developments of the teacher as researcher movement may be possible within the IT-INSET pattern, where practising teachers, tutors and initial trainees engage together in practical problem-solving. Those from the academic community need to work in such situations to see to it that the local is also seen as a reflection of the wider structure of education. Groups of teachers such as the one discussed here need to form alliances across the system for collective strength. Perhaps we also need to look outside the profession of teaching to see how others assert a critical tradition.

References

ADELMAN, C., JENKINS, D. and KEMMIS, S. (1976) 'Rethinking Case Study: Notes from the Second Cambridge Conference', *Cambridge Journal of Education*, 6, 3, pp. 139–50.

CHANAN, G. (1977) *What School Is For*, London, Methuen.

ELTON, G. (1967) *The Practice of History*, Sydney, Sydney University Press.

GOLBY, M. (1985) *Caught in the Act: Teachers and Governors after 1980*, Perspectives 21, School of Education, University of Exeter.

KENNY, W.W. and GROTELEUSCHEN, A. (1984) 'Making the Case for Case Study', *Journal of Curriculum Studies*, 16, 1, pp. 37–51.

PRING, R.A. and WILSON, P.S. (eds) (1972) 'From Practice to Theory: an Approach through Case Study', Special Edition of *London Educational Review*.

SHAW, K. (1978) 'Understanding the Curriculum: The Approach through Case Study', *Journal of Curriculum Studies*, 10, 1, p. 117.

STENHOUSE, L.A. (1975) *Introduction to Curriculum Research and Development*, London, Heinemann.

STENHOUSE, L.A. (1978) 'Case Study and Case Records: Towards a Contemporary History of Education', *British Educational Research Journal*, 4, 2, pp. 21–39.

STENHOUSE, L.A. (1980) 'The Study of Samples and the Study of Cases', *British Educational Research Journal*, 6, 1, pp. 1–6.

TRIPP, D. (1985) 'Case Study Generalisation: The Agenda for Action', *British Educational Research Journal*, 11, 1, pp. 33–43.

Chapter 10

The Practical Ethic Takes Priority over Methodology

Clem Adelman

> Methodology is too important to be left to methodologists.
>
> (H.S. Becker)

In their everyday work teachers, nurses, social workers and members of other caring professions act partly on their training, partly on their experience and partly on their judgments of what is in the best interests of their 'client', 'patient' and 'student'. These actions have direct consequences for the lives of others and eventually for the professionals themselves. These actions are informed by, or based on, an amalgam of caselore, statute, claims of efficacy and theory. With the introduction of new technologies, administrative structures, lines of accountability, legislation and statutes, the context of such actions is prone to rapid change. It is thus hardly surprising that some professionals plead that they are too busy to think reflectively about the consequences of their actions or the changing contexts in which they occur. They carry out the tasks for which they have been trained as well as they are able, and leave the critical commentaries on their practice to boards of enquiry, government agencies, academics and the media. In short, many professionals do not engage in practical reasoning with regard to the changing context of their work. They take their training, the claims of efficiency and theories upon which it is based, for granted. Such professionals are in no position to make adjustments or changes in their practice, based upon informed judgment.

This chapter examines the extent to which action research has, and potentially can, contribute to the development of informed judgments which may lead to a review of existing claims, theories and conventions, and ultimately to a rethinking of teacher professionalism. Can action research provide the kind of information essential to practical reasoning about the consequences of our actions on others' lives?

Teaching was, and still is, regarded primarily as a craft or art rather than as a science or technology. From this 'craft' tradition come episodic accounts (Blishen, 1966; Neill, 1915) which could be taken as exemplars to be emulated with some regard for the particular context of one's own work. Unfortunately teacher educators have appropriated these craft accounts for different purposes. Some, as Stones and Morris (1972) observe, have transformed them into little more than prescriptions for tutees. Others, however, approach teaching not as a craft but as a cause-effect rule-governed activity. This quest to establish a 'science' of teaching has comprised attempts to find the rules and principles of effective, that is, learning maximized, teaching. The 'science of teaching' literature, dating from the 1920s, has been summarized by Dunkin and Biddle (1974), Tom (1984), Shalveson (1988).

As a means of teacher preparation, both the craft and science theories are deficient. The former provides particular cases without general rules or principles, the latter rules and principles without particular cases. An analogy is that excellent musicians cannot necessarily formulate the rules or principles guiding their performance, whereas excellent music teachers may know these rules but may be unable to realize them in performance. So it is with teaching; what we need to know is by what process the musician develops from potential, through student to quality musician. Is the process audible and visible to the observer? To a considerable extent the process of development of teachers or musicians is neither visible nor audible. For the researcher to make inferences as to how the changes in performance have arisen in the thought, priorities and topics of the developing teacher is to lose validity in the study. The researcher asks the developing teacher or musician to give an account of what led to a perceptible change in performance. If the teacher or musician finds it difficult to recall, then he or she may be asked to keep a diary of thoughts during practice. The researcher and practitioners, by jointly collecting data on the process of development, are now in a position to make the relationships between observed performance and the cognitive and instrumental actions that led to the perceptible changes in performance.

Such a process of joint research and theorizing was used by Louis Smith and William Geoffrey in their pioneering work, *Complexities of an Urban Classroom* (1968). Instead of applying a technical 'rules into action' approach, as sought in positivistic studies of teaching, Smith and Geoffrey revealed the goals and values that underlay actions. Actions have consequences which can be monitored, and the analysis of consequences and comparison with goals and values constitute a process of reflection from which options for further action may be devised. Through their joint work Geoffrey was encouraged to *intervene* in his own teaching by means of reflection, or rather joint theorizing, on the extent of success or failure of the action in terms of general values, desired goals and perceived consequences. Through this theorizing or reflecting on actions and consequences in relation to stated values and goals, the teaching issue under consideration become clearer. Geoffrey had to think hard about these relationships; he 'theorized' in the sense that he took as little as possible for granted. Similar 'theorizing' towards clarification of an issue, that is a real or apparent discrepancy between aspiration and practice, can be seen in some of the Ford *Teachers Case Studies* (1974), in some of the case studies in *A Fair Hearing for All* (Adelman *et al.*, 1983) and in *Assessment and Evaluation in the Arts* (Treacher, 1989).

Teaching, like nursing, engineering, journalism, politics, design, playing musical instruments or painting, is an activity which entails reflection on what one has done in order to become more accomplished. This kind of reflection on doing has been called 'practical reasoning'. It is a form of reasoning in which envisaged ends and practical means are considered jointly in order to improve practice. Whatever our criteria for judging effectiveness, such practical reasoning cannot be spelt out in operational terms, but only in terms of teachers' reflective understanding of their own practices with regard to specific areas of curriculum, assessment and pedagogy.

The application of practical reasoning to teaching involves more than a calculation of the most efficient means to achieve a desired end. Work in these areas impinges on the lives of others, who may be influenced, guided or manipulated by the means chosen to undertake particular tasks. For this reason the *ethical* as well as the technical desirability of the means becomes an issue. For example, teachers decide how they will talk to pupils, what access they will allow them to the knowledge required to make progress through a series of tasks and what criteria they will use to evaluate or assess pupils' performance. Each of these decisions involves ethical as well as technical judgments. Practical reasoning on the ethical consequences of actions is what Schwab (1969) calls a 'practical ethic'.

Schwab argued that the field of curriculum in the 1960s had become dominated by 'theoretic' (technical) thinking. The field had developed a reliance on theories drawn from sociology, psychology, economics and even philosophy, which provided frameworks for developing and implementing curricula in schools. It was hoped that curricula and curriculum development projects could simply apply these theories as a means to attaining defined and agreed curriculum objectives. Thus the large science education curriculum development projects of the 1960s, for example, could take their content as given from contemporary academic scientists, and this content could be organized and sequenced by curriculum specialists (expert in educational psychology, especially the design of teaching/learning activities and methods of assessment) into materials for teachers and students. The work of educators was, under this conception, technical work: implementing in practice the ideas and objectives of theorists outside the classroom, the school and often outside the education system (for example, implementing the ideas of politicians, scientists or academic theorists).

In English, or rather Anglo-Saxon culture, the innovative ('art') or repetitive ('work') are long established, whereas the practical ethic professions spread across structural categories, sometimes appearing more like art as with photographers, sometimes like repetitive work as with teaching, nursing and musical performance. However, the integrity of the practical ethic professions comes from reflection on consequences of known practices in new contexts and the freedom to propose and try alternative options for action. But this kind of practical reasoning on ethical consequences can only be reliable, valid and refutable if the isssue is clarified through the hard work of theorizing and testing alternatives by intervening in the life of practice. Quality action research offers the means whereby this kind of process can be implemented. It can be the methodology of enquiry for the practical ethic professions — nursing, teaching, social work, design — which are neither repetitive in terms of cause-effect nor innovative, or even iconoclastic, as in living creative art.

The methodology of action research was originally conceived by Lewin (1946) as one means to foster democratic access to knowledge in the pursuit of power sharing. He objected to conventional psychostatistical research, sponsored by agencies and carried out by those with privileged access to the language and concepts and funds of educational research. But since the late 1970s an uncritical celebration of the methodology of action research has developed which obscures the essential concerns with quality, relevance and integrity in the practical ethic of teaching that were initially sought by Schwab and later by Stenhouse. Teachers doing research on their own practice, in collaboration with those from higher education and agencies, does not ensure that the issues researched are any less innocuous, even when they relate to concerns in pedagogy, curriculum, assessment or educational management. Ironically, a democratic methodology such as action research may be used to promote and exacerbate inequalities of opportunity, process and outcome.

Thus the disappointment on reading teachers' action research reports as purveyed by Hustler *et al.* (1986), McNiff (1988), Ebbut and Elliott (1985). Without attributing any blame or incompetence to the teachers involved, what these accounts reflect is the belief that an aspect of teaching can be improved if it more effectively achieves a desired outcome. What these cases lack is the hard, joint theorizing on the relationships of values, action and consequences prior to the devising of fresh options for action. An understanding of teaching as a species of practical ethic is lacking. These accounts read like the pursuit of certitude, of effectiveness or predictability and in this sense are indistinguishable from the positivistic, single-item, cause-effect research which the promulgation of teaching as a practical ethic has tried to replace. The medium (action research) has become confused with the message (teacher development towards autonomy). Conducted in this way, 'doing' action research may have no more intrinsic educational significance than much of the psychostatistical research to which action research is seen as a radical popular alternative (Silver, 1987; Adelman, 1987).

We now have well argued theoretical rationales (Carr and Kemmis, 1986; Winter, 1987; Elliott, 1987) for the democratization of educational research but a paucity of high quality case studies by teachers, and collaborators, displaying the sources and the practical outcomes of reflection on curriculum, pedagogy, assessment or educational management. The published studies, most of which seem to be summaries of master's dissertations, rarely extend beyond personal awareness. They lack the wider contexts of organization, politics and policy. In brief, we know and understand *why* action research could be an important means to democratize educational research, but are disappointed, if not dismayed, by the published studies. It may be that the arguments for action research as an acceptable means of educational research have been won, but there is no reason for complacency, a malaise that may be encapsulated by the response, 'well, you've got to let teachers start somewhere'. Action research stands or falls by its demonstrable relevance to the practical ethic of education, as well as whether it is reliable, valid and refutable as a methodology.

As readers of action research studies, we need to know what is the educational *issue*, its context, how reflection has prevailed and what 'conclusions' for intervention in action were reached. The display of a practical ethic by practitioners is more convincing when practitioners collaborate on how an issue 'manifests' in the different contexts of their classrooms and schools. Collaboration on a common issue also provides the possibility of comparison and the opportunity to extend the validity of the research.

Collaboration and joint action have been central to action research since Lewin devised action research essentially as community self-study. This was a voluntary intervention in which the members of the community, themselves under the expert guidance of applied social psychologists, would be responsible for the collection and analysis of community data. The data were to be used in the planning of a programme of action. The community would, Lewin thought, more readily accept the data and their applications from its own survey than from an outside agency. The professional researchers, through their face-to-face collaboration with the community, would see whether their theories of social action and change and their methodologies of enquiry were adequate to meet the complexities of their social problem.

Like Lewin, Stenhouse (1983) also spoke for educational reconstruction informed and powered by systematic reflective enquiry into the practical ethic of teaching. But for Stenhouse, teachers' research into their understandings and actions was only part of the process of reconstruction. As with Lewin, Stenhouse saw democratization through power sharing, informed by a process of practitioner research at every level. This aspiration, so clearly conceptualized and expressed by Stenhouse, was never fulfilled in his lifetime. The Humanities Curriculum Project was the nearest realization, but its potential impact was countered by reaction of the political Left and Right and the conservatism of schools (Rudduck, 1976). The unpublished Sheffield 'SAFARI' case study, an evaluation of the medium-term impact of the curriculum reform materials of the 1960s, did not foster reflective reconstruction at the time. SAFARI's sister project, the Ford Teaching project, demonstrated that teachers could research their own teaching as a means to elucidate their own educational values and the extent to which these were consonantly realized in practice.

Stenhouse considered the Ford project as too narrowly focused on the intricacies of only part of the process of reconstruction. 'Tinkering with the fine tuning' was his (1980) judgment; one that I would accept only in relation to the larger cultural context of reconstruction. The Ford project tested the claim that teachers could conduct research and theorize, initially about their own and eventually about others' teaching. Teachers could also devise interventions in their teaching and monitor the consequences as part of an action research cycle. Elliott and I researched the teachers' problems in conducting reflective enquiry. From joint analysis with the teachers of their teaching actions and the terms used by teachers to label these actions, a relationship between teachers' categories for describing their teaching was constructed. Teachers were able to show that they have a theory of their own practice which is not haphazard, reactive or one-dimensional. Although richer action research case studies have now been published

(Treacher, 1989) and much has been written on the democratic principles that action research can engender with regard to research and to the planning of change (Carr and Kemmis, 1986; Winter, 1987), the Ford project publications, albeit dispersed, have not been superseded with regard to the process of action research and its problems as a practitioner endeavour.

According to McNiff (1988), there is a proliferation of 'styles' of classroom action research among which that of her former tutor, Jack Whitehead, is superior. This, like the published conversation between Whitehead and Lomax (1987), prompts the question: What in terms of the wider reconstruction of education has this preferred 'style' of action research actually achieved? Why is the educational action research 'movement', of which it claims to be a major part, so inward looking and ahistorical? Why did Carr and Kemmis not cite Schon (1983) alongside Freire (1970)? Why is no celebration of the exemplary teachers' studies of their own teaching provided by Armstrong (1980) and Rowlands (1984)? Where is any mention of Smith and Geoffrey? The exceptions to this demise are few. They are redolent with fresh thinking and insight into clearly conceptualized issues in curriculum, pedagogy or assessment. Pollard and Tann (1987), Easen (1985) and Treacher (1989) are examples that begin to fulfil the quest to understand the practical ethic, as clearly stated by Schwab (1969) and Stenhouse (1975), practised by Hawkins (1974), Armstrong (1980) and Rowlands (1984), tested by the Ford project and advocated as a means to realize democratic critical communities (Carr and Kemmis, 1986) and the pursuit of greater self-understanding (Elliott, 1987).

Overbearing claims are being made for action research as an alternative research paradigm, as a democratizing force and means of achieving informed, practical change arising from issues at the grass roots. Many of these claims are uncorroborated by cases, by applications to wider programmes of change or in a shared understanding of teaching voiced as concerted criticism of, say, recent DES and HMI tracts and invocations. Where is action research in the National Curriculum and assessment, let alone teacher moderation and institutional accreditation? Frankly, classroom action research with all its adherents and latter-day 'converts' (e.g., Bennett, 1986) has not shown any sign that teacher researchers share vocabulary, concepts and understandings about teaching and classrooms in any degree sufficient to respond to, let alone initiate, change. The sad truth is that some academics have highjacked action research and, in an effort to demonstrate direct relevance to classroom practice and efficiency, unwittingly promoted the positivistic and normative stance that is clearly antithetical to furthering understanding of teaching as a practical ethic.

I have cited the well argued rationales for educational action research, and we should note that the methodologies described by various authors, whether or not they have taken part in action research, are similar. The important differences among the literature pertain to the experience and understanding of how difficult practitioners find the clarification of the issue, the setting of the problem. The real or apparent discrepancy between aspiration and practice is not given at the outset. Teachers may be able vaguely to identify a 'concern' or 'trouble' (Wright Mills, 1959), but that is only a beginning. The hard work of reflection on research data that raises questions about one's own teaching competence and consequences cannot be lightly addressed in favour of following through a prescribed methodology of action research. Reflection is theorizing about one's own practice in action; reflection on what is learnt by doing — in other words the practical ethic. If you accept teaching as a practical ethic, then action research into teaching must include theorizing about what is learnt through research on one's own teaching. Furthermore, the theorizing cannot be delimited to specific items, events, phenomena, but must try to make explicit relationships between the categories used by the action researcher in trying to make sense of the knowledge gained by data collection from the social, objective and subjective worlds. These qualities are lacking in most of the published practitioners' studies that are themselves not case studies in the developed sense (see Simons, 1980).

To gain credibility, educational action researchers must make greater demands on themselves and those with whom they collaborate in their theorizing about issues of the practical ethic of professions. We should be reluctant to publish studies that do not show understanding of the practical ethic, of theorizing or of issue clarification. We should identify practitioners' case studies that fulfil these criteria and build our understanding of issues from there. Such studies are presently few in number.

References

ADELMAN, C. (1987) Proposal for the Motion in *The State of Education Today*, Norwich, Centre for Applied Research in Education.

ADELMAN, C., BOXALL, W., PARSONS, I., RANSON, P., THEBAULT, Y., TREACHER, V. and RICHARDSON, R. (1983) *A Fair Hearing for All*, Bulmershe Research Publication No. 2, Reading.

ARMSTRONG, M. (1980) *Closely Observed Children*. London, Chameleon Books.

BENNETT, N. (1986) in Hustler *et al.* (1986).

BLISHEN, E. (1966) *Roaring Boys: A Schoolmaster's Agony*, London, Panther Books.

CARR, W. and KEMMIS, S. (1986) *Becoming Critical: Education, Knowledge and Action Research*, Lewes, Falmer Press.

CHERNS, A. (1971) 'Models for the Use of Research', *Human Relations*, 22, 1, pp. 25–33.

DUNKIN, M. and BIDDLE, B. (1974) *The Study of Teaching*, New York, Holt, Rinehart and Winston.

EASEN, P. (1985) *Making School Centred INSET Work*, London, Croom Helm.

EBBUT, D. and ELLIOTT, J. (1985) *Issues in Teaching for Understanding*, London, Longmans.

ELLIOTT, J. (1987) 'Educational Theory, Practical Philosophy and Action Research', *British Journal of Educational Studies*, 25, 2, pp. 149–69.

ELLIOTT, J. and ADELMAN, C. (1976) *Innovation at the Classroom Level: A Case Study of the Ford Teaching Project*, Milton Keynes, Open University Press.

FORD TEACHING PROJECT (1974) *Teachers Case Studies*, particularly *The Castles Group*, Norwich, CARE, University of East Anglia (Orders to Cambridge Institute of Education).

FREIRE, P. (1970) *Cultural Action for Freedom*, Cambridge, Mass., Centre for the Study of Change.

HAWKINS, D. (1974) *The Informed Vision: Essays on Learning and Human Nature*, New York, Agamon Press.

HUSTLER, D., CASSIDY, A. and CUFF, E.C. (eds) (1986) *Action Research in Classroom and Schools*, London, Allen and Unwin.

LEWIN, K. (1946) 'Action Research and Minority Problems', *Journal of Social Issues*, 2, pp. 34–36.

MCNIFF, J. (1988) *Action Research: Principles and Practice*, London, Macmillan Education.

NEILL, A.S. (1915) *A Domnies Log*, Glasgow, Hubert Jenkins.

POLLARD, A. and TANN, S. (1987) *Reflective Teaching in the Primary School*, London, Cassell.

ROWLANDS, S. (1984) *The Enquiring Classroom*, Lewes, Falmer Press.

RUDDUCK, J. (1976) *Dissemination of Innovation: The Humanities Curriculum Project*, London, Evans/Methuen Educational.

SAFARI: Theory in Practice (1977) Occasional Publication No. 2, Norwich, CARE, University of East Anglia.

SCHON, D. (1983) *The Reflective Practitioner*, London, Temple Smith.

SCHWAB, J. (1969) *The Practical: A Language for Curriculum*, School Review, Vol. 78, pp. 1–24.

SHALVESON, R. (1988) 'Contributions of Educational Research to Policy and Practice: Constructing, Challenging, Changing Cognition', *Educational Researcher*, 17, 7, pp. 4–22.

SILVER, H. (1987) *Research in CNAA Validated Institutions*, London, Council for National Academic Awards.

SIMONS, H. (ed.) (1980) *Towards a Science of the Singular*, Norwich, CARE, University of East Anglia.

SMITH, L. and GEOFFREY, W. (1968) *Complexities of an Urban Classroom*, New York, Holt, Rinehart and Winston.

STENHOUSE, L. (1975) *An Introduction to Curriculum Research and Development*, London, Heinemann.

STENHOUSE, L. (1983) *Authority, Education and Emancipation*, London, Heinemann.

STONES, E. and MORRIS, S.I. (1972) *Teaching Practice: Problems and Perspectives*, London, Methuen.

TOM, A. (1984) *Teaching as a Moral Craft*, New York, Longmans.

TREACHER, V. (ed.) (1989) *Assessment and Evaluation in the Arts*, Reading, Berkshire Education Authority.

WHITEHEAD, J. and LOMAX, P. (1987) 'Action Research and the Politics of Educational Knowledge', *British Educational Research Journal*, 13, 2, pp. 175–90.

WINTER, R. (1987) *Action Research and the Nature of Social Inquiry: Professional Innovation and Educational Work*, Aldershot, Gower.

WRIGHT MILLS, C. (1959) *The Sociological Imagination*, Oxford, Oxford University Press.

Chapter 11

Teacher Appraisal and the Development of Professional Knowledge

Richard Winter

In this chapter it is argued that the appraisal schemes currently proposed for the teaching profession depend on a fundamentally untenable theory of knowledge, and that in consequence such schemes are both unrealistic and incoherent. In particular, it is argued that there is a confusion within appraisal schemes between a desire for managerial control and a desire to create 'objective information'. This rests on a simplistic 'means-ends' model of rational action and an implicit claim that human situations may be understood by means of analogies with the methods of natural science. A contrasting theory of knowledge and consequently an alternative model of the relationship between professional knowledge and the development of professional practice are proposed.

The Contradictions of 'Appraisal': Understanding and Control

'Appraisal' ('an official valuation' — *Shorter Oxford English Dictionary*) necessarily concerns the making of judgments, and thus involves choosing to compare one thing with another by means of a further choice of criteria for similarity and difference. But even though such judgments may claim to be 'official', they are nevertheless open to question, being inevitably based on the differing assumptions and values of those who make them. For example, Geoffrey Samuel (a headteacher), describing 'an established appraisal scheme', begins by quoting Sir David Orr, 'Chairman of Unilever', on the importance of 'making the right key appointments. We spend a great deal of time trying to get right the appointment of the top man [sic] and the top team.' He goes on to cite Sir Michael Edwardes: 'Good men [sic] prefer to be accountable,'[1] In the same volume of readings, however, Stan Bunnell (a headteacher) and Erika Stephens (a member of his staff), writing *jointly* of 'a democratic approach to the introduction of a teacher appraisal scheme', observe:

> Committed and professional people do not take kindly to a model of appraisal which . . . now seems incredibly alien and naive, namely the 'one-way' or linear model of appraisal favoured by industry, where the more senior one judges the less senior one against performance targets and desirable qualities.[2]

Alien and naive though it may seem to some, this is exactly what is proposed in David Trethowan's recently published book, based on his many contributions to 'Education for Industrial Society'[3] and (apparently) his lengthy experience on a frigate in the Royal Navy,[4] a context where, as Plato noted, the democratic decision-making espoused by Bunnell and Stephens does not easily flourish.

Can the staff of educational establishments be judged in 'the same way' as those in business corporations or frigates? This is a judgment on which there will be different views, just as there will be different views as to whether or not the criteria for 'desirable qualities' have been met. Thus some might agree with Trethowan that it is desirable for a teacher to 'maintain professional dress and appearance',[5] but Trethowan might object to that person's Peace badge; similarly it might be agreed that we should 'maintain a high standard of professional conduct in all matters',[6] but some might object to Trethowan publishing anti-Irish jokes.[7] So even if two people agreed on general criteria, each might still contest the detailed judgments of the other as an authoritative appraiser, just as many female colleagues would be suspicious of being appraised by Sir David Orr, Sir Michael Edwardes, or Geoffrey Samuel. In other words, acts of appraisal may seek to be 'official' valuations, but they are unlikely to be able to avoid the general ideological debates in which such valuations are always situated.

This raises the problem of what is to count as 'valid' knowledge. In most modern societies social authority attempts to legitimate itself by showing that it is based on 'valid' knowledge (rather than *mere* economic or military power), so there is a link between rival claims as to the source of valid knowledge and debates as to the nature of political legitimacy. In the above examples the claims of the hierarchical principle (knowledge from *above*) confront those of democracy (knowledge through cooperation), but the rival principles do not simply coincide with the different authors cited.

On the one hand, Trethowan's generally hierarchical approach does not prevent his emphasizing 'joint setting of targets, identified, monitored, and achieved by agreement between the teacher and the appraiser, [and] . . . the opportunity . . . for most teachers . . . to participate in departmental policy making.'[8] On the other hand, Bunnell and Stephens found that 'the two-way development . . . was something of a disappointment': most staff chose to be appraised by a superior, and few suggestions were made by appraisee teachers for general school policy changes.[9] We have here, therefore, within appraisal schemes, a general contradiction (between hierarchy and participation) which goes much deeper than the differing values and statuses of individuals.

This contradiction concerns the nature of the processes by which valid knowledge in created. Most appraisal schemes put forward three basic processes: (1) *self-appraisal* by the person whose knowledge and practice are supposed to develop; (2) *observation* of the appraisee's work-related behaviour; (3) *interaction* between the appraisee and another, during which alternative views of the appraisee's work are exchanged. This interaction may be (3a) set within a *hierarchical* relationship, where appraisers might be advised to 'explain on what evidence a judgment is being made'[10] in order to persuade the appraisee to accept it, or (3b) it may be a voluntary 'two-way' process of '*mutual assessment*'.[11] Each of these basic processes points to a particular problem concerning the development of knowledge, viz:

(1) *self-appraisal*: how can a self-review yield *new* outcomes?
(2) *observation*: how can the findings of an outsider be either objective or usable?
(3a) *hierarchical judgment*: what is the relationship between a social, institutional authority and an ability to make valid interpretive judgments?
(3b) *mutual assessment*: how is it possible to go beyond the frameworks for everyday interaction (politeness, self-defence, bias, etc.)?

By putting all of these processes together (albeit with varying emphases) appraisal schemes implicitly recognize the need to resolve two fundamental issues which haunt attempts to investigate human activities: first, how can knowledge of human beings be objective? (cf. the process of 'observation'), and second, how can such knowledge be of practical benefit? (cf. the setting and monitoring of 'targets'). Since all the questions noted in the previous paragraph remain unanswered, the overall process of appraisal (as currently proposed), far from resolving these issues, merely serves to sharpen up the contradictions, since the four elements in the process all tend to undermine each other. Why bother to engage in self-appraisal if you are going to be 'observed'? What is the point of mutual assessment if a hierarchical superior can make an authoritative judgment? How can observation not be affected by the network of social relationships within which it takes place?

The issue can be put even more sharply. Appraisal is proposed as necessary and valuable on two counts: that it will provide a 'record'[12] of 'reliable information',[13] and that it will lead to professional 'development'[14] or 'improvement'.[15] In other words, appraisal is intended to be *both* an objective account of professional activity *and* an effective managerial tool for motivating professional workers towards the achievement of institutional goals. Thus within the one concept of appraisal we have two distinct notions whose relationship is highly problematic: effective manipulation and accurate description — control and understanding. To see why appraisal schemes are so widely proposed in this inherently disparate form, let us begin by considering one central aspect of its underlying ideological function.

The Ideology of Means-Ends Rationality

It is no accident that Max Weber is known as the theorist both of bureaucracy and of instrumental rationality: the two ideas complement each other. The theory of bureaucracy is that institutions can be understood as hierarchies, in which each level in the hierarchy sets the goals for the levels below, and each level is accountable for the achievement of its goals to the level above. This fits in neatly with a theory that human actions may be understood by seeing how far those actions are instrumentally effective in bringing about the goals to which (in principle) they are 'rationally' directed. What is easily forgotten, however, is that these theories were not put forward by Weber as *descriptions* (as suggestions that institutions actually do work like this or that human actions actually are of this nature) but as analytical devices which provide a sort of measuring rod, against which any actual institution (or action) may be compared, in terms of how far and in what ways it (inevitably) differs from the abstract concept. The theories of bureaucratic hierarchy and of instrumental rationality are *only* useful for analytical purposes because *no* real phenomenon can ever correspond to them.[16]

This enables us to see the ideological effect of linking appraisal with 'target-setting': it involves treating the abstract theories of bureaucratic hierarchy and instrumental rationality as though they were practicable ideals which ought to be attainable, that is, as descriptions of possible and desirable states of affairs. As an ideological manoeuvre by managers and management theorists, this is quite straightforward: it constructs a model of human situations which serves to legitimate their own interests and concerns. We can clarify this point by reminding ourselves of the fundamental and widely known *unreality* of both theories. Since the writings of Selznick, at least, it has been widely realized that formal hierarchical structures are always modified by an 'informal order' of semi-private redefinitions of priority and concern which make the instutution workable for those who work in it.[17] Since the writings of Freud, at least, it has been widely accepted that our rational pursuit of justifiable goals is greatly modified by displaced emotions, childish fixations and semi-neurotic distortions.

What is more interesting, though, is how the ideology of rational goal achievement (as a theory both of institutions and of individual behaviour) is linked with a theory of knowledge. We are not merely dealing here with a management theory of effective control (of team-building, of motivation, of morale creation) but a theory of how *at the same time* to create 'reliable information' based on the evidence of observation. One is tempted to ask: why try to link the two? It is not surprising that workers in schools, like those in frigates, commercial organizations, the Civil Service, etc., have a problem of low morale. So it is not surprising that managers in those establishments are looking for techniques for improving the morale of those for whose activities they may be held accountable. Where better to look for such techniques than among those of the professional *counsellor*, whose job is precisely to raise the morale of people in difficult circumstances.

In counselling, the processes of agreeing short-term and medium-term targets, reviewing progress towards those targets, listing strengths and weaknesses, etc. have long been established and familiar practices, and it seems that some aspects of appraisal schemes are tacitly borrowed from this body of expertise.[18] But the counselling process makes no claim to create objective descriptions or evaluations of the individual concerned. Why, then, when a perfectly plausible case could be made for 'management-as-morale-boosting' or management as 'hard-edged' counselling, are we confronted with something called 'appraisal', which makes a claim not simply for effective psychological manipulation but also for accurate description and evaluation?

One important reason has already been suggested: that in democratic societies social authority seeks to legitimate itself not merely as technically effective but also as possessing a basis in 'valid' knowledge. On this basis the exercise of social power can more easily present itself as not only efficient but as *just*, that is, as 'justifiable' to those to whom those exercising power are accountable. Bureaucracies *document* their activities in such a way that they can always show sufficient 'evidence' for any decision that they may have to take. 'Information', therefore, must be gathered, with a range of possible purposes in mind (promoting or redeploying staff, passing or failing students, paying or withholding welfare benefits, etc.), and this information must be stored in a form which could be used not only by the official who gathered it but by *any* other official with access to the relevant files. ('Official' judgments are 'impersonal'.)[19]

In this way a theory about the form of our knowledge of human beings ('the gathering of objective information'), derived from an analogy with our knowledge of natural objects, joins a theory of institutions ('bureaucracy') and a theory of behaviour ('instrumental rationality') as parts of a complex ideology which justifies the exercise of authority *by* one group of people (those who collect and possess information) *over* another group (those about whom information has been collected). It is exactly this combination of effects and purposes which undermines the pretensions of 'positivist' social science. Its use of the methods of natural science does not simply constitute an approximation to 'objectivity' but an implicit programme of 'control'[20] in which 'populations' and 'sub-populations' become statistical entities to be manipulated as 'variables'. However, the claims of social science to create reliable laws and accurate predictions, as effective practical instruments of social control, are not sustainable,[21] except in those extremely rare (and usually quite uninteresting) cases where the purposes of the work *and* the categories used are entirely non-contentious. Thus concerning teachers, one might agree that 'information' could be collected about, say, their average height and weight, but to suggest that judgments as to their professional effectiveness could be collected in this way is intellectually untenable (even though we can see by now the reasons why such suggestions are made). To examine exactly why it is untenable will involve considering the crucial differences between our understanding of people and our understanding of the natural world.

The Theoretical Impossibility of 'Information' about Teacher Quality

First of all we can note that no one collects raw information about anything without classifying it under general categories. This is just as true when we observe butterflies or the movement patterns of sub-molecular particles as when we observe teachers' interactions with pupils. (Indeed, as soon as we put our individual experiences into words we immediately *classify* them under the *general* meanings provided by those words. Nevertheless, there is a widespread commonsense notion that one gains understanding by directly observing particular phenomena, a view which Popper dismisses as 'utterly naive and mistaken', and 'devastating' in its influence on our theories of investigation.[22]

The question then becomes: what general categories shall we use, and how shall we decide on them? To begin with, generalizations cannot be derived from, or erected upon, repeated particular observations by the process of 'induction'. We can only assume that our future observations will continue the general pattern we think we have discerned in our past observations if we make an *assumption* about the regularity and stability of our experience, which is, of course, a circular argument. The assumption itself may serve an important practical need, but as a theory, says Popper, it is no more than a 'myth'.[23] Therefore, for the investigator, as for the bureaucrat, the categories under which information is collected must always depend on a set of *prior* purposes. This is because any phenomenon has a theoretically infinite number of constituent elements on which our perceptions might focus during an act of observation. We cannot observe several phenomena and generalize about what they have in common unless we already have a theory as to which of these elements are more significant than others (for our purposes), and thus worth picking out as the basis for a general category under which these several phenomena may be classified. Hence Popper's well known sequence for the process of enquiry, in which one first makes a 'conjecture' (a hypothesis derived from a theory) and then attempts to make observations which are designed to be capable of 'refuting' it. For Popper, 'no theory has been shown to be true, or can be shown to be true'; rather, 'not only are all theories conjectural, but also all appraisals of theories.' Hence 'the quest for certainty, for a secure basis of knowledge, has to be abandoned.'[24]

Where does this leave the appraisal of teacher effectiveness? Basically one is left with an insoluble dilemma. If we ignore Popper's critique of induction, and seek to erect generalizations upon repeated observations, we end up with Byrne's problem: the phenomenon of teacher effectiveness has such a massive number of variables that, practically speaking, we *cannot* generalize about it:

> We should therefore hesitate to speak of a teacher's effectiveness except in relation to particular situations. Teacher rating-scales or other appraisal procedures designed for use across a wide range of subjects and types of pupils . . . in many cases . . . cannot be taken seriously at all . . . . On the basis of the evidence, the more closely

an appraisal procedure is designed for use in a particular teaching situation, the more valid it can be expected to be. Furthermore, the lack of stability of teacher effects with the same group of pupils over similar topics . . . suggests that the same procedures may suffer a significant deterioration in validity when applied to situations which are not very dissimilar.[25]

Byrne goes on to propose the development of 'a multiplicity of appraisal procedures',[26] but his own emphasis on 'particular situations' suggests that the variety may be infinite, which casts doubt on the feasibility of such a proposal. The point is neatly made by Kitwood and Macey, writing of Neville Bennett's notorious attempt to investigate teacher effectiveness in the mid-1970s:

The results, as we have shown, are not very convincing. A thorough investigation which could claim even to approximate to the self-imposed canons of the (research) paradigm would probably take the same team, working at the same rate, about fifty years to complete, and might well cost as much as the whole primary education budget for a year![27]

Should we, therefore, follow Popper, abandon the 'quest for certainty' based on repeated empirical observations, and accept that our theories of teacher effectiveness must remain conjectural. If conjectural knowledge is an acceptable basis for the natural sciences, why not for the social sciences? Popper's ideas have found a ready welcome in writing on social science methodology,[28] but there are several powerful arguments why Popper's theory of knowledge cannot be transferred from the investigation of the natural world to the investigation of social affairs.

First, according to Popper, conjectures are 'refuted' by being shown to be 'in contradiction with facts'.[29] Habermas suggests that this means that Popper is contradicting himself: if facts can only be observed in the light of theories, then how can facts *in themselves* refute those theories?[30] Admittedly Popper is concerned with *experimental* methods of investigation, which (perhaps) can be set up quite precisely to *construct* 'facts' in relation to particular theories. But this is only possible where physical phenomena are concerned; it is impossible where the investigation concerns human beings, whose moral and political *rights* will drastically curtail the number and type of experimental manipulations which can be carried out. In social investigation, therefore, facts can never be so rigorously constructed as to refute theories.

Second, if social investigation cannot conform to the strict procedures of experimental natural science, 'refutation' becomes a matter of interpreting rather questionable 'evidence' which is always, in principle, open to various interpretations. Would-be 'refutations' are thus themselves no more than further conjectures, so Popper's 'dialectic' between conjecture and refutation lapses into circularity.

Third, the processes of the natural world change on a much slower time-scale than the processes of scientific investigation, which means that criticism of theories in natural science can utilize the *replication* of experiments. This is not so in the investigation of social affairs: a social situation is inherently likely to change quite substantially before the results of any investigation have been published, and these changes will also be affected by the processes of the investigation itself.

Fourth, whereas the human observer confronts the natural world as a subject observing and interpreting objects, in social science the person being observed is interpreting the investigator; the events of a social investigation are always an *interaction*, whose effects are thus never entirely within the control or awareness of the observer. Therefore, the observer must not only be content with less than full 'certainty' as to the activities of the observed, but the observed may (consciously *or unconsciously*) disagree with, and even seek to frustrate, the activities of the observer by subterfuge, non-cooperation, or masquerade. To attempt to understand this aspect of an investigation would require a further investigation, leading to an infinite regress.

Fifth, the limited certainty of our understanding of the natural world merely presents us with a technical problem: we cannot as yet colonize Venus, but this does not prevent our exploiting to the full our current ability to put communications satellites into space. In contrast, the limitations of our certainty in understanding human beings present us with a moral problem: if we can have no certainty concerning our current (or possible) theories of teacher effectiveness, we cannot justifiably promote and demote teachers in the light of what we know to be merely a structure of inter-locking conjectures.

We can thus see the nature of the problem. The paradigm for the creation of knowledge (derived from the procedures of natural science), which serves important ideological functions for institutional managers, is fundamentally flawed as a basis for understanding the events over which managers claim responsibility. The question then becomes: what procedures for understanding *would* be appropriate?

Professionalism: The Coincidence of Understanding and Development

In contrast to the theory of bureaucratic institutions, the theory of professional expertise offers an alternative account of how human affairs may be rationally ordered. Whereas the theory of bureaucracy emphasizes general rules applying to all officials and all cases, the theory of professionalism emphasizes the particularity of individual cases, which always present professional workers with the problem of how their expertise is to be applied on each and every occasion. This is especially so where the profession is concerned with human needs (e.g., education, social work, psychotherapy, counselling, nursing, law, journalism, planning, personnel management), and where the professional expertise involved is not an 'exact science' (in contrast to, say, engineering), or where the outcome is a human process rather than a material product (in contrast to, say, architecture), or where precise measurement of desirable outcomes is difficult (in contrast to, say, marketing).

In professions concerned with ordering human affairs, the problem of making a decision 'for the best' in the individual case is dramatized in popular books, films and TV series about a 'professional-as-hero', engaged in a quest for justice and truth in spite of widespread misunderstanding, 'red tape', lack of resources, political pressures from on high, etc. This genre presents the professional-as-investigator, who refuses to take conventional interpretations at face value, and thus represents expertise in a mode of critical autonomy, dedicated to the complex needs of the individual client, usually in opposition to the would-be prescriptive rules of the bureaucratized institutions within which the professional practice is situated.

While appreciating the significance of this mythological theme, we must not be taken in by it. Professional work is also enmeshed in a crucial contradiction between its expert *authority* (based on an official body of knowledge which legitimates the right to practise) and the *inability* of that expertise to prescribe (except tentatively) for the individual case. This has an important consequence: professional workers in human affairs can only practise effectively and justly if they *learn* from the individual cases in which they are involved, since their expertise, as a body of knowledge, is always inadequate and incomplete with respect to its objects and purposes. This presents professional workers not so much with an opportunity for self-righteous heroism as with an obligatory stance of critically questioning their expertise in the face of the complex needs of the individual client. The *temptation* for professional workers (usually hard-pressed, overworked, underresourced) is to treat their expertise as though it *could* be used like a natural science, and to simplify issues and to save time by treating clients as objects who can be immediately classified under pre-existing categories and explained by pre-existing theories. The critical function of the professional is not essentially directed towards others (as in the popular genre, which makes the professional-as-hero into yet another mythic authority figure) but towards the inevitable limits of their own knowledge and understanding. In this way the professional role may be defined as the form of activity where the improvement of effective practice *coincides* with the development of understanding.

However, this is easier said than done. 'Criticism' is a slippery word. What does it entail? Most appraisal schemes make reference to 'self-appraisal' but go on to treat it as a preliminary to an interview with the head and 'classroom observation'.[31] The difficulty is (as has been suggested earlier) that our theories of knowledge, dominated as they are by natural science analogies, tend to provide procedures whereby one person observes, categorizes and gathers evidence about *another*, which thereby divorces the seeking of understanding from the development of practice. What is needed, in order to support the model of the professional role outlined above, is an alternative theory of knowledge, which does not rely on natural science analogies, which coherently provides procedures for critique and for the linking of theoretical and practical development into a single process. Such an alternative is outlined in the next section.

Action Research: Collaboration and Critique, Dialectics and Reflexivity

As the term implies, 'action research' is more than 'observation' or 'self-appraisal'; it is an activity in which the development of professional practice and the development of understanding are inseparably linked in a process where one supports the other. In action research practitioners reflect upon their work in such a way as to generate insights which will open up new practical developments, and from these new practical developments fresh insights are derived which subsequently open up further practical innovation, in a theoretically endless spiral.

Action research is not merely a concept. Over the last decade or so the practical activities of groups and organizations of teachers such as the Classroom Action Research Network (originally led by John Elliott and now coordinated from the University of East Anglia by Bridget Somekh) have radically transformed the curriculum of in-service courses for teachers, at every level from week-end conferences to higher degrees, towards a research-based format. As a result of this action research movement (which is both international and local) there exist numerous groups of teachers who are experienced in the process of developing their practice and their understanding through the combination of systematic reflection and strategic innovation.

The basic process of action research expresses the professional mode of expertise, and is fundamentally opposed to the natural science model of knowledge which separates knowledge from action and the active knower from the passive object of knowledge. In this way action research not only offers a format for effective professional development, but also a solution to fundamental problems of social science, and hence an appropriate format for the understanding of social (including educational) realities.[32] It is worth spelling out the nature of this solution in some detail, since — as we have seen — the natural science model of enquiry (whether as crude positivist 'observation' and 'fact-finding' or in its more sophisticated Popperian version) has enormous ideological appeal. Four fundamental principles concerning the development of knowledge about social events are compatible with, implicit in and required by action research. Together they form a coherent alternative rationale by means of which the natural science paradigm can be avoided.[33]

Collaboration.   Our investigation of people cannot take the form of seeking an accurate description which corresponds to an external reality because that reality does not have the form of a static external object. So we cannot carry out repeated experiments to improve upon the accuracy of any preliminary interpretation. Our descriptions *might* be accurate, but we cannot know this, and so we cannot claim it. Instead we must conceive of investigation as an interaction between two parties (investigator and investigated), where the actions of the investigated inevitably change alongside or even in response to the interpretations of the investigator. Instead of the observer and the observed (a metaphor from biology) we have collaborative work, either between colleagues, who in terms of the investigative process have equal status and who may well be playing both roles, or between facilitators and practitioners, where, of course, it is *the latter* who determine purposes, agendas and timing. In this way we can see that 'self-appraisal' is not mere introspection, but empirical study of one's working practices, using one's clients (pupils, students, etc.) as collaborators.

Critique.   The result of collaboration is not certainty (nor even hypothetical conjecture) but critique, that is, a movement beyond whatever had been the state of understanding previously taken for granted (as a set of categories or explanations). This point takes up part of Popper's argument: whereas perceptions of events (observations, experimental results) are always subjective, the *objectivity* of knowledge resides in the 'logical' process of criticism by which observations and results are questioned, and new investigations proposed.[34] But the notion of critique in social investigation draws strength from two further arguments. First, unlike natural objects, human situations are not static entities which can be described 'as they are'. Rather they must be understood within a general and inevitable process of *change* (at the level of the individual, institutions, communities, the balance of economic and political forces in the state, etc.), which makes clear the need for continuous revision of any given state of understanding. Second, this revision is nothing like receiving the latest 'update' batch of 'information'. Our deep-seated need to believe in the stability of our environment, as well as the practical requirements of orderly interaction, require us to treat our current state of understanding as 'good enough for present purposes'.[35] This combination of practical motives, familiar actions and apparently adequate grasp of our situation functions (permanently) as an 'ideology' in which we live.[36] Hence to treat our current understanding and our current practices as matters for investigation entails a specific act of overcoming resistance, that is, a 'critique' of what we otherwise take for granted.

But this is where we have to part company with Popper, because if (as is the case in the social sciences) we can have no valid experimentally constructed data which could 'refute' our current understanding (see the quotation from Kitwood and Macey above), what could 'critique' consist of, as an *objective* rational process (as Popper would hope) as opposed to the exchange of subjective judgments? Two suggestions can be made here, as further basic procedural principles concerning social enquiry in general and (in particular) the development of professional knowledge.

Dialectical Analysis.   The value of dialectical analysis is that it creates theoretical criteria for making selections from potentially infinite amounts of data and interpretation.[37] These criteria are as follows. (a) Events and situations may appear to be separable, isolated phenomena, but they must be analyzed as part of a *necessary* context of relationships, that is, the *other* events and situations in relation to which they have meaning. For example, an evaluation of the effectiveness of an assessment procedure could not simply compare a set of results with a norm, but would need to consider carefully, say, the objectives of the assessment and the various attitudes towards those objectives of the teachers and learners involved. (b) Events, situations, communications, personalities, etc. may appear to be coherent and unified, but they must be analyzed as sets of contradictions between their constituent elements, and so we will be looking for diversity concealed by apparent unity, as well as for the unity behind apparent diversity. To pursue our example concerning assessment procedures, we would look for wide divergencies concealed by overall averages, and for discrepancies between and within expressions of attitude. (c) The apparent unity of events, situations, etc. gives an appearance that they are static, but the recognition that they include contradictory elements enables us to concentrate our analysis on the ways in which they are unstable, and thus inevitably *changing*. In the case of our assessment example, the discrepancies in result and attitude will indicate those points of friction within the procedures which will be creating pressure for change, so that those frictions will be reduced (at the cost, of course, of creating others). (d) Within a dialectical approach theory is not a final, accurate explanation, and practice is not a determined sequence of cause and effect. Theory changes alongside practice (since the theorist also is within the practical world), and practice is continuously self-transformative (since the practitioner is a decision-maker concerned with events which are in process of change). Hence theory-as-critique opens up hitherto ignored possibilities for practice, and practice selects one or some of these possibilities as a provisional basis for innovation, but then this new level of practice is still open to further critique. Our evaluation of an assessment process will, therefore, not only lead to changes in specific assessment practices, but also to a more precise understanding of the ways in which assessment practices in general are always open to question, that is, to a greater theoretical grasp of the nature of assessment. (The process is thus an unending circle between critical interpretation ('hermeneutics') and practice. One could term the epistemological principle for action research 'practical hermeneutics'.)[38]

Reflexive Analysis. A similar dialectic between analytical opening up and practical closure operates in respect of the crucial process of making judgments. In practical affairs we have to treat judgments as though they were accounts of an external state of affairs ('this pupil has special educational needs'; 'this student's work is not up to standard', etc.). A tradition of work directly inspired by Harold Garfinkel and more indirectly by the later writing of Wittgenstein reminds us that this is an oversimplification. First, following Wittgenstein, behind any set of rules for assigning meaning lies another set of rules for how the first set of rules is to be applied.[39] Second, in making judgmental statements I am not using language as a set of labels;

rather I am taking part in a highly complex structure of shared assumptions: that you and I both know the 'sort of thing' I am referring to, even though I have not defined it with absolute precision, that if you said it, I would make sense of your words in the same way that I hope you can make sense of mine; that you will gloss over the (inevitable) gaps in my meaning structure by filling in those gaps from your own experience, as I do from mine. In other words, in trying to communicate with you, I must first construct my meaning for myself. In this sense communications in general and judgments in particular are 'reflexive' — bent back into the set of experiences (those of the writer/speaker and subsequently those of the reader/hearer) in terms of which they are significant. To analyze the reflexive basis of judgments is to note the inevitable fragility of the process involved. The basis of judgments is always 'good enough' for someone's practical purpose at this moment, but always open to question later, and thus to the suggestion that various other interpretations might have been made, equally compatible with the (never quite complete) evidence on which at that time they were made. (Hence, for example, the fragility of judgments concerning 'professional appearance' and 'professional behaviour' referred to in the opening pages of this chapter.)

Conclusion

The previous section presents a sketch of an alternative approach to the analysis of social affairs freed from the assumptions of the natural science paradigm of knowledge which dominates the academic, political and instititional life of bureaucratized societies by means of a series of metaphors: understanding as 'information', enquiry as 'observation', evidence as 'indicators' and human activity (including teaching and learning) as 'performances'. As educators, our professional expertise includes a concern for the nature of knowledge and insight into the processes by which it is acquired. We, therefore, rather than any other group, are in a position to take a lead in educating our managers and paymasters into a realization that these *are* metaphors. Understanding the actions of people cannot be conducted by means of procedures whose intelligibility relies on analogies with understanding the behaviour of objects, unless we are prepared to violate essential moral, intellectual and political principles.

Concerning teacher appraisal schemes, let us, as a first practical step, propose that the time resource to be made available for the process of enhancing the professional work of teachers should be distributed to teachers themselves, so that they can engage in collaborative action research. This must be part of an overall recognition that what is currently being sought through the single process of 'appraisal' can only be achieved through three quite separate processes: first, widespread opportunity for practitioner action research, to improve professional practice generally; second, specific procedures for rational decision-making concerning promotion and career development; third, specific procedures to deal with cases of professional inadequacy.[40] It is a delusion to think that one can achieve all three of these simultaneously by means of a single process based on the collection of 'information' concerning the quality of teachers in general. This chapter is an attempt to expose the nature and origin of that delusion.

Notes

1 G. Samuel, 'An Established Appraisal Scheme', in S. Bunnell (ed.), *Teacher Appraisal in Practice*, London, Heinemann, 1987, p. 69.
2 S. Bunnell and E. Stephens: 'A Democratic Approach to the Introduction of a Teacher Appraisal Scheme', in S. Bunnell (ed.), *ibid.*, p. 56.
3 D. Trethowan, *Appraisal and Target Setting*, London, Harper and Row, 1987, p. 213.
4 *Ibid.*, p. i.
5 *Ibid.*, p. 190.
6 *Ibid.*
7 *Ibid.*, p. 18.
8 *Ibid.*, p. 6.
9 Bunnell and Stephens, *op. cit.*, p. 67.
10 Trethowan, *op. cit.*, p. 79.
11 Bunnell and Stephens, *op. cit.*, p. 59.
12 *Ibid.*
13 Trethowan, *op. cit.*, p. 11, quoting DES, *Better Schools*, London, HMSO, 1985.
14 Bunnell and Stephens, *op. cit.*, p. 59.
15 Trethowan, *op. cit.*, p. 15.
16 M. Weber, 'The Ideal Type', 'Bureaucracy' and 'Social Action', in K. Thompson and J. Tunstall (eds), *Sociological Perspectives*, Harmondsworth, Penguin, 1971, pp. 63, 69, 128.
17 P. Selznick, 'An Approach to a Theory of Bureaucracy', *American Sociological Review*, 8, 1943, reprinted in L. Coser and B. Rosenberg (eds), *Sociological Theory*, New York, Collier-Macmillan, 1967.
18 See, for example, G. Egan, *The Skilled Helper*, Monterey, Calif., Brooks/Cole Publishing Co., 1982.
19 See H. Garfinkel, 'Good Organizational Reasons for "Bad" Clinic Records,' in *Studies in Ethnomethodology*, Cambridge, Polity Press, 1984, and also R. Winter, 'Keeping Files: Aspects of Bureaucracy and Education', in G. Whitty and M.F.D. Young (eds), *Explorations in the Politics of School Knowledge*, Driffield, Nafferton Books, 1976.
20 See B. Fay, *Social Theory and Political Practice*, London, Unwin, 1975.
21 See A. MacIntyre, *After Virtue: A Study in Moral Theory*, London, Duckworth, 1981, Ch 8.
22 K. Popper, *Objective Knowledge*, London, Oxford University Press, 1972, p. 61.

23 *Ibid*, p. 23.
24 *Ibid*, pp. 21, 58, 37.
25 C. Byrne, 'Can Teachers Be Validly Appraised?' in S. Bunnell (ed.), *op. cit.*, pp. 37–9.
26 *Ibid.*, p. 39.
27 T. Kitwood and M. Macey, 'Teaching Styles or Research Styles: The Implications of the Bennett Report', *Education for Teaching*, No. 101, 1976, p. 35.
28 See, for example, J. Ford, *Paradigms and Fairy-Tales*, London, Routledge and Kegan Paul, 1975, and D.C. Phillips, *Philosophy, Science, and Social Inquiry*, Oxford, Pergamon Press, 1987.
29 K. Popper, *Conjectures and Refutations*, London, Routledge and Kegan Paul, 1963, p. 327.
30 J. Habermas, 'Rationality Divided in Two', in A. Giddens (ed.), *Positivism and Sociology*, London, Heinemann, 1974, p. 201.
31 M. Marland, 'Appraisal and Evaluation: Chimera, Fantasy, or Practicality,' in S. Bunnell (ed.), *op. cit.*, pp. 17–18.
32 The full argument for this is presented in R. Winter, *Action-Research and the Nature of Social Inquiry*, Aldershot, Gower, 1987.
33 Fuller explanations and examples are presented in R. Winter, *The Practice of Action-Research: Learning From Experience: Principles and Practice*, 1989, Lewes, Falmer Press.
34 K. Popper, *op. cit.*, pp. 146–8.
35 See Popper, *ibid.*, p. 90; Garfinkel, *op. cit.*, pp. 13–14.
36 See L. Althusser, *Lenin and Philosophy*, London, NLB, 1971, pp. 149–70 and also *For Marx*, London, NKB, 1977, p. 232.
37 See notes 32 and 33 above. Of the general accounts of dialectical method the following are particularly helpful: E.V. Ilyenkov, *Dialectial Logic*, Moscow, Progress Publishers, 1977; J. Israel, *The Language of Dialectics and the Dialectics of Language*, Brighton, Harvester Press, 1979; M. Fisk, 'Dialectic and Ontology', in J. Mepham and D-H. Ruben (eds), *Issues in Marxist Philosophy, Vol. 1: Dialectics and Method*, Brighton, Harvester Press, 1979; M. Markovic, *Dialectical Theory of Meaning*, Dordrecht, Reidel, 1984, Introduction.
38 See R. Winter, 'The Contradictions of Teacher Appraisal: An Action-Research Solution?', presented to the BERA national conference, 1987, reprinted in J. Elliott and H. Simons (eds), *New Directions in Teacher Appraisal*, Milton Keynes, Open University Press, 1989. This emphasis on dialectical understanding as empirical, critical *and* exploratory suggests a way forward from the dilemma posed by John Elliott's recent paper ('Educational Theory, Practical Philosophy, and Action Research', *British Journal of Educational Studies*, 25, 2, 1987) in which he presents a fundamental opposition between understanding derived from the interpretation of particular practical contexts and the critique of contextually derived understanding from an independent basis in social science theory.
39 See P. Winch, *The Idea of a Social Science*, London, Routledge and Kegan Paul, 1958, pp. 24ff.
40 See R. Winter, 'The Contradictions of Teacher Appraisal: An Action-Research Solution?', *op. cit.*

Chapter 12

Knowledge, Power and Teacher Appraisal

John Elliott

Power produces knowledge (and not simply by encouraging it because it serves power or by applying it because it is useful); power and knowledge directly imply one another; there is no power relation without the correlative constitution of a field of knowledge, nor any knowledge that does not presuppose and constitute at the same time power relations. (Michel Foucault, *Discipline and Punish: The Birth of the Prison*, p. 27)

The subjection of those who are perceived as objects and the objectification of those who are subjected . . . in this slender technique are to be found a whole domain of knowledge, a whole domain of power. (Michel Foucault, *The History of Sexuality*, Vol. 1, p. 95)

No science can create its own conditions of possibility: these are to be found in the transformation of power relations . . . . Knowledge is not so much true or false as legitimate or illegitimate for a particular set of power relations. (Alan Sheridan, *Michel Foucault: The Will to Truth*, p. 220)

Prologue: An Autobiographical Excursion into Questions of Knowledge and Power

The relationship between teacher appraisal and educational research is a matter of personal and professional concern which has its roots in my own biography. The relation between knowledge and power constitutes a major theme in that biography and accounts for my continuing concern with the relationship between educational research (the creation of educational knowledge) and educational practice (the exercise of educative power). The phenomenon of teacher appraisal impinges upon those concerns because it raises fundamental issues about the relationship between knowledge and power in the educational process. I have decided to approach these issues by reflecting on my own professional biography in the light of Michel Foucault's analysis of the relationship between knowledge and power. The quotations cited above provide me with an initial structure of ideas around which to weave my story, and the reflections about knowledge and power it stimulates. In this way I hope to establish a framework for discussing the relationship between teacher appraisal and educational research.

For reasons which are still obscure to me, I have always fancied myself as both action-man and contemplative-man; as someone who makes a powerful impact on events and as someone who contemplates their meaning and significance from a position of detachment. One aspect of this divided self has never completely overshadowed the other. Between the ages of 18 and 21, I was a horticultural researcher contemplating the mysteries of magnesium and iron deficiency in apple trees through the lens of the agricultural-botany paradigm which, unknown to me at the time, had been adopted by educational researchers as the model for studying educational processes. I was not aware that terms familiar to me like 'deficiencies', 'treatments', 'gross yields' were also being used to describe aspects of education; namely the states of pupils, curricula and methods, and pupils' learning. If I had been so aware, perhaps I would have reflected more about my own motivation for becoming a horticultural researcher.

I had contemplated becoming a farmer (action-man) but chose research into farming instead. The research techniques I employed were techniques of control. The agricultural-botany paradigm yielded knowledge by establishing a power relationship between the researcher and his/her subject. I was not simply contemplating nature, but changing and shaping it to serve its marketability. My 'power motivation' was an integral, if unacknowledged, aspect of my career as a horticultural researcher. In doing this kind of research one is not simply engaged in applied research, yielding knowledge which practising farmers can use. One is doing farming — albeit 'scientifically'.

Of course, there is a sense in which those action-men and women who base their farming on research knowledge are engaged in 'scientific farming'. But perhaps we should make a distinction between this sort of farming and 'farming scientifically'. It is the latter which generates knowledge, and we cannot have all farmers doing it. 'Farming scientifically' is not an effective strategy for maximizing the market value of the produce. Experiment necessarily restricts productivity. It is 'scientific farming' which maximizes the productive value of nature in the marketplace. This is the strategy which subjugates nature to the requirements of 'the market' and constitutes a particular form of power relation between the farmer and nature. But the techniques of 'scientific farming' are constructed by those who 'farm scientifically'. It is agricultural/horticultural research which creates power.

'Farming scientifically' is the source of 'scientific farming's' power. The knowledge it produces is not neutral with respect to power, something which can be used or not used to establish power relations. In as much as it is knowledge, it establishes a power relation. It is the achievement of a certain form of power relation to nature's products, which itself constitutes the test for truth. Both the methods and the outcomes of the agricultural-botany paradigm are conditioned by the possibility of this achievement — a possibility which emerges as market values increasingly shape the process of social change.

I left horticultural research to train as a teacher, not least because the contemplative part of me was not satisfied by the subject-matter. Evenings and weekends had been spent reading books on philosophy, religion and psychology, exploring ideas about human nature. Action-man had not been satisfied either. I wanted to make an impact on people's lives rather than plants. Teaching offered a better possibility of bringing these two aspects of myself together. Education, I felt, was about helping people to realize their human capacities and potential and, therefore, presupposed a theory of human nature.

My teacher training was a partial success in satisfying contemplative-man, but it did not give me a clue about how to reconcile him with action-man in real classrooms and schools. The theories of human nature we discussed in the college did not exactly match human nature as it appeared in the secondary modern classrooms where I did my teaching practice. This did not present me with too much of a problem in an instrumental sense. Action-man always saved the day. If contemplative-man held an optimistic and idealistic view of human nature, this was countered in practice by the pessimism and realism of action-man. From the perspective of the former, education was about giving children opportunities to discover and develop their natural powers and capabilities. Children may be wicked and destructive at times but this is caused by the frustration of their natural powers. Remove the frustrating conditions and you unlock their potential for good. *Give control* and do not *take control*. From the perspective of action-man, human destructiveness has its roots in nature rather than nurture. It must be contained and suppressed through externally imposed discipline. Therefore, *take control* and do not *give control*. My contemplative-man treated children as he wanted them to become, as self-actualizing individuals. But he had no way of coping with them as they were.

If these two aspects of myself were not exactly reconciled in the teacher role, they were at least both operating in it to counterbalance each other. So it remained as I entered a full-time teaching career in a secondary modern school. I was lucky in the point of entry. It was 1962. Kids in the secondary modern school were no longer passively conforming to the schooling on offer to those who had failed the entrance examination for a grammar school. They were generally switch-off and rebelling. Teachers were finding it difficult to cope and some survived only by turning their schools into 'concentration camps' devoted to solving a problem they had defined as one of containment and control. Others created what David Hargreaves described as the 'innovatory secondary modern'. I started my teaching career in one. They had a clearly defined ethos and were easily identified. In our school we knew where the other innovatory secondary moderns were in the LEA, and we knew many of the teachers in them. We attended the same conferences and sometimes set them up for each other. The LEA was not simply tolerant, but positively supportive. The problem of 'pupil disaffection' was difficult to ignore, and any teachers who felt there was an educational response to it were to be welcomed. It was widely acknowledged to be a very urgent, immediate and practical problem.

There was very little abstract discussion about the aims of education. The heads of these schools, and the key staff they gathered around them, were action men and women (but of a different species from the traditional disciplinarian). They had a broad vision of the direction they wanted to move in, but there was no blueprint, no detailed list of objectives specifying desirable learning outcomes. The vision was of the educational *process* rather than its outcomes. It was of a process which helped children to make sense of their lives, themselves, their relationships and their society. Its central elements were the curriculum and the manner of its transmission. The key words in the discourse were those of 'relevance', 'integration', 'interest' and 'responsibility'. The vision was vague; few sat back and contemplated it in abstract form. It was clarified in action and reflection on action in the context of practical discourse.

No teacher in the innovatory secondary modern could escape this context. You could not make the curriculum more 'relevant' to children's lives by respecting the traditional subject boundaries or without raising controversial issues about where these boundaries should and should not be controversial issues about where these boundaries should and should not be drawn. You could not make the curriculum more 'interesting' without raising controversial issues about teaching methods. You could not foster in pupils a sense of 'responsibility' for their own learning in classrooms without raising controversial issues about school rules in general.

Controversy stimulates self-reflection. The alternative interpretations of actions expressed in the sort of practical discourse I described provide the context in which one renders one's own actions problematic and searches for evidence to legitimate them to colleagues. The evidence was to be found in the pupils' perceptions of the curriculum and teaching strategies. No curriculum could be justified as 'relevant' unless it was experienced as such by pupils, or justifiably claim to 'integrate' knowledge and understanding if pupils could not perceive relationships between its contents. No teaching method could be justified as stimulating an 'interest' in the subject-matter if pupils could not perceive anything of interest in it, or as helping them to take 'responsibility' for their own learning if they did not perceive it as helpful in this respect. Teachers legitimated their actions to each other on the basis of subjective data elicited from pupils. Pupils were also drawn into a practical discourse in which their education was continuously constructed, critiqued and reconstructed. Faced with alternative accounts of our actions from our colleagues and pupils, we not only reassessed them but refined and modified our understanding of the process values which underpinned them; namely concepts of 'relevance', 'integration', 'interests', etc. If we evaluated our actions in the light of our vision, we also clarified the vision in the light of the actions we took to realize it. In practical discourse focused on curriculum processes, aims and methods were objects of joint reflection. The tension in me between contemplative-man and action-man was largely resolved by my very relevant, but not very recent, experience in an innovatory secondary modern, and with it my problem of linking educational practice to educational theory. If my educational theorizing has anything to say to teachers today, I owe it largely to my experience in a school over two decades ago.

It was in the innovatory project of a now nearly dead institution (the secondary modern) that a new paradigm of educational research emerged in the UK. It is now known as action research. What we now recognize as the methodology of action research — the focus on processes rather than products; the study of a practical problem in relation to its context (case study); looking at the problem from different points of view (triangulation methods); monitoring the effects of action strategies on pupils' experience of classrooms and schools; deliberating about problems, actions and consequences with peers and pupils — was all part and parcel of the curriculum prise defied any job description or division of labour. Individual teachers were researchers, theorists, pedagogues, policy-makers. Some contributed more to one aspect than others, but all had opportunities to contribute to each according to his or her particular talents and abilities. The enterprise required an open democratic system. It allowed a creative interaction between person and role. The multifaceted professional role enabled teachers to develop as persons, and in doing so enabled them to develop their professional role. Personal and professional developments were inseparable. It was a never-to-be-forgotten educative experience for me and my colleagues. It empowered us as persons and as teachers and, in doing so, educated us both personally and professionally. It taught us that there can be no empowerment (education) of pupils without the empowerment of teachers. And so I return to the theme of power and knowledge.

In the early part of my teaching career the contemplative-man in me could not cope with the discrepancy between his educational ideals and classroom reality. He *gave control* to pupils and *lost control over himself*. So I had tended in practice to rely on the action-man part of me to exercise the kind of disciplinary power which enabled me to *take control* of the situation and thereby stay in control within it. What I learned in my innovatory secondary modern, through action research-based curriculum development, was how to *be in control* in the situation without *taking control*. I came to a tacit understanding of the way in which educational ideals and aims link to practice. They provide criteria for assessing the *educational quality* of the learning environment rather than states of the pupils. Since this environment is mediated and often constituted by educational aims, teachers focus their reflection on their own actions and conduct. By self-monitoring the educational quality of their actions, teachers take control of the learning environment, and (by implication) of themselves rather than of their pupils. Like all forms of educational knowledge, this kind of professional self-knowledge creates a particular form of power and presupposes a certain power relation between teachers and pupils. The form of power it creates is *educative power*, which is an enabling rather than constraining power. Through educational action research, teachers transform the learning environment (curricula, teaching methods and school ethos) into one which enables pupils to discover and develop their powers and capacities themselves. In creating educative power, action research not only professionally empowers teachers, it empowers pupils.

The curriculum development enterprise I have depicted was a response to a situation in which pupils were increasingly hostile to their schooling. Teachers were finding it difficult to cope, and the enterprise was about giving teachers the power to cope again, but so was the transformation of some secondary moderns into 'concentration camps'. (I exaggerate, of course, and will apologize later.) In the innovatory school teachers coped by creating educative power in the learning environment, and, since they were part of it, in themselves. In the 'concentration camps' they coped by creating systems of domination. Before explaining this alternative coping strategy, let me describe the departure point of both.

Traditionally, the power of the teacher was legitimated by the authority invested in his or her role. It was because (s)he was perceived as a legitimate authority on the subject-matter (s)he taught that (s)he was obeyed and that when (s)he was disobeyed the resulting punishment was accepted as the exercise of legitimate power. What might be called disciplinary power was traditionally mediated by the authority pupils invested in the teacher's role. It was an aspect of the individual teacher's relationship to his or her pupils. The teacher who sent a pupil elsewhere to be disciplined (e.g. to the head or deputy) tacitly acknowledged a breakdown in his/her authority. The crisis in the secondary modern school stemmed from the widespread refusal of pupils in these schools to invest authority in their teachers.

My metaphor of the 'concentration camp' indicates some of the features of one response to this situation. First, the exercise of disciplinary power is transformed. It is no longer mediated by the recognition of rights of authority on the part of those subject to it. It lacks the quality of voluntariness present in the traditional power relation between teachers and pupils in schools. It is a relation of the *domination* of the will of one group by the will of another group. The legitimate exercise of disciplinary power had been transformed into a form of coercion.

This transformation of teacher-pupil power relations opened up new possibilities for the use of strategies and techniques of social control on a scale not previously witnessed in state schools. Relations of domination need a system of *surveillance* covering as many aspects of the lives to be dominated as possible. Such a system is necessary to exert the kind of detailed control of individual behaviour which domination requires. Its main features are techniques for observing that behaviour and thereby rendering it visible; for recording, collating and reporting information about it; and for assessing it and deciding whether and what 'remedial' action is necessary. Disciplinary power which takes the form of domination is mediated by a 'system' rather than authority invested in individuals.

Many secondary modern schools began to develop systems of surveillance and control as they re-established disciplinary power by transforming its mode of operation. Discipline was decreasingly the responsibility of individual teachers and more that of 'the system'. Some individuals were given special roles in maintaining the system. It was in such secondary modern schools that the so-called 'pastoral care system' was spawned, and that hierarchical system of specialist roles we now dignify with the title of 'management'. In the innovatory secondary modern there were 'leadership' roles, but not 'management' roles.

Implicit in the development of such hierarchical systems of control in schools is the view that human nature is infinitely 'plastic'. Traditional authority presupposed the possibility of resistance by a fixed human nature whose destructive manifestations could be contained and suppressed but not eliminated. When it broke down, the 'progressive' teacher in the innovatory secondary modern also presupposed a fixed human nature, but its destructive manifestations were regarded as frustrated expressions of intrinsically good powers. They could be eliminated only by transforming the frustrating conditions into enabling ones. However, the systems of domination and control which evolved in schools did not aim to eliminate destructive behaviour by transforming its context, but by moulding and reshaping it at will. Such behaviour was not so much interpreted as the manifestation of a 'wicked', 'wilful', 'obstinate', 'irresponsible' or 'uncaring' subject, but as a 'deficiency in the material'. Such an interpretation assumed an infinitely 'plastic' human nature.

The transformation of traditional power relations into systems of domination, which began in some secondary modern schools during the 1950s and 1960s, continued after comprehensive reorganization with the development of even more sophisticated management techniques of surveillance and control. This particular transformation must be seen against a much broader social process: the transformation of individuals into 'plastic men and women' who were adaptable, flexible and compliant enough to meet the requirements of a constantly changing labour market. It is in this context that we should understand the large-scale transfer of the agricultural-botany paradigm of research to the study of educational processes and programmes during the last three decades. Its employment in educational settings presupposes the possibility of transforming power relations in schools into a perfect system of technical control over human nature in the service of market forces. In many ways the Education Reform Act of 1988 is simply a set of mechanisms for effecting this transformation.

Such research is not unbiased with respect to the aims and values of education; nor is the knowledge it generates unbiased about the uses of disciplinary power. A research paradigm which necessarily views the aims of education as quantifiable 'products', educational programmes and processes as 'treatments', and the educational needs of pupils as 'deficiencies', is hardly unbiased. Knowledge which is only valid if it creates new possibilities of technical control over behaviour is hardly unbiased about the nature and uses of power in educational settings. Such knowledge necessarily creates the power to extend and refine systems of surveillance and control in schools. It is the basis of scientific management not only with respect to the application of the knowledge it generates, but also with respect to the application of the techniques of observation and analysis it employs as instruments of surveillance and assessment.

The 'concentration camp' metaphor greatly exaggerates the ethos of schooling today and the influence of the agricultural-botany paradigm on it. Schools are not perfect systems of domination, and never were. Their ethos was and remains mixed, with a tendency for one sort of climate to dominate. Traditional authority still permeates the power relations between teachers and pupils, as does the kind of climate generated in the innovatory secondary modern. Both provide teachers with 'cultures of resistance' to the pressures from the marketplace for schools to perfect their systems of domination and control. The crisis of authority referred to was itself a necessary stage in the transformation of schooling into a manufacturing process. Traditional uses of disciplinary power were ill-equipped to meet the economic requirements of a late twentieth century capitalist society. But they persist. And what of the innovatory climate transmitted into comprehensive schools from the innovatory secondary moderns?

The crisis of authority in the late 1950s and 1960s created the possibility of truly educative power relations between teachers and pupils. But humanist ideals are not without utility in a free market economy. The ideals of 'self-realization' and 'self-direction' can easily be distorted by re-interpreting them in the categories of a liberal individualism which defines human beings as 'marketing man'. 'Self-direction' comes to mean being directed by one's wants and desires, while 'self-realization' means having them satisfied. Wants and desires, unlike innate powers and capacities, can be products of human conditioning and the exercise of coercive power. If selves are simply the sum total of their wants and desires, then their nature is infinitely 'plastic'. The manufacture of 'autonomous beings' is not an inconceivable enterprise for a power-coercive educational system, when viewed from the standpoint of liberal individualism.

In government the 'New Right' has appropriated and, in the process, distorted those progressive educational ideas it raved against in opposition. Witness, for example, the MSC's support for progressive rather than traditional methods in its TVEI scheme. The scheme not only further undermines traditional authority in schools, but in its deceptive appearance, threatens to disarm that other pocket of resistance to the growth of coercive power in schools, namely the climate emanating from the innovatory secondary modern. Not all innovatory teachers are deceived, but prefer a strategy of creative conformity to one of outright rebellion. They comply with the official rhetoric in accounting for their actions, while resisting its distorting influence on their practice. By so doing, they continue to create and maintain educative power relations with pupils.

Teacher Appraisal: The Pathology or the Triumph of Educational Research?

And so to teacher appraisal and its relationship to educational research. The appraisal of teachers could be interpreted as another strategy in the exercise of coercive power over the lives of pupils. Does a form of appraisal which creates a sub-system of surveillance and control over teachers constitute a strategy for eliminating those pockets of professional culture which still resist the transformation of schooling into a manufacturing process? I believe it does because it is essentially a strategy for controlling the conditions under which the practical knowledge of teachers is constructed.

In the craft tradition of teaching, disciplinary power operates through the authority teachers possess by virtue of tacit knowledge they acquire through experience. Practice based on craft knowledge is highly resistant to any bureaucratic standardization of performance, because such knowledge is not only largely tacit, but also bound to particular contexts of experience. It cannot be used as a basis for defining general performance standards. The criteria of 'good practice' vary according to the context (see Bridges, Elliott and Klass, 1986; Brown and McIntyre, 1986 for a careful explication of the structural characteristics of such criteria). This is why appraisal from the point of view of the craft culture is largely construed as an informal self-appraisal process.

The resistance to bureaucratic standardization which the possession of craft knowledge generates in teachers can only be overcome by eliminating the conditions under which this knowledge is constructed and transmitted, that is, the conditions of professional privacy and freedom from external regulation. Any form of teacher appraisal which changes these conditions, by establishing a hierarchical system of surveillance and control over teachers' activities, constitutes a strategy for eliminating the craft culture.

The practical knowledge, of which the innovatory progressive culture consists, is generated through a process in which teachers reflect about their own and each other's actions in situations where tacit craft knowledge is too problematic to serve as a basis for action. This action research process develops teachers' conscious awareness of what constitutes educative teaching in particular contexts: an awareness which empowers them as educators. The innovatory progressive culture is also resistant to bureaucratic standardization. The practical insights it consists of, although not tacit, are grounded in the experience and reflection of teachers in particular contexts. What constitutes an educative practice in one context may not apply to another. This has to be determined afresh as contexts of action change, although insights developed in one context can serve as fruitful sources of action hypotheses to be tested in others. Generalizations can be developed across contexts, but only through reflective comparisons of a finite number of experiences. As a basis for future action, such general insights provide intimation of possibilities rather than predictions. Moreover, even judgments of what constitutes an educative practice in a particular context are intrinsically problematic because the meanings of the criteria of educational quality they employ are never unambiguously fixed and settled by attempts to define them. Within the innovatory progressive culture, criteria of 'good practice' are not only context-bound but infinitely contestable. For both these reasons the insights embedded in this professional culture are always provisional, controversial and changing.

The innovatory progressive culture, like the traditional craft culture, can only be eliminated by changing the conditions under which it is constructed, that is, those social conditions which enable teachers to participate in reflective discourse about their own and each other's practices. Any form of appraisal which restricts teachers' opportunities to reflect about their practices in free and open discourse with each other constitutes a strategy for eliminating the innovatory progressive culture in schools.

We can, therefore, assess the extent to which appraisal schemes are power strategies for eliminating resistant professional cultures by considering the ways in which they shape the creation and construction of teachers' practical knowledge. If they transfer responsibility for generating practical knowledge from teachers to outsiders, then they undermine that paradigm of educational action research spawned in the innovatory secondary modern. It is in this sense that teacher appraisal may constitute the *pathology* of educational research. But it may also constitute the *triumph* of that other paradigm: the agricultural-botany model. This will have implications for the future development of educational research and teacher education in universities and other institutions of higher education. In order to explain why I need to resort to a little more autobiography.

I left teaching in 1967 to join the Schools Council/Nuffield Humanities Project led by Lawrence Stenhouse. The project's brief was to support innovation in an area where teachers experienced the full strength of pupil disaffection: the humanities subjects in secondary schools with young adolescents. The raising of the school leaving age to 16 had been planned for 1970. The Schools Council, through its early working papers, had already begun to support and disseminate ideas and curricula coming out of the innovatory secondary moderns. The Humanities Project developed, refined and articulated the progressive professional culture which had emerged in these schools, and attempted to disseminate it more widely. It gave progressive innovators an explicit curriculum theory in the form of 'the process model' and an explicit theory of teacher development centred on Lawrence Stenhouse's idea of 'teachers as researchers' (Stenhouse, 1975).

Stenhouse's idea was highly original. Teachers were not viewed as targets in a curriculum sales campaign. It was their professional responsibility to realize a worthwhile curriculum process for their particular pupils, the 'outsider's' task was to enable teachers to reflect about what constituted such a process and how it might be realized in their practical situation. Here we have a distinction between the curriculum development role of the insider and the teacher development role of the outsider. In the Humanities Project I made the transition from a developer of a curriculum for schools to a developer of a curriculum for teachers. But it was a very different sort of curriculum from the traditional courses on offer to teachers. It focused on the curriculum problems and issues which arise in particular educational settings, rather than on general theories about educational practice. Its methods aimed, not to transmit information, but to establish conditions which enabled teachers reflectively to develop solutions to the curriculum problems they identified. This conception of teacher education as the facilitation of teachers' action research was entirely consistent with the culture of progressive innovation which had emerged in the innovatory secondary modern. Indeed, it presupposed such a culture.

In the context of the Humanities Project, the roles of curriculum developers in schools and teacher developers overlapped. The latter designed a curriculum project, but viewed it as a vehicle for helping teachers to reflect about the relationship between educational values and practice. The project was designed as a set of action hypotheses (about how to realize an educationally worthwhile humanities curriculum) which teachers could test in practice. From our point of view the success of the project rested not so much on its widespread adoption in pure form, as on its power to foster reflective practice. Although it embodied curriculum strategies for teachers to test, the project as a whole constituted a teacher development strategy for the project team to test. It involved two levels of action research: the first-order level of facilitating a worthwhile educational process in schools; and the second-order level of facilitating a worthwhile process of teacher education. The first level was primarily the responsibility of teachers, while the second level was primarily the responsibility of the project team.

In the Humanities Project, I made the transition from a first-order action researcher to a second-order action researcher. In my subsequent 'academic' career I have attempted, through a number of projects (Elliott, 1976, 1985), to integrate the 'outsider' roles of teacher educator and educational researcher in the form of second-order action research; aimed at facilitating teachers' action research in schools. Indeed, I would claim that the growth of this integrated conception of educational research and teacher education in institutions of higher education has in no small measure supported and sustained the innovatory progressive culture among schoolteachers. But the relationship is reciprocal. Teacher education as a form of educational action research, aimed at fostering reflective curriculum development, presupposes the continuing existence of the innovatory progressive culture in schools. If teacher appraisal constitutes a strategy for eliminating this culture, then it also constitutes a strategy which threatens the continuing integration of teacher education and educational research in the form of the action research paradigm.

If the formal appraisal system is a strategy for standardizing teachers' practices, then it will control the nature of in-service training and who has access to it. The in-service curriculum will tend to focus on the acquisition of specific competencies and skills, defined as measurable performances. Only those who are assessed as deficient in, or in need of, such skills will be given access to this curriculum. Under these conditions, the action research paradigm of teacher development and educational research would be unable to operate. On this scenario, the future of teacher training belongs to the 'skill trainers', and the future of educational research to the 'agricultural-botanists' whose process-product studies will discover the necessary skills. Academics in education will have a 'choice' of two careers: as part of an élite core of educational researchers or as humble technologists manufacturing skills in teachers.

So how is the development of a national system of teacher appraisal shaping up, and what are its implications for the relationship between power and knowledge in our educational system?

From *Teaching Quality* to ACAS: The Negotiation of Relations between Knowledge and Power in Education

Proposals to establish a formal system of appraisal for teachers in England and Wales have met with considerable opposition from teachers and their unions. At the heart of the controversy there are fundamental issues about power. But I do not see the issue in quite the same way as some teachers and their representatives: as another strategy in central government's bid for more power over education. Like them, I see appraisal as part of a much broader strategy for transforming power relations in our educational system. However, I do not see this broader strategy as simply an attempt on the part of central government to possess more power over educational processes. This is important because a simple treatment of appraisal issues focuses attention on the wrong enemy. The enemy, if there is one, is not central government but the form of power at work in the educational system generally, and the form of educational research which helps to create that power. The problem about seeing the issues in terms of government power is that it blinds ordinary teachers to the ways in which the foundations of formal appraisal are being laid in the subtle transformations of power relations taking place day by day in their own classrooms, schools and LEAs.

I remember feeling furious with a major union which advised its members not to get involved in the development of appraisal schemes at the local level until the national pilots had been evaluated. Some LEAs had wanted to involve teachers in the development of a 'professional' form of appraisal. The advice was probably well intentioned, but it was based on a false diagnosis of the power issue. The advice assumed that teachers at the local level were unable to influence the future of appraisal because it was a power strategy of central government and could only be modified and changed by negotiation at the national level. Following Foucault's concept of power, I would see appraisal as part of a complex strategic situation operating at different levels and locations in society. On this view, a particular form of teacher appraisal is emerging and permeating the educational system, and the interventions of central government on its behalf are simply one aspect of the phenomenon which has to be addressed. Teachers at every level need to reflect about, and respond to, the operations of this broad strategy as it impinges upon their professional practices.

If formal appraisal is part of such a broad strategy for transforming schools into systems of coercive power, I am optimistic enough to believe that it can be successfully resisted. This optimism is, of course, based on the view that neither pupils nor teachers have infinitely plastic natures; that

their need to develop themselves in action, both personally and professionally, will always impose limits on the extent to which they will conform to
coercive power strategies.

Outright rebellion and obstructionism are not necessarily the most
effective forms of resistance, particularly in a society which still requires
policies to be legitimated in terms of democratic rhetoric. This rhetoric
gives considerable leverage to 'creative conformists' who are able to
negotiate sufficient trade-offs from the proponents of a power-coercive
policy to protect their own values and interests. In the process of democratic legitimation, policies become transformed.

The government's attempts to legitimate teacher appraisal provide an
excellent illustration of this process. Sir Keith Joseph's 1983 White Paper on
Teaching Quality quite unambiguously proposes appraisal as a strategy of
hierarchical surveillance and control over the activities of teachers. The
paper contrasts the desired form of appraisal with self-appraisal, and
damns the latter with faint praise.

> The government welcome recent moves towards self-assessment
> by schools and teachers, and believe these should help to improve
> school standards and curricula. But employers can manage their
> teacher force effectively only if they have accurate knowledge of
> each teacher's performance. The government believe that for this
> purpose formal assessment of teacher performance is necessary
> and should be based on classroom visiting by the teacher's head or
> head of department; and an appraisal of both pupils' work and of
> the teacher's contribution to the life of the school.

Note how the teacher is reduced to an object of scrutiny. The focus is on
observable performances, rather than the subjective and personal qualities
teachers bring to them. When teaching competence is construed as performance rather than the exercise of personal qualities, it can be standardized. But as Doll (1984) argued, this understanding of 'competence' is a
departure from customary usage: 'Competence refers essentially to a state
of being or to a capacity . . . . Performance is the outward and public manifestation of underlying and internal powers.' Understood in these terms,
teaching 'competence' refers to the inner quality of teaching as manifest in
outward performances: to the realization of teachers' 'underlying and
internal powers' as educators and their 'capacity' to translate educational
values into educative forms of practice. This sort of 'competence' is
developed and assessed through practical deliberation and discourse with
professional peers (action research).

The passage cited from the White Paper also suggests that appraisal should attempt to assess teacher performance against learning outcomes. Hence the reference to pupils' work. It implies the possibility of standardizing performance against desired learning outcomes, and thus construes teaching as a technology, applying standardized treatments in a manufacturing process (Elliott, 1985). It is certainly not construed as either a craft or as the reflective practice of translating educational values into educational practice.

What are the functions of the form of appraisal proposed in the White Paper? These are clearly stated as those of guiding management decisions about the deployment, training and dismissal of teachers. If appraisal fulfilled such functions, it would effectively leave teachers with very little professional control over their practices, their professional development, or their careers. In effect it would deprofessionalize them and eliminate professional cultures.

But the whole enterprise depends upon the ability of the agricultural-botany paradigm of educational research to discover the performance indicators of competence, and develop the instruments for measuring them. Many claims to discoveries have been made. The DES evidently constantly reviews the research evidence, and it will not be long before a consensus is distilled from this kind of 'educational' research. The search for demonstrable performance indicators of teaching competence is not in vain if teaching is construed as a form of technical control over learning construed as behaviour. It is always possible to discover standard techniques for controlling performance. But one cannot control the development of innate and fixed human powers; one can only establish the conditions which enable these states of being to develop and grow. This is the task of the educator as opposed to the technologist.

The reaction of teachers to Sir Keith's proposals brought a gradual shift in government rhetoric. In an address to the Education for Industry Society in February 1985, Permanent Secretary Hancock made the following statements:

> The assessor must possess the range and quality of teaching knowledge towards which the (assessed) teacher is working and will thus be a senior colleague . . . .

> It must be an open, two-way, process . . . .

> The (assessed) teacher . . . will have the opportunity to add any comment or reservation (to the assessor's report) considered necessary.

The purpose of assessment is to encourage and monitor the professional development of the teacher.

No one has ever suggested that a school should be run exactly like a business. The idea of appraisal is to identify the qualities that make a good teacher.

. . . we have in mind the achievement of consensus as the basis for any regulations and not the imposition of ideas nurtured in Elizabeth House.

Although this speech acknowledged no significant changes in the original proposal, there is a marked shift in the way appraisal is legitimated and described. The emphasis was now placed on 'professional development' as the aim of appraisal (although what this means was not explained), in contrast to management functions which could be interpreted in a less positive light. Hierarchical appraisal was toned down by talk of 'senior colleagues' and a 'two-way' process. The significance of context for appraisal was also acknowledged in a shift of focus from performance to the qualities of the teacher. The intention that teachers will have a major say in how they are to be assessed and the denial of power-coercive motives was stressed. The rhetoric, if not the substance, of the proposals went some way to accommodating the professional cultures of teachers.

Over a year later, the Secretary of State, Kenneth Baker, in a speech to the Industrial Society (April 1986) elaborated the rhetoric of professional development and teacher participation in the operationalization of appraisal. The hierarchical control over the process was reaffirmed but softened. Appraisal was now to operate at all levels of the hierarchy, and, in the 'personal opinion' of Mr Baker, 'a measure of peer review and reciprocity should be involved'. The head was no longer seen as a classroom observer. This task was simply described as one for senior colleagues (even possibly more than one), rather than as a management task. In this speech it is not only the rhetoric which shifted in the direction of a collegial and reflective form of appraisal, but procedures were proposed (albeit as a matter of personal opinion) to match the shift.

And so we come to the ACAS agreement of 1986, between government, employers and teacher associations. This agreement is now the framework for the national pilots in selected LEAs. It incorporated most of Mr Baker's anticipatory rhetoric and proposed procedures. It accommodated possibilities for developing collegial forms of appraisal, involving self-appraisal, peer observation and safeguards to appraisees with respect to access to, and use of, appraisal records.

The agreement did not prescribe a form of appraisal which is equally balanced between managerial and professional cultures, but allowed for different emphases. On the one hand, it allowed for a strong element of hierarchical surveillance with some restrictions on the process and outcomes (for example, that a formal appraisal should be preceded and informed by self-appraisal, and that appraisees should have a right to appeal over both substantive judgments and procedures). On the other hand, it allowed for a strong element of self- and peer appraisal, with some concessions to hierarchical access to, and use of, records.

What we witnessed during the period between *Teaching Quality* and the ACAS agreement was the transformation of a coercive model of teacher appraisal into a model which accommodated elements of existing professional cultures. As it stands, the framework leaves plenty of space in which to develop appraisal in schools as a form of classroom action research, and for people like myself to participate in this development as a second-order action research enterprise. If the opportunity is not grasped by reflective teachers and teacher educators, if we shrink from creative compromise, then we have no cause to moan when the spaces provided by ACAS are filled with managerialism, skill training and techniques of control supplied by the 'agricultural-botany' paradigm. The matter is urgent, for this paradigm is now being reinforced by the requirement to implement the Education Reform Act of 1988: yet another part of that broad strategy now operating in our society to transform schools into systems of coercive power, and schooling into a process for manufacturing passive and possessive individuals in the shape of the market economy.

References

ACAS INDEPENDENT PANEL (1986) *Report of the Appraisal and Training Working Group*, Mimeo.

BRIDGES, D., ELLIOTT, J. and KLASS, C. (1986) 'Performance Appraisal as Naturalistic Inquiry', *Cambridge Journal of Education*, 16, 3, pp. 221–33.

BROWN, S. and MCINTYRE, D. (1986) 'The Qualities of Teachers: Building on Professional Craft Knowledge,' Mimeo, Scottish Council for Research in Education.

DES (1983) *Teaching Quality*, White Paper, London, HMSO.

DES (1985) Text of Mr D. Hancock's speech on 'Appraisal: Opportunities, Not a Threat', Press Notice 34/85, 25 February.

DES (1986) Text of Secretary of State's speech to the Industrial Society Conference on the Education Bill, 14 April.

DOLL, W.E., Jr. (1984) 'Developing Competence', in Short, E.C. (ed.), *Competence*, Lanham, Md, University Press of America.

ELLIOTT, J. (1976) 'Developing Hypotheses from Teachers' Practical Constructs', *Interchange*, 72, pp. 2–22.

ELLIOTT, J. (1985) 'Facilitating Educational Action-Research in Schools: Some Dilemmas', in Burgess, R. G. (ed.), *Field Methods in the Study of Education*, Lewes, Falmer Press.

ELLIOTT, J., HUNTER, C., MARLAND, D. and WORMALD, E. (1985) 'Teacher Education and Teaching Quality', *British Journal of Sociology of Education*, 6, 1, pp. 97–116.

FOUCAULT, M. (1977) *Discipline and Punish: The Birth of the Prison*, London, Allen Lane, Penguin Press.

FOUCAULT, M. (1979) *The History of Sexuality. Vol. 1: An Introduction*, London, Allen Lane, Penguin Press.

SHERIDAN, A. (1980) *Michel Foucault: The Will to Truth*, London and New York, Tavistock Publications.

STENHOUSE, L. (1975) *An Introduction to Curriculum Research and Development*, London, Heinemann Educational.

Notes on Contributors

Clem Adelman is a Professor in Education at the University of Reading. His major contributions have been in the areas of qualitative research methodology, evaluation, pedagogic theory and practice and action research.

Wilfred Carr is a Senior Lecturer in Education at the University of Sheffield. He has published extensively on the theory–practice relationship, the role of educational research in teacher education and educational action research. He is co-author, with Stephen Kemmis, of *Becoming Critical: Education, Knowledge and Action Research.*

John Elliott is Professor of Education at the Centre for Applied Research in Education, University of East Anglia. He directed the Ford Teaching Project, which has been a major stimulus to the development of the theory and practice of action research in the UK and worldwide. His publications have dealt with topics such as educational action research, curriculum planning and evaluation and accountability.

Peter Gilroy has taught a range of subjects at secondary school level. He studied philosophy at Birkbeck College and later at the London University Institute of Education. He is at present Director of the Advanced Studies Programme in Sheffield University's Division of Education.

Michael Golby is a Senior Lecturer in Education at the University of Exeter. His research interests centre on the philosophy of education. He directed the Leverhulme sponsored project, *Parents as School Governors.*

Shirley Grundy is a Senior Lecturer in Curriculum Studies at the University of New England, New South Wales, Australia. Originally a primary school teacher, she undertook her university education as a mature aged student.

She has written extensively in areas relating to teacher professionalism, curriculum theory and action research. Her book, *Curriculum: Product or Praxis?*, was recently published by Falmer Press.

Fred Inglis is a Reader in Education at the University of Warwick, having been an English teacher before teaching for seventeen years in the Division of Advanced Studies at Bristol. His most recent book is *Popular Culture and Political Power* (Harvester Wheatsheaf, 1988).

Maurice Kogan is Professor of Government and Social Administration and Dean of the Faculty of Social Sciences at Brunel University. His main areas of concern have been the government and politics of education and higher education. His most recent books include *Education Accountability: The Use of Performance Indicators in Higher Education* (with Martin Cave and others) and *School Governing Bodies* (with Daphne Johnson and others).

Glenn Langford has been teaching philosophy at the University of Exeter since 1965. A principal interest during that time has been that of gaining a philosophical understanding of education.

Martin Lawn is a Senior Lecturer in Teaching Studies at Westhill College, Birmingham. He has published widely in the fields of teacher professionalism, the labour process of teaching and curriculum policy. Recent publications include *Teachers: The Culture and Politics of Work* (with Gerald Grice).

Fazal Rizvi is a Senior Lecturer in Education at Deakin University, Australia. He has published papers on multiculturalism as an educational policy, the politics of democratic reforms in education and ethical issues in educational administration.

Hugh Sockett is Director of the Center for Applied Research and Development in Education at George Mason University, Fairfax, Virginia. He is author of a number of papers on professionalism and accountability in teaching.

Richard Winter is a Senior Lecturer in Education at the Essex Institute of Higher Education. He has published articles on action research, on teacher appraisal and on the relation between aesthetics and social theory. A longer theoretical study, *Action Research and the Nature of Social Inquiry: Professional Innovation and Educational Work*, was published by Gower in 1987.

Index